S0-BYN-936

On the Philosophy of Law

David A. Reidy
University of Tennessee

WADSWORTH
CENGAGE Learning·

Australia • Brazil • Japan • Korea • Mexico • Singapore • Spain • United Kingdom • United States

WADSWORTH
CENGAGE Learning™

On the Philosophy of Law
David A. Reidy

Philosophy Editor:
Steve Wainwright

Assistant Editors:
Lee McCracken,
Barbara Hillaker

Editorial Assistant:
Patrick Stockstill

Technology Project Manager:
Julie Aguilar

Marketing Manager:
Worth Hawes

Marketing Assistant:
Kathleen Tosiello

Marketing Communications
Manager: Stacey Purviance

Creative Director: Rob Hugel

Executive Art Director:
Maria Epes

Print Buyer: Linda Hsu

Permissions Editor: Bob Kauser

Production Service/Compositor:
Integra Software Services

Copy Editor: Tara Joffe

© 2007 Wadsworth, Cengage Learning

ALL RIGHTS RESERVED. No part of this work covered by the copyright herein may be reproduced, transmitted, stored, or used in any form or by any means graphic, electronic, or mechanical, including but not limited to photocopying, recording, scanning, digitizing, taping, Web distribution, information networks, or information storage and retrieval systems, except as permitted under Section 107 or 108 of the 1976 United States Copyright Act, without the prior written permission of the publisher.

For product information and technology assistance, contact us at **Cengage Learning Customer & Sales Support, 1-800-354-9706**

For permission to use material from this text or product, submit all requests online at
www.cengage.com/permissions
Further permissions questions can be e-mailed to
permissionrequest@cengage.com

Library of Congress Control Number: 2006932738

ISBN-13: 978-0-495-00421-9
ISBN-10: 0-495-00421-9

Wadsworth Cengage Learning
20 Davis Drive
Belmont, CA 94002-3098
USA

Cengage Learning is a leading provider of customized learning solutions with office locations around the globe, including Singapore, the United Kingdom, Australia, Mexico, Brazil, and Japan. Locate your local office at
www.cengage.com/global

Cengage Learning products are represented in Canada by Nelson Education, Ltd.

To learn more about Wadsworth, visit
www.cengage.com/wadsworth

Purchase any of our products at your local college store or at our preferred online store **www.cengagebrain.com**

Printed in the United States of America
3 4 5 6 7   21 20 19 18 17

Dedication

For my children, Kiyoko Cecelia Reidy and
Kame Benjamin Reidy

Acknowledgments

I owe many thanks to Mr. Jeppe von Platz for his exceptional research and editorial assistance and to Mr. Walter Riker for many helpful comments on early drafts of each chapter. Without their assistance, I could not have written this book in timely fashion without interrupting my other publishing projects. I owe many thanks to Professor Rex Martin for sharing his time and learning over the years and for encouraging me to take on this project. I owe perhaps the greatest thanks to my wife, Kathy Saunders, and my children, Kiyoko and Kame. They were extraordinarily patient and understanding as I spent weekends and evenings in the office. I also want to thank Professor John Davis and an anonymous reviewer for Wadsworth for valuable comments given upon a read of the penultimate draft of the manuscript. Last but not least, I want to thank Robert Talisse for asking me to write this book; I have enjoyed doing so.

I hope this book will prove useful and stimulating to students of all sorts, as well as to faculty wishing to orient themselves quickly with respect to some of the central issues around which the philosophy of law is organized.

Contents

1

Brief Introduction

In this book, I offer what I hope is an accessible and inviting, but not simplistic, introduction to some of the main issues and debates constituting the philosophy of law. It is neither possible nor desirable in a book like this to examine all the topics that fall under the big tent of the philosophy of law. Nor is it possible or desirable to cover every aspect of the topics examined. And so I have had to make choices. I have tried to choose topics likely to leave those who are approaching the philosophy of law for the first time hungry for more. And I have tried to cover those topics in a manner sufficient to sustain informed conversation and guide further inquiry. I have aimed to stimulate interest in problems, not solve them or survey every proposed solution. Accordingly, I have allowed my own viewpoint and, in some cases my own concrete views, to shape the text to some degree.

Chapters 2–4 concern the many relationships among law, morality, and power or politics. In particular, these chapters set out to assess three different ways in which philosophers have thought about the nature, validity or existence conditions, and normative authority of law in general. Chapter 2 takes up various versions of legal positivism. Chapter 3 takes up various versions of natural law theory. And Chapter 4 takes up various legal realisms—or, as the chapter's title puts it, legal realism and its progeny. Chapters 2–4 set the stage for Chapter 5's inquiry into issues raised by the practice of judicial review in a constitutional democracy, issues increasingly center stage in American political and legal discourse and practice. By the end of Chapter 5, the institutional and normative density and complexity of constitutional rule-of-law democratic government should be plain to all readers. Chapter 6 turns to the problem of legal punishment. Notwithstanding F.H. Bradley's claim a century ago that the philosophy of legal punishment is never more than the giving of bad reasons for what we know must be justified anyway, many philosophers of law today have begun to consider the possibility that if all we can turn up are bad reasons, then perhaps legal punishment in anything like its present form is, in fact, unjustified. This, in turn, raises deep questions about the social role or function of law, or at least a good deal of law. Chapter 7 completes the book with an inquiry into the nature of international law, a topic too long ignored by philosophers of law and no longer ignorable.

What have I left out? A great deal. In the chapter on legal realism and its progeny, I do not discuss critical race theory, nor do I give critical legal studies or feminist jurisprudence the attention they deserve. Each of these subjects deserves at least a chapter of attention, but space constraints prevent that here without dropping other topics. What I have tried to do is say enough in the chapter on legal realism to orient students so they might profitably follow out their interests in these other matters on their own.

In the chapter on punishment, I do not take up the important issue of the limits of criminal liability: How do we draw the boundary between criminal and civil liability? How ought we draw it? Should pot smoking by fully informed, mentally competent adults be eligible for criminalization? What about consensual homosexual sex? Or prostitution? Or cruelty to animals? These issues—issues of legal paternalism and legal moralism—also deserve at least a chapter of attention, but giving them the attention they deserve would mean dropping other topics covered in this book. I have chosen to address here the more basic issue of legal punishment, again with the hope that I will have said enough to orient students so they might profitably follow out their interests in these other matters on their own.

I do not examine the nature of legal rights in this book. This is a fundamental issue in the philosophy of law. What are rights in general? What distinguishes legal rights from other sorts of rights— say, moral rights? Do legal rights necessarily always "trump" other legal considerations in adjudicative contexts? If so, are some kinds of rights necessarily weightier than others? I also do not examine the key philosophical issues that arise within the various core domains of private law, contract, tort, and property. I venture in this book no analysis or justification for the law of contract. I omit discussion of legal conceptions of causation and responsibility, central issues within tort law. And I leave to the side the many fundamental issues raised by the legal recognition of property: What is it to have a legal property right? Are legal property rights purely conventional, or do they necessarily have a moral foundation? And so on.

Finally, I do not take up the many issues concerning other substantive legal doctrines within public law that are commonly discussed in philosophy of law classes. There is no analysis of affirmative action law, or sexual harassment law, or the law governing freedom of speech and association, and so on. All these matters are set to the side, not because they are unimportant but rather so the more basic matters discussed in this book may be taken up in a serious and sustained, instead of a cursory and somewhat superficial, way. Those wanting to reach beyond the topics covered in this book will find no shortage of sources. I list some general resources at the end of this brief introductory chapter. And topically focused select bibliographies follow each chapter. My hope is that this book will function as a stepping stool, enabling those who wish to reach beyond it higher and further and with greater accuracy than they might otherwise be able to do on their own.

WHAT IS THE PHILOSOPHY OF LAW?

There are many reasons to study the law. The most obvious is to know the content and procedures of the law within some existing legal system to which one has a practical relation, as, say, a person subject to the law or an official within the legal system. For the most part, the study of the law in this sense is undertaken in law schools or other institutions aimed at professional training and education.

A slightly less obvious reason to study the law is to try to understand the law as a special kind of institutional and social practice, either within a particular human society or across human societies in general. Understanding the law in this sense is a complex endeavor. It requires a good grasp of the descriptive facts and the best explanations of them. It also requires a clearheaded sense of the meaning of such concepts as law, legal obligation and authority, punishment, and so on, as well as their relationships to such related but distinct concepts as power, politics, sanction, morality, and so on. For the most part, philosophers of law make only modest contributions to the task of accurately describing and then explaining the nature and development of

3

particular legal institutions or practices or legal systems in general. This work is mainly done by those working in other disciplines—political science, sociology, anthropology, economics, history, and so forth. Philosophers of law have made substantial contributions, on the other hand, to our understanding of the meaning of such concepts as law, legal obligation, legal authority, legal punishment, and so on. Their work on this front constitutes one major component of the philosophy of law, known as analytic jurisprudence.

Another important reason to study the law is to try to figure out whether legal institutions in general or particular legal systems or laws are morally acceptable—and if not, how to make them so. Here, too, philosophers of law have made substantial contributions. Their work on this front constitutes a second major component of the philosophy of law, known as normative jurisprudence.

To be sure, neither analytic nor normative jurisprudence belongs exclusively to the philosophers of law. But they both constitute the two branches of the systematic study of law, or jurisprudence, to which philosophers of law have made the most substantial contributions. Philosophers of law have also made important contributions to sociological jurisprudence, the systematic description and explanation of law as an institutional social practice. But here their contributions typically pale in comparison to those made by persons working in other intellectual disciplines.

While philosophers of law make use of methods and conclusions drawn from all, or nearly all, the other branches of philosophy—metaphysics, epistemology, philosophy of language and mind, and so on—the philosophy of law is conventionally understood as a subdiscipline within political philosophy. Bodies politic are the objects of study within political philosophy, and one important kind of body politic is that constituted through and subject to the rule of law. Accordingly, the philosophy of law is usually organized around, or at least takes as its point of departure, the analytic and normative inquiry into the rule of law.

Human societies are, or should be, systems of cooperation, mutually advantageous for all members. Sustained cooperation requires rules and settled expectations. It will almost always also require an asymmetrical distribution of some forms of authority. There will be rulers and the ruled, even if the ruled select the rulers. The rule of law refers to the organization and governance of societies as cooperative ventures through legal rules. Ideally, the rule of law ensures that the exercise of authority, and in particular coercive authority, is always rule-governed and never arbitrary; that those who are ruled are always informed in advance of the rules with which they are expected to comply and given a reasonable opportunity to comply with them; that the rules are fairly and impartially enforced; and that the rulers and the ruled stand equally under a common, publicly promulgated law that governs them both, even if it assigns them different rights and responsibilities. Within a society organized under and governed by the rule of law, no one is above the law. Yet the law remains, or should remain, subject to human needs, interests, moral demands, and so forth. It is for us; we are not for it. It is this political and institutional possibility that the philosophy of law inquires into, both analytically and normatively.

In this book, I presuppose, at least as a starting point, that the rule of law is both possible and desirable. If that presupposition is correct, then a complete and adequate political philosophy must include a well-developed philosophy of law. And no political philosopher or theorist can long afford to ignore the philosophy of law.

Of course, no political philosopher is likely to make much progress in the philosophy of law without a decent empirical, historical, and institutional understanding of bodies politic and the legal systems and practices through which they manage their affairs. Neither political philosophy nor the philosophy of law is an a priori discipline. I have, in this book, necessarily presupposed a certain basic familiarity with the American political and legal system or modern liberal democratic systems similar to it. Where more than such a basic familiarity seemed necessary, I have tried to provide sufficient empirical, historical, or institutional background to keep the reader on track.

If none of the foregoing counts for you as a reason to study the philosophy of law, then perhaps you will be moved by two final considerations. It's a great way to sharpen your philosophical skills. And it's a lot of fun.

SELECTED BIBLIOGRAPHY

General Philosophy of Law Sources

Altman, Andrew. *Arguing About Law,* 2nd ed. (Belmont, CA: Wadsworth), 2001.

Bix, Brian. *Jurisprudence: Theory and Context,* 3rd ed. (Boulder, CO: Westview Press), 2003.

————. *A Dictionary of Legal Theory*. (Oxford, UK: Oxford University Press), 2004.

Carter, Leif and Burke, Thomas. *Reason in Law*, 7th ed. (New York, NY: Pearson Longman), 2005.

Coleman, Jules, et al., eds. *Oxford Handbook of Jurisprudence and Philosophy of Law*. (Oxford, UK: Oxford University Press), 2002.

D'Amato, Anthony, ed. *Analytic Jurisprudence Anthology*. (Cincinatti, OH: Anderson Publishing), 1996.

Fletcher, George. *Basic Concepts of Legal Thought*. (Oxford, UK: Oxford University Press), 1996.

Golding, Martin, et al., eds. *The Blackwell Guide to Philosophy of Law and Legal Theory*. (Oxford, UK: Blackwell Publishers), 2005.

Kelly, J.M. *A Short History of Western Legal Theory*. (Oxford, UK: Oxford University Press), 1992.

Murphy, Jeffrie, et al. *Philosophy of Law: An Introduction to Jurisprudence*. (Boulder, CO: Westview Press), 1990.

Patterson, Dennis. *Law and Truth*. (Oxford, UK: Oxford University Press), 1996.

————, ed. *A Companion to Philosophy of Law and Legal Theory*. (Oxford, UK: Blackwell Publishers), 1999.

2

On Legal Positivisms

The law purports to bind or obligate those subject to it. Or, if that seems too strong, it at least purports to give normative direction to those subject to it, to constitute by itself a reason for acting one way rather than another. As a social institution or practice, it aspires to or claims for itself normativity. It tells those subject to it what they ought to do. It gives them reasons for doing one thing rather than another, reasons intended to override considerations of narrow self-interest. In this respect, the law is like morality. It asserts a kind of normative authority over us. The legal "ought" is familiar.

But unlike morality, the law has, or at least claims to have, normative force simply because it is the law, and not because of the moral merits of its content. That this is so is clear enough. Many laws concern matters about which morality is silent or indifferent. Their normative authority must arise from something other than the moral merits of their content. Some laws require or allow things that morality forbids or condemns, while others forbid things that morality allows or requires. This is sometimes because it does not make sense legally to prohibit everything morality condemns or to require every-thing morality demands. But it is also sometimes because humans mistakenly legally forbid things that are in fact morally permissible or legally allow things that are in fact morally impermissible. In any case, the point is that even laws that legally require what is morally forbidden or forbid what is morally permissible have or claim norma-tive force as laws.

Depending on what is at stake, the normative force of some laws might be outweighed by other moral considerations. But nevertheless,

7

all laws have, or at least claim for themselves, normative force simply as laws. They give us reasons to act one way rather than another, even if those reasons are finally outweighed, all things considered. This normative force must arise, it would seem, out of something other than the moral content of the law in question. The normative authority of valid laws appears to arise simply out of the fact that they are "valid" laws. This makes the legal "ought" very different from the moral "ought." It also means it is important to be able to distinguish valid laws from other rules or norms to which the legal "ought" does not attach.

But how do valid laws have normative authority for us if not through the moral merits of their content? Perhaps the normative authority of valid laws derives simply from our rational self-interest. After all, the law is often backed by sanctions coercively imposed by the state for noncompliance. Immoral conduct might get you criticized or cost you friends or even your eternal salvation. But unless it is also illegal conduct, you're not likely to find the state coercively taking your property, liberty, or life. Illegal conduct, on the other hand, may get you just that. It may seem that this aspect of the law, its connection to state-imposed sanctions for noncompliance, accounts for its normative authority. Why must you do as the law requires? Because if you don't, you'll be fined, imprisoned, or worse. What more reason does one need to obey the law? The legal "ought" may seem to be just the "ought" of prudence or self-interest.

This is a common thought. If the law were not coercively enforced, the mere fact that it was the law would seem to give no one a reason to do as it demands. Coercive enforcement may seem necessary not simply to motivate compliance when it might not be forthcoming for one reason or another, but also to ensure that the law gives us reasons to act as it requires simply by virtue of its validity or being the law, regardless of its moral content. If this is correct, then perhaps morality and law are not only distinct but also fully separate and independent systems of normative authority. Morality derives its normative force from what our reason tells us about the right, the good, virtue, and so on. Law derives its normative force from our self-interested fear of the sanctions it threatens to impose for non-compliance.

Notwithstanding its familiarity, we ought to be careful not to endorse this line of thinking too quickly. For one thing, the normative authority of the law is generally understood to override considerations of narrow self-interest. Those rationally willing to risk being sanctioned for illegal conduct so as to have a good shot at securing some gain, or those simply unmoved by fears of sanction, are just as bound by valid laws as are others. There are also many laws for which there is no obvious sanction for noncompliance. So, it would seem, a self-interested fear of sanction alone could hardly account for the law's authority. If the normative authority of the law derives from rational self-interest alone, then the derivation is vastly more complex than that suggested by the self-interested desire to avoid sanctions.

This should not surprise. We don't usually think that might alone can make right or give rise to genuine obligations, and taken alone, sanctions look like little more than the manifestation of might. After all, you would have no legal obligation to obey an invalid or a repealed law, *even if* the state credibly threatened to enforce it against you (though such a threat might make it in your rational self-interest to obey). So, it would seem that threat of sanction alone cannot account for the normative authority of the law. The normative authority of the law must derive at least in part from its validity as law. But how? And how could the validity of a law account, by itself, for its normative authority without reference to the law's moral content or the threat of sanction for noncompliance?

To begin, we need a richer understanding of what it is for a law to be valid or genuine—to exist—as a law. Only with this understanding in hand can we determine whether and how the validity or genuineness or existence of a law as a law underwrites its peculiar normative authority, its ability to underwrite legal obligations.

THE NATURE OF LAW: TWO PERSPECTIVES

It is hard to think about the law without thinking also about both force or power and morality. But the relationships among law, power or force, and morality is a puzzle, indeed a core puzzle, within the philosophy of law. One reason philosophers of law have not been able to solve this puzzle once and for all is that its central questions— questions about the validity and normative force of law—may be raised from more than one point of view. And depending on the point of view from which the puzzle is viewed, different solutions suggest themselves. Accordingly, philosophers of law sometimes appear merely to disagree with one another, each giving a different solution to the puzzle, when in fact they're actually giving different solutions to different puzzles or to the same puzzle viewed from very different perspectives and sets of concerns.

The first point of view is that of the nonparticipant in or external observer of the law. This is the point of view of someone concerned with determining—simply as a matter of theoretical understanding, or what Aristotle called the contemplative aspect of our reason—how it is that the law comes, just by virtue of being the law, to bind, obligate, or give normative direction to those subject to it. Imagine a Martian sociologist concerned with understanding, as a matter of social science, the strange thing Earthlings call law or legal systems. It is the Martian's point of view. She wants to describe, analyze, and explain observable legal practices, common talk about the law, and so on. She also wants a descriptive theory of law consistent with her descriptive theories of moral discourse and practice, on the one hand, and brute power relations, on the other. She regards all simply as phenomena to be described, analyzed, and explained in a scientific way.

The second point of view is that of the participant in or subject of the law. It is the internal point of view of a person or agent concerned with determining, as a matter of practical reason oriented toward action, whether and to what extent the law really does bind, obligate, or give normative direction. What such a person or agent wants to know is whether he really should do some particular thing said to be required by the law, and if so, why. His interests aren't theoretical or speculative; they're practical. He must act one way rather than another, and he needs reasons, reasons decisive for him from his practical point of view. A descriptive theory of law given from the point of view of a nonparticipant observer is not what he needs. What he needs to know is whether and what kind of practical reason he has to act as the law requires.

Getting clear on the relationships among law, morality, and coercive force (or the relationship between the validity or existence of the law and its normative authority) is hard enough if we take up matters from just one or the other of the two foregoing points of view. It's even more difficult if we set ourselves the task of giving a coherent account that makes sense from both perspectives. It's probably impossible if we fail to distinguish consistently between the two perspectives and instead run them together and equivocate between them in our reasoning. Yet, it is easy to do just that. To engage profitably with the philosophical debates over these matters, we shall need to keep the foregoing in mind and remain always attentive to the task engaged (is it descriptive and explanatory or practical and normative?) and the point of view from which it is being executed (is it the nonparticipant observer or the participant actor?).

Debate over the nature of legal validity and its relationship to the normative authority of law as law has been dominated by the contest between two rival schools of thought—legal positivism and natural law theory. These two schools are said to divide over whether there is a necessary conceptual connection between law and morality. Legal positivists are said to deny this claim; natural law theorists, to affirm it. Legal positivists are said to claim that whether X is a genuine legal system or Y is a valid law is always and only a matter of social fact and that the normative authority of real or valid laws simply as laws depends in no way on morality. Natural law theorists are said to claim that the genuineness or validity, and thus the normative authority, of all laws is always, at least in part, a matter of moral evaluation. Both agree that law and morality are distinct systems of normative authority. What they divide over is whether they're fully separate and independent. But notwithstanding the apparently clear and significant divide between them, legal positivist and natural law theories of law may be less starkly opposed to one another than may at first appear. How and where they conflict, if they do, is a question left to the reader after having read this and the following chapter.

CLASSICAL LEGAL POSITIVISM: AUSTIN'S COMMAND THEORY OF LAW

Like his near contemporary, neighbor, teacher, and friend Jeremy Bentham, the nineteenth-century legal philosopher John Austin was interested in the moral reform of the law in England. He was convinced by Bentham that a clear, objective, and descriptively accurate understanding of the law was, both in terms of its specific content and as a social institution or practice, a necessary precondition to any sensible reform of the law. Accordingly, Austin took up the sort of "objective" and "scientific" point of view toward human institutions pioneered by Machiavelli and Hobbes, and later embodied in the nineteenth-century "positivist" movement in the social sciences: the external point of view of a nonparticipant observer concerned simply with describing, analyzing, and explaining the law and legal institutions and practice. (Legal positivism takes its name from the fact that it studies positive human law—law made law by virtue of its being posited—from the point of view of a nonparticipant observer who is keen simply to describe, analyze, and explain so as to arrive at a social science of law.)

From this point of view, Austin claimed, the law is best understood simply as that set of general and prospective commands issued by the sovereign of a state to the subjects of that state. A command, in turn, is an expressed general and prospective desire for determinate conduct backed by a credible threat of coercive sanction for noncompliance. The sovereign of a state is simply that person or persons to whom the bulk of the population is habitually obedient and who in turn is habitually obedient to no other. As an objective, descriptive matter of social scientific fact, a legal system exists wherever there is a sovereign issuing general and prospective commands, with credible threats of sanction for noncompliance attached, to a habitually obedient population. And the content of the law is given by those commands. Valid laws are those that can be traced back to the sovereign; they're identifiable by their pedigree. The law is made binding or obligatory or gives genuine normative direction by virtue of the sovereign's credible threats of sanction for noncompliance.

According to this view, law is a system of normative authority with no necessary connection to morality. When we talk about the law (or a legal system or legal obligations or the authority of law) simply as it is, we are not talking about anything necessarily involving morality. Of course, when we talk about whether the law is good or bad, in need of this or that reform, and so on, we will be talking in part about morality, for it is morality that gives us our evaluative standards. But what the law is and what it ought to be are two separate matters, Austin insisted.

To be sure, most legal systems will require many things that are also required by morality. The law and morality may both prohibit murder. This overlap between law and morality is desirable and to be expected. But it is contingent rather than conceptually necessary; it is unnecessary to the existence or normative authority of the law as law. The existence and normative authority of the law is best understood, Austin maintained, in terms of general and prospective commands given by a sovereign. At least this is how it is best understood from the external point of view of a nonparticipant observer.

Although the law stands in no necessary relation to morality, on Austin's view, it does stand in a necessary relation to coercive force.

Expressed desires count as commands only if they include a credible threat of sanction for noncompliance. The threat of sanction is not an accidental but rather an essential property of all genuine commands. It is what enables commands to generate obligations or duties to obey, on Austin's view, thereby distinguishing commands from mere requests. If the law obligates, and Austin assumed that it does, then it must be a system or set of commands. Of course, not every command is a law. Laws arise out of only general and prospective commands issued by sovereigns. Still, to qualify as commands at all, credible threats of sanction must be attached.

There is, then, on Austin's view, a necessary connection between law and coercive force, even a necessary conceptual connection. Yet, as just noted, not every command counts as a law. There is a difference, for example, between the law and the commands given by a playground bully. This is not just because most playground bullies do not seek to command an entire population in a general and prospective way. It's also because any sanctions threatened by a playground bully will prove of limited credibility. Playground bullies and the sanctions they threaten are subject to all sorts of constraints arising out of the authority or power of others: parents, recess monitors, teachers, older students, and so on. Playground bullies are not sovereigns, usually not even over the playground. They habitually obey others, even as they bully and boss their fellow playmates. Accordingly, they cannot make law, not even a law of the playground. Commands count as law only when given by an agent habitually obedient to no one and to whom others are habitually obedient in turn. Only within the context of the relationship between such a political superior and political inferiors is it possible for general and prospective commands, with credible threats of sanction attached, to constitute law. Although the law is necessarily connected to brute coercion, it is distinct as a system of brute coercion. It is the most basic or primary system of coercion operative at the level of a body politic. At least that is how it appeared to Austin from his external nonparticipant observer point of view.

Austin's view resembles familiar voluntarist views regarding the authority of divine law. Voluntarists maintain that the authority of divine law flows not from the wisdom or reasonableness of God's commands but rather from the fact that they are God's commands, expressions of God's will, coupled with God's supreme power over us. In this way, voluntarists reduce the normative authority of divine law—the "ought" built into divine commands—to facts about God's

power over us coupled with facts about the content of God's will. In the same way, Austin reduced the normative authority of, or "ought" built into, the positive law of the state to facts about the sovereign's power over subjects coupled with facts about the content of the sovereign's will. The existence, authority, and content of the law are, for Austin, matters of social fact concerning the pedigree or origin of the law, or its genesis in the will of the sovereign. Whether you have a legal obligation to do or not do something is not a question to be settled through any form of moral inquiry or reasoning. It is a question of social fact to be determined through empirical investigation: Is there a sovereign? Has the sovereign issued a general and prospective command regarding the matter at issue? What is the content of that command?

Austin thought humans, as a matter of fact, to be generally subject to three primary systems of law, each possessed of its own distinct normative authority: the positive law of the state (which we've just described), divine law, and the conventional (or positive) moral law. Divine law is the system or set of general and prospective commands God gives to humans (and other intelligent creatures capable of choice). Austin thought the principle of utility—that actions and institutions are morally right to the extent that they maximize the welfare of all those they impact—a good summation of the divine law. But he maintained that the authority of God's commands does not derive from their mirroring the principle of utility taken as an independent moral standard given by reason or from their moral soundness more generally. The authority of God's commands derives simply from God's will and power over humankind.

The conventional (or positive) moral law is the system or set of general and prospective commands enforced by social pressure and given by the "indeterminate many" participating in custom, traditions, and shared historical practices over time, rather than by any determinate political superior. The authority of the conventional moral law derives from the superior will and power of the many engaged in common patterns of behavior over time and united by shared expectations.

Notwithstanding his treatment of these three systems of normative authority as descriptively and analytically distinct, Austin did not regard them as wholly unrelated. Both sovereigns and subjects are bound by divine law and the conventional moral law. Thus, sovereigns are subject to both divine law and the conventional moral law when making positive law (of the state) binding on their subjects.

They should make the positive law (of the state) consistent with both divine law and the conventional moral law.

But Austin recognized that no human sovereign would ever fulfill this obligation fully or perfectly. Thus, it is always possible for subjects to find themselves with a genuine legal obligation that, all things considered (e.g., divine law and conventional morality), they have an obligation not to fulfill. For example, a subject might find herself with a legal obligation to do something forbidden by divine law. In this case, there is no escaping the internal point of view of the agent subject to (at least here) competing systems of normative authority and concerned to determine what she ought to do. From this point of view, the internal point of view of conscience, an agent subject to legal obligations can determine what to do only through critical, reflective moral inquiry and reasoning. Austin allowed that from this point of view one could be obligated by divine law to violate the positive law of the state, but he was clear: a conflict between divine law and the positive law of the state does not negate, invalidate, or destroy the legal obligation arising from the positive law of the state. The legal obligation exists as a matter of social fact discernible from the external point of view, even if one has, from the internal point of view of conscience, overriding moral reasons to violate it.

Austin pressed this point, in large part, as an antidote to the kind of thinking exemplified by William Blackstone. Blackstone, an influential eighteenth-century teacher of and commentator on the law in England, had argued that positive laws (of the state) contrary to the natural and moral law of reason were invalid as positive laws and were not really laws at all. Austin thought this view not only mistaken but dangerous. It invited one of two further thoughts: The first was that the enduring common law of England must be morally right and reasonable, because it has for generations been recognized and enforced as valid positive law. This thought led to an unacceptable conservatism and moral passivity. The second was that every citizen must judge the legal validity of each law for him- or herself. This thought led to an unacceptable radicalism and/or tendency toward anarchy. Austin sought to establish the existence and authority of the law as a matter of social fact, but in a manner that left the law open to reasonable critical moral evaluation, dissent, and reform—something most likely to be engendered when there arose conflicts between the law and either divine commands or conventional morality.

FROM COMMANDS TO RULES: INTRODUCING HART'S LEGAL POSITIVISM

H.L.A. Hart's *The Concept of Law* is perhaps the most important work of legal philosophy in the twentieth century. It would be difficult to overstate its importance and influence. It is the one book in the philosophy of law that is still routinely required reading of both philosophy and law students around the world. It is to the philosophy of law what John Rawls's *A Theory of Justice* is to political philosophy: something of a North Star in terms of which philosophers locate their own positions.

In *The Concept of Law*, Hart takes on two basic tasks. The first is to make a decisive case against Austin's command theory of law, or the classical version of legal positivism. The second is to set out a more compelling version of legal positivism. According to this new version, the law and legal systems are best described, analyzed, and explained not in terms of commands, sanctions, and a sovereign but rather in terms of systematic relations between different kinds of rules and the internal beliefs and attitudes of agents following them. The difference may at first seem slight, but it is not. For on Hart's account, what is essential to the law is not that there is a sovereign issuing commands with the will and power to enforce its desires against a subject population. Rather, what is essential is that there are agents who make, adjudicate, and enforce the law by participating in a system of rules and thus acting for reasons. On Hart's account, both the validity or existence and the normative authority of the law are functions of the law's essential connection to rules and reasons rather than to will and power. Against Austin, Hart insists that mere might or power alone can never make legal right or obligation. With Austin, however, Hart insists that both the existence or validity and the normative authority of the law as law are always matters of social fact available to the external nonparticipant observer.

Like Austin, Hart sets himself the task of giving a philosophically sound description, analysis, and explanation of law and legal systems from the external point of view of the nonparticipant observer. He maintains, with Austin, that there is no necessary connection between law and morality, even if there are, in most legal systems, various contingent connections and even if moral criteria are always relevant to determining what the law ought to be. So, Hart and Austin agree that what the law is is one thing and what it ought to be is another. Hart ultimately rejects Austin's command theory of law, but he does so in the name of an improved legal positivism rather than any anti-positivist alternative. *The Concept of Law* belongs, therefore, to the tradition initiated by Bentham and Austin.

Hart's *The Concept of Law* reflects debts to at least two other significant philosophical influences. The first is Hans Kelsen, a twentieth-century legal philosopher from Austria. Kelsen shared Austin's aspiration to describe, analyze, and explain law and legal systems from the external point of view and thereby to advance a "science" of law or jurisprudence. He also agreed with Austin that from this point of view there is no necessary connection between law and morality. But Kelsen rejected Austin's attempt to reduce the law and its normative authority to some set of facts about commands, sanctions, and habits of obedience. On Kelsen's view, within every legal system, individual laws necessarily derive their existence or validity, and thus their normative authority, from a fundamental norm at the foundation of and presupposed by the legal system as a whole. This norm is, on Kelsen's view, just a function of the logic of legal reasoning and legal norms. Laws are merely the institutional manifestation of legal norms, directing officials to act in particular ways, imposing sanctions, and so on in light of certain circumstances. For the officials following such norms, the norms are necessarily validated or justified through their relationship to deeper and more general norms. The law against murder, then, is to be understood as a norm directing officials to sanction those who murder. And the norm directing officials to sanction those who murder is validated or justified by reference to a deeper and more general norm concerning official responses to conduct contrary to specified statutes. And that norm is validated or justified, in turn, by reference to some deeper and more general norm concerning statutes themselves. And so on. At a certain point, this chain of justification or normative reasoning must come to an end. It necessarily terminates, Kelsen maintained, not in some fact about the world but in a fundamental norm presupposed by and constituting the foundation of the legal system as a whole. This *grundnorm*, as Kelsen called it, need not be moral. It may be no more than "everyone ought to do what the king commands" or "those who do not do as the king commands must be sanctioned," but it must be a norm. Laws within any legal system are valid by virtue of their logical relationship to this *grundnorm*, it underwrites the normative authority of all the laws it validates.

The aim of legal science or analytic jurisprudence is to identify the fundamental norm in each legal system and then to map the logical relationships between it and all the subordinate norms. Ultimately, this makes it possible to understand the system's legal rules as institutional manifestations of a complex and integrated system of norms.

For Kelsen, legal science or analytic jurisprudence ought not concern itself with the causal relationships through which law comes to exist and operate. The study of such matters of fact belongs to the sociology of law. Nor ought it concern itself with the moral merits of the law. The study of such matters belongs to ethics and other disciplines devoted to critical moral reflection on law. Legal science ought to concern itself solely with describing, analyzing, and explaining legal systems as systems of norms. Through a careful study of legal reasoning, the philosopher of law deduces the fundamental norm presupposed by and grounding the unity of (or logically constituting, as Kelsen might say) any given legal system as a system of and with normative authority.

Hart draws several ideas from Kelsen. One is that the philosophy of law properly focuses on the law not as a natural social phenomenon to be studied in terms of causes and effects, but rather as a normative social phenomenon to be studied in terms of norms and reasons. Another is that legal systems, in general, have a sort of two-level structure: there are valid laws, and then there are the criteria in terms of which those laws are ultimately judged to be valid. The latter, however, are not valid laws, even though they are essential to the existence of any legal system. They are the prelegal or extralegal soil from which valid laws arise— something closer to normative (though not necessarily moral) presuppositions. Unlike Kelsen, however, Hart does not try to deduce the normative criteria of legal validity in any given legal system from the logical relations of the norms within it. Rather, he tries to identify them through empirical observation of the normative behavior of the officials and other participants in the legal system.

The second significant influence on Hart was John Austin, a twentieth-century philosopher of language (not to be confused with the nineteenth-century John Austin discussed above). This second Austin emphasized that careful attention to ordinary linguistic use often revealed important and stable conceptual distinctions that philosophers, being inclined to jargon far removed from everyday life, often missed. Austin also emphasized the importance of first getting a clear view of the central, or paradigm, cases of particular terms or concepts and not trying always to generate a neat unified definition that would cover every possible case. Nonparadigm cases might be related to a paradigm case in many ways and need not fall under the same definition taken as a set of necessary and sufficient conditions.

Like the nineteenth-century Austin, Hart aims to describe, analyze, and explain the law from the external point of view. But he follows the twentieth-century Austin insofar as he arrives at many of the essential elements of his theory only after a careful study of the ordinary linguistic use of terms like *law, legal obligation, rule, sanction,* and so on in their paradigm cases. In this way, he identifies important conceptual distinctions between, for example, being obliged and having an obligation, acting as a rule and acting because of a rule, having the final say on some question and being infallible with respect to, or having unlimited discretion on, that question, and so on. Hart's own version of legal positivism relies heavily on these distinctions. So, though Hart sets himself the task of giving a descriptive theory of law, he does not rely only on observation. Rather, he relies also heavily on conceptual analysis, with the thought that by getting clear on the relevant concepts he can shed light on the relevant phenomena and thus deliver a more fully adequate description.

Hart's legal positivism constitutes an important development in positivist thinking in two related senses. First, he offers a legal positivism cut free of voluntarist assumptions shared by Austin and others. Hart's positivism does not depend on the controversial claim that the existence and normative authority of the law depends on the will of a sovereign. Second, Hart gives a novel account of the legal "ought." Once stripped down, it is the "ought" of neither morality nor mere prudence or self-interest. Rather, it is an "ought" of social convention, of rule-following, or of reasons arising out of rule-following conventions. It is like the "ought" associated with the rules of games. So long as they are the rules, they have normative authority over those keen to play the game, and they do so just because they are the rules.

HART'S INITIAL CRITICISMS OF AUSTIN

Hart's criticisms of Austin's command theory of law are clear and generally powerful. To be sure, Austin contemplated and addressed some of these criticisms. But, in general, Hart shows Austin's responses to be inadequate. Hart's first complaint concerns the range of rules qualifying as genuine laws on Austin's view. For Austin, a law is a general and prospective command by the sovereign, with a threat of sanction for noncompliance attached. This account best fits criminal law. It does not fit very well the law of contracts or of wills and trusts or the public law creating and governing various legal offices. These areas of the law do not command or forbid conduct on pain of sanction for noncompliance. Rather, they permit various kinds of conduct and make it possible for persons to acquire certain legal rights or powers or statuses, provided they follow a defined procedure. These laws are more like recipes than commands. Hart calls them power-conferring rules that tell persons how to do things if they want to do them in an officially recognized or legal way.

Suppose you want to make a legally valid contract to sell your house. Contract law tells you that you'll need to reduce the contract to writing, execute it in such and such a way, and so on. It doesn't tell you that you are forbidden to sell your house without a contract or to make a legally invalid contract. You're legally free to do these things. Contract law simply tells you that if you want to have a valid, legally recognized contract for the sale of your house, if you want the legal power to enforce your contract or claim damages for its breach, you must jump through certain specified hoops. There is no command and no sanction for noncompliance. On Austin's account, that means there is no law. But that's silly. The law of contract is as much real law as is criminal law. If Austin's theory suggests otherwise, so much the worse for Austin's theory, on Hart's view.

The same argument pattern may be extended to the law of wills and trusts, property law, the public law governing election and powers of government officials, the creation of boards and commissions, and so on, including, in the United States, the Constitution. If only commands with sanctions attached count as real law, then only the criminal (and perhaps some administrative and regulatory) law is real law.

Austin anticipated this difficulty and suggested that there is a kind of hidden command and sanction built into contract law, the law of wills and trusts, and so on. It's true that if you don't follow the law in these areas you won't be punished, but you also won't achieve your goals. And the failure to achieve your goals is itself a kind of sanction, or so Austin argued. But this is nonsense. First, you might choose not to follow the relevant rules in these areas precisely because you don't want, or don't care whether you manage, to create a legally valid contract, will, trust, public commission, and so on. In that case, your failure to do so can hardly count as a sanction; you got what you wanted, or at least did not suffer anything unwanted.

Second, treating the failure to secure a desired result as a kind of sanction distorts both our ordinary understanding of sanctions and the internal structure of Austin's view. On Austin's account, as well as in ordinary linguistic use, although sanctions may be essential to the existence of commands (they distinguish commands from mere requests), they are logically independent of the content of the commands to which they're attached. A sovereign commands her subjects to do X and then threatens Y as a sanction if they don't do X. The subjects need to know that their sovereign threatens Y to know that she has commanded (rather than merely requested) X. But they don't need to know that the sovereign threatens Y to know what it is, X, that she has commanded. What the sovereign commands is just some determinate conduct, general and prospective. Do not murder, or do not drive faster than 55 miles per hour on this stretch of highway, or some such thing. The nature of the sanctions for noncompliance is a separate matter. It makes perfect sense to ask, "But what is the sanction if I don't comply?" This is how sanctions operate—both in Austin's theory and in ordinary linguistic use.

But now consider Austin's suggestion that your failure to make a valid contract, for example, is your sanction for failing to follow the law of contracts. This suggestion departs significantly from the standard model. To understand what is required to make a legally valid contract, you must already understand that if you fail to do what is required, you will not make a legally valid contract. You must understand the alleged "sanction" in order to understand the content of what is commanded. The sanction is not logically independent of the content of the command. (Just think how stupid you would sound if after being told how to make a legally valid contract, you asked, "But what happens if I do it some other way?" The reply is likely to be, "Duh, you don't make a legally valid contract!") When a court fails to give legal effect to the "contract" you tried unsuccessfully to make, it is not sanctioning you for not complying with the law, at least not on any ordinary understanding of what it means to sanction. It is simply declaring that though you may have tried to follow the law's recipe for making a valid contract, you failed. Only a person dogmatically committed to the idea that there must be a necessary connection between law and sanctions would argue otherwise. But there need be no such connection. Threats of sanction are attached to the law not for the purposes of establishing its validity or its normative authority. They are attached for the purpose of giving at least some, perhaps many, persons an additional self-interested reason to comply with the law, just in case its normative authority as valid law by itself is not enough. Law without sanction is a conceptually coherent notion instantiated in various domains of many legal systems.

The law of contract, wills and trusts, and so on is problematic for Austin's theory not only because it carries no sanctions for noncompliance but also because it does not seem to command anyone to do anything. For example, contract law does not require anyone to make a contract or to do so in the valid way. It just states the conditions that must be met by those who wish to make legally valid contracts. But on Austin's view, contract law isn't law, because all law commands determinate conduct.

It's no good here to suggest that contract law at least requires officials to act in certain ways depending on whether the contract presented to them satisfies or fails to satisfy the relevant conditions. If we take contract law to be commands directed at officials, what then are the sanctions for noncompliance? In any case, it seems implausible to take contract law to be commands directed at officials. Surely, contract law is meant primarily to guide and direct legal subjects (those of us wanting to make legally valid contracts), not officials. Hart concludes that Austin's theory fails with respect to all those areas of law constituted by power-conferring rules.

Austin's theory also fails with respect to those laws established as laws simply by customary practice. In many legal systems, as well as in international law, customary practice can have the force of law simply because it is custom. Many customary business practices are still enforced as law in the United States, and much of international law is simply customary practice recognized as law. The trouble with customary law for Austin is that it is law, notwithstanding the fact that it does not originate from a command given by the sovereign. To his credit, Austin recognized this. He tried to accommodate customary law within his theory by arguing that although this law was not expressly commanded by the sovereign, it was nevertheless tacitly commanded. By not blocking its enforcement by judicial and other subordinate officials, the sovereign tacitly commanded fidelity to the customs recognized by those officials as law.

But Hart argues that this attempt to stretch the command theory of law to account for customary law fails. In most cases, the sovereign will have little or no idea what customs are being enforced by courts and other subordinate officials; thus, the sovereign could not possibly, merely through inaction, be said to command tacitly the enforcement of such customs as law. Inaction signals a tacit command only if the agent not acting has some general knowledge of what it is he or she is not reacting to. Further, when courts or other subordinate officials enforce customs as law, they do so because they already recognize the customs as law, not because they expect the sovereign to acquiesce to their conduct and thus transform the customs into law, ex post facto, through a tacit command. To accommodate customary law, Austin's command theory must be stretched to the point of distorting experienced reality and ordinary linguistic use. The alternative is to give up the idea of laws as commands given by sovereigns. Hart argues that the latter is the better path. But what is the alternative to Austin's view?

HART ON SOVEREIGNS AND RULES

The core of Hart's own view begins to emerge in his discussion of another objection to Austin's theory. On Austin's view, a sovereign is always, necessarily and conceptually, beyond the reach of the positive law of the state. Sovereigns stand outside the legal systems they create. They are never subjects under the positive law. They are only lawmakers. It is tempting here to suggest that a sovereign could at least be a subject under the positive law of the state over which it is sovereign. But on Austin's view, this is not possible. A sovereign cannot credibly threaten to sanction itself for failing to comply with a command it gives itself. On Austin's view, then, wherever there is a system of positive law, there is also a sovereign (a lawmaker) standing outside and beyond the reach of that law.

This may seem noncontroversial. But if it is correct, then all constitutional systems of government and law are really illusory. They must be, because in a constitutional system, whether it is a monarchy or a representative democracy, the authority of the "sovereign" (the king, parliament, even "we the people") is politically and legally constituted and thus subject to the terms of its constitution. Austin's view cannot accommodate this familiar fact about constitutional systems. For if there is law at all, on Austin's view, then there must be a sovereign who stands, or whose will stands, outside the positive law of the state, unconstrained by any constitutive conditions on its authority—it is a prelegal source of the law that binds. On Austin's view, you can have law or you can have constitutionalism, but you cannot have both. An unconstrained power to make law is inconsistent with constitutionalism. Within a constitutional order, the authority to make law is always itself constituted and thus subject to constitutional limits. So if Austin was right about the nature of law, then what we call the rule of law is not realizable. Ultimately, it always collapses into a particular form of the rule of man. But the rule of law is realizable, or at least it would seem to be. It is, or seems to be, realized (at least to a very high degree) in many contemporary constitutional states: England, the United States, Japan, Costa Rica, and so on. If it is realizable, then Austin's theory of law must be rejected as an inaccurate description and explanation of law. Or so Hart argues.

Someone eager to defend Austin might argue that even in a genuine constitutional system, there is still a sovereign standing beyond the reach of positive law or constitutional limit. The positive law, including constitutional law, might be said to extend to the sovereign's private identity or personal capacities but not to his or her official identity or public capacities as sovereign. As the official public lawmaker, the sovereign might be said to stand beyond the law, outside the legal system, subject perhaps to divine law, but not to the positive or constitutional law of the state.

But as Hart points out, this argument won't do. It presupposes some legal, presumably constitutional, basis for distinguishing the official identity and public capacities of the sovereign from his or her private identity and personal capacities. But how is one to describe and explain the basis for this distinction? If the distinction is grounded in the law—say, constitutional law—then there is no Austinian sovereign standing outside and beyond the reach of the legal system. If the distinction is not grounded in the law, then constitutionalism really is—our everyday experience of contemporary constitutional states notwithstanding—just an illusion. Neither alternative leaves Austin with a very plausible theory.

Convinced that Austin's conception of the sovereign and its relationship to law constitutes the Achilles heel of his view, Hart presses his criticism with a kind of thought experiment. Imagine a simple society within which Rex I is the Austinian sovereign. Rex I makes many laws, unconstrained by any constitutional limits. What he commands is recognized by all and enforced by officials as law. After many years of ruling, he dies. His son, Rex II, ascends to the throne. Suppose Rex II ascends on a Tuesday. Is he the new sovereign capable of making law on that day? On Austin's view, he cannot be. On the day he ascends to the throne, the bulk of the population cannot yet be in the habit of obeying him, and he cannot yet be in the habit of obeying no one else. (He was, presumably, just the day before in the habit of obeying Rex I.) Habits of obedience arise and exist only over stretches of time, and when Rex II first ascends to the throne, not enough time will have passed for any habits of obedience to develop, whether of the population to him or of him to anyone else. So, on Austin's account, it looks like there can be no new sovereign immediately or shortly after Rex I dies. Only after new habits of obedience develop can there be a new sovereign. But then no new law can be made immediately or shortly after Rex I dies. With no sovereign, lawmaking must come to a stop.

In fact, all law must cease to exist after Rex I dies. Once Rex I is dead, the sanctions he threatened for noncompliance with his commands are no longer credible. He's dead. And neither Rex II nor anyone else can recommand Rex I's commands after his death, thereby securing their continued existence as law. This is because after Rex I's death, neither Rex II nor anyone else is sovereign. Even if Rex II could make a credible threat of sanction for noncompliance with his commands, no one is yet in the habit of obeying him. Furthermore, even if there were a new sovereign immediately after Rex I's death, recommanding all his commands is not something that can be done in an afternoon. Rex I's commands could continue as law after his death only if the new sovereign could be said to command them tacitly. But we've already seen why such appeals to tacit commands are suspect.

The upshot here is that on Austin's view there seems no way of avoiding the conclusion that after Rex I's death, his kingdom necessarily must pass through a period of lawlessness and anarchy until some new sovereign emerges out of the habits of obedience manifest in observable behavior. As a matter of description and explanation, this claim cannot be right. It flies in the face of too much experience. Within constitutional states, the law continues in its existence through such changes in ruler(s) all the time.

Even in a simple society ruled by a powerful monarch, there is typically an orderly succession upon the death of the king or queen to the next monarch in line. But Austin's theory leaves this phenomenon unexplained and unexplainable. What might explain it? How about this: The authority of the monarch to rule is not a function simply of his or her brute power over subjects as an Austinian sovereign, but rather of his or her satisfying the conditions of some general rule that picks out who, in fact, is the monarch and that invests the monarch with constituted lawmaking authority. It is the existence of such a rule—essentially a constitutional rule—that explains why even simple monarchies typically manage an orderly succession upon the death of the king or queen and why they do not necessarily pass through a period of lawlessness and anarchy.

But then, what is fundamental to the existence of law is not the will, commands, or power of some Austinian sovereign but rather a general rule constituting and determining who, in fact, has legitimate lawmaking authority, whether king, queen, parliament, or what-have-you. It is the existence of some such rule that explains how within nearly all legal systems, both the authority to make law and the validity of the laws previously made typically endure, notwithstanding changes in the identity of the lawmaker(s). "Sovereigns" exist only through such rules. Because such rules are more basic than the "sovereigns" they constitute, we can explain the evident fact of constitutional states and the continuity of their legal systems by appeal to them. Of course, we'll have to give up the Austinian idea that the law arises out of the unconstrained will of a sovereign. We'll also have to explain the nature of such foundational rules and their relationship to ordinary legal rules, the laws made by those with lawmaking authority.

It is tempting to say in Austin's defense that neither Rex I nor Rex II is sovereign as an individual person. Rather, the office they each occupy in succession is sovereign. This office remains continuous, even as the individuals occupying it change. Thus, there is no necessary period of lawlessness and anarchy after Rex I's death. This is a plausible thing to say, but not as a defense of Austin. If it is the office that is sovereign and not Rex I and II as individual persons, then neither Rex I nor Rex II as individual persons can create the office that is sovereign. But then we need an account of how the office of sovereign is legally created. It can't be both legally constituted and the office from and through which all law is created.

Perhaps it is time to give up on the Austinian command theory of law and to see whether a better theory might be constructed out of the idea of law arising out of some sort of interplay between various kinds of rules and rule-following behavior.

THE NATURE OF RULES AND RULE-FOLLOWING

Convinced that the Austinian account of law in terms of commands, sanctions, and sovereigns cannot be made good, Hart proposes an alternative account in terms of rules and rule-following behavior. He remains committed, with Austin, to developing a theory of law from the external point of view. And he has the same phenomena in view: the legal systems of England, the United States, France, and so on. But Hart describes, analyzes, and explains these phenomena not in terms of a subject population habitually obeying a sovereign *as a rule*, as if perhaps by blind habit or merely out of fear of the sovereign's power, but rather in terms of both rulers and ruled acting as they do *because there is a rule* that tells them to do so. If we want to understand what law is, Hart argues, we must refer to rules and rule-following behavior, or to rules as reasons for acting.

But what is a rule? What is rule-following behavior? How do we know the difference between a population behaving a certain way merely *as a rule* or out of habit and a population behaving the same way *because there is a rule* and thus with reason? Suppose we see a population within which members always give one another a hug when they first see each other on any given day. What determines whether this population is behaving as it does merely as a rule (out of habit) or because there is a rule (and thus a reason) that its members are following? The answer, Hart claims, is that the internal beliefs or normative attitudes of the members of the population determine the nature of their conduct. If they think of themselves as bound, obligated, or normatively directed to give one another hugs when they first see one another on any given day, then they're acting as they do because they are following a rule that requires such hugging. They are not simply acting out of habit, behaving as a rule in a regular and predictable way. They are acting as they do because there is a rule and therefore *a reason*.

But how do we know the internal beliefs or normative attitudes of the members of our hugging population? We must infer them, Hart maintains, from observable conduct. If failures to hug in the described manner generate offense, harsh words, condemnatory judgments, shame, social sanction, and so on, then that is evidence that the regular hugging is being done because there is a rule the members of the population are following, and they regard that rule as giving them a reason to hug and are not hugging merely out of habit. If inquiries about whether it is okay not to hug generate long lectures on the obligation to hug, that is further evidence. On the other hand, if such failures to hug generate only surprise, head scratching, and a bit of social awkwardness, but no negative judgments or harsh words, then that is evidence of there being no rule requiring hugging and no reason to hug—thus, the behavior is being done merely as out of habit. There may be an explanation for such habitual behavior—perhaps people hug as they do because of some primitive instinct—but the explanation will have, for those engaged in it, no normative force. It won't count as a reason.

The key point Hart makes is that it's not possible to understand the nature of rules and rule-following behavior without making reference to the internal or normative point of view of those subject to the rules or engaged in the rule-following behavior. This doesn't mean that one must take up or occupy that point of view to describe, analyze, and explain the existence of rules or rule-following behavior. It just means one must make reference to it.

Austin tried to describe, analyze, and explain law as a social phenomenon without making any reference to the internal or normative point of view of those whose conduct constituted the phenomenon. This left him unable to conceptualize law—both its validity or existence and its normative authority—in terms of rules and rule-following behavior. For Hart, neither the existence or validity nor the normative authority of the law can be accounted for from the external point of view without reference to rules and rule-following. And that means any adequate account of law from the external point of view must make a necessary reference to the internal, normative point of view of those participating in the legal system. Hart does not think we need necessarily to know why those participating in the legal system understand themselves to be bound by the rules or to engage in the rule-following behavior essential to their legal order. We need only know that they do, and this we can determine as an empirical matter of social fact simply through careful observation of their behavior.

On Hart's view, all rules give normative direction, but not all rules bind or obligate. Some give only loose normative direction. Rules bind or obligate only when they require conduct usually thought to be important to some significant social good, when they are generally followed, and when violations are regularly and strongly criticized (or worse) in relatively robust, normative language. For many social and moral rules, such as the rules regarding inappropriate physical contact or promise keeping, these conditions are met. These rules, then, give rise to social and moral obligations or duties. In contrast, if there is today a general social rule requiring men to remove their hats upon entering a church, it probably only gives loose normative direction. Were we to observe general social behavior, we'd probably find that the conditions necessary to an obligation or duty for men to remove their hats in church are not met, even if the conditions necessary to there being a rule that they remove their hats in church are met. Men usually remove their hats when they enter a church. And we can see that they do so because there is a social rule requiring them to do so and not merely because they do it out of habit. But we can also see that that social rule is not now regarded as important to some significant social good, and although noncompliance is met with reminders to remove the cap or disappointed looks, it is not met with very strong and sustained social criticism and pressure to conform.

LAW AS A SYSTEM OF RULES

So much for the nature of rules and rule-following behavior in general. What does all this have to do with law, legal obligations, and so on? At first blush, the answer is not altogether clear. After all, we generally don't think we need to observe the behavior of a population to determine whether a particular legal rule exists. We need only consult the relevant law books or a competent legal official. And we generally don't think that whether the members of a given population have a specific legal obligation turns on how widely the relevant rule is internalized or internally accepted or how important the required conduct is to a significant social good. There are many laws requiring or forbidding conduct about which people are largely indifferent as a matter of their internal beliefs or attitudes. There are also many laws concerning matters of little social significance. Yet these laws presumably still give rise to legal obligations. Indeed, if ignorance is no excuse, then we recognize that we might have legal obligations arising out of rules with respect to which we have no internal beliefs or attitudes at all. This makes legal rules and obligations look very different from moral or social rules and obligations. Thus, if Hart is correct that law is fundamentally a matter of rules and rule-following behavior, it must be so in a distinctive and complex way. Legal rules must be different from moral or social rules more generally. But how?

Hart draws out the difference by contrasting mature legal systems with systems of only moral and social rules. Imagine a very primitive prelegal society. There are many moral and social rules, some of which give rise to duties or obligations. The existence of these rules is made manifest through convergent patterns of behavior, evidencing the internal beliefs and attitudes essential to rule-following. About such a society we can say the following: First, the rules in this society can change only through changes in the behavior patterns and internal beliefs and attitudes of its members. This means the rules can change only slowly and incrementally. The society has no mechanism for quickly and decisively changing its moral and social rules. Second, the only way to determine what the rules are in this society is to observe general patterns of social behavior over time. So long as members manage to use their rules in relatively stable ways, this may not prove a serious problem. But suppose members find themselves in a situation in which two rules seem to conflict, or in which it's unclear whether any rule applies, or in which they disagree among themselves over what a rule requires. In these cases, they'll want to know what the governing rule is. But they have no mechanism for determining what the governing rule is. Although they certainly follow and use moral and social rules, they have no authoritative way of validating the existence of these rules, settling conflicts between them, and so on. Third, the only way to enforce the rules in this society is through ad hoc acts of criticism, censure, punishment, and so on. There is no official, institutional, regular procedure for the consistent general or collective enforcement of the rules.

So, in this prelegal society with only moral and social rules, the rules exist only in and through the behavior of the society's members. The rules have no "official" existence. There is no authoritative way to validate the rules and thus no authoritative way to settle conflicts between them. There is also no authoritative way to change the rules or to adopt new rules on short notice. The rules arise and change only as the society's members adopt the necessary beliefs and normative attitudes toward shared patterns of behavior. Finally, the normative authority of the rules is purely a function of those beliefs and attitudes. As they weaken, the rules lose their normative authority—first giving loose direction (as the pirate captain in the movie *Pirates of the Caribbean* says of the pirate code, " 'Tis more like guidelines than rules"), then losing normative force altogether.

Now, compare the foregoing to a society with a legal system. With the introduction of law or a legal system, it becomes possible to validate the legal rules authoritatively, to change them quickly as needed, to determine their content and to resolve conflicts between them, and to enforce them in a consistent institutionalized manner through designated officials. Further, with the introduction of law or

30

a legal system, the normative authority of the legal rules depends only on their status as valid legal rules and thus remains consistent through changing beliefs and attitudes within the subject population. The law binds or obligates until it is revoked or repealed, regardless of how those subject to it feel about it. In terms of securing social order and giving normative direction in anything other than very small primitive societies, Hart argues, the advantages of law or a legal system should be evident. The law cannot replace moral and social rules; these rules are always necessary. But the development of the law is a major step forward when it comes to the organization and normative structure of social life.

So a system of legal rules is very different from any set of moral or social rules. But what precisely accounts for this difference? It is the two-tiered structure and systemic unity of legal rules. The law exists always through a union of two kinds of rules that exist and operate at different levels. This is what distinguishes the law from social and moral rules more generally. Within the law, there are primary rules that require, forbid, or recommend behavior. There are also secondary rules that govern the authoritative identification, the making and changing, and the adjudication and enforcement of the primary rules. With respect to social and moral rules, there are only primary rules. There are no secondary rules governing how the primary rules of social etiquette or morality are to be validated, changed, adjudicated, or enforced. Unlike social and moral rules, which can exist purely as primary rules, legal rules always and only exist where there is a systemic union of primary and secondary rules, on Hart's view. It is this systemic union of two kinds of rules, not commands given by sovereigns, that is the foundation or essential core of law.

THE RULE OF RECOGNITION

The most basic of the secondary rules within any legal system is what Hart calls the rule of recognition. It is the rule that sets the criterion or criteria that must be met for any other rule to count as a real or valid legal rule and thus to give rise to genuine legal obligations. If the rule of recognition sets out multiple criteria, they must be ordered hierarchically, with one criterion supreme. Without a supreme criterion, the rule of recognition could not authoritatively determine which rules are the valid legal rules within the system. Rules regarding the making, changing, adjudicating, and enforcing of the law are all subject or subordinate to the rule of recognition. The rule of recognition is the master rule.

Every legal system depends on or presupposes a rule of recognition. However, the rule of recognition is never itself a valid legal rule. It does not exist as a *legal* rule. Rather, it is the rule in terms of which other rules are identified or validated as legal rules. It identifies the sources of valid law. If the rule of recognition is "whatever the king says is law," then it is the king's utterances to which we look for valid law. But the rule of recognition itself—the rule "whatever the king says is law"—is not and cannot be itself a valid law. It does not and cannot validate itself. It is like Kelsen's *grundnorm*. So what kind of a rule is it?

The rule of recognition is, Hart insists, a social rule. It does not exist by virtue of satisfying any particular criterion of legal validity. Rather, it exists in the way any social rule exists, through the convergent behavior and internal beliefs and normative attitudes of those engaged in that behavior. Here the relevant behavior is that of those who assert official authority within the legal system. The rule of recognition exists as part of the internalized norms governing their shared practice of validating, making, adjudicating, and enforcing law in particular ways.

Suppose, in a given population, that most people claiming to exercise official or legal power treat whatever the king says as law in a way that suggests they are doing so because there is a rule or because they are following a rule, namely the rule that whatever the king says is law. "That the king said it" is for them a reason for thinking that "it" is valid or authoritative as law. In this context, there exists a rule of recognition—namely, "whatever the king says is law." But this rule exists only as a social rule. It is not itself a valid legal rule. And no one participating in the legal system would ever cite *its existence* as a reason or justification for any particular judgment. They would simply *use* the rule. When asked why they think a particular law is valid, they would say "because the king said so." In saying this, they would *use* the rule of recognition as a guide to their reasoning about law. When asked why they think a particular law is valid, they would not say "because we have a rule of recognition according to which whatever the king says is law." That response would cite *the existence* of the rule as a reason, which would immediately invite inquiries into the legal validity or authoritative status of the alleged rule of recognition—What makes it legally valid? Ultimately, to avoid an infinite regress, the validity of legal rules must be a function of something other than a valid legal rule.

So, from the internal point of view of participants in a legal practice, such as the legal officials, the rule of recognition is something they use. It exists, and can be seen from the external point of view to exist, by virtue of their beliefs and attitudes toward their shared practice. But it's not something they can point to from their internal point of view as participants in that practice as something that is legally valid or that exists as a legal rule.

The existence or validity of all the legal rules within any legal system, then, is a function of their relationship to the rule of recognition presupposed by the system as a whole and used by participants within it, at least the officials. What is fundamental to see here is that the existence or validity of the legal rules within the system is determined purely by the rule of recognition. The rule of recognition depends for its existence on the behavior, beliefs, and attitudes of participants—at least officials—in the legal system. But the legal rules depend for their existence or validity only on the rule of recognition, which exists as a matter of social fact.

As a social rule, the rule of recognition, unlike the legal rules it validates, cannot be changed at a moment's notice. It can change only slowly and over time as the behaviors, beliefs, and attitudes (of officials and others) through which it exists shift and change. If the rule of recognition is "whatever the king says is law," then the king can change the law on Tuesday morning. But on Tuesday morning, neither the king nor anyone else can make it no longer the case that "whatever the king says is law." That can be accomplished only through manifest changes over time in the behavior, beliefs, and attitudes of those participating in the legal system, especially officials.

The rule of recognition must vest some determinate official (the king, parliament, the court, etc.) with final authority over questions regarding the validity of legal rules. It is tempting to think that to have final authority is to have unlimited authority. But this is false. In a baseball game, there is an official who has final say over whether a pitch is a strike. But it doesn't follow that the official can say whatever he wants. He must follow the rule. Of course, he might get things wrong and declare a strike what was really a ball. But we generally know the difference between a standard baseball game within which officials follow the rules regarding strikes, even if they sometimes make mistakes, and a "game" within which officials follow no rule and simply declare strikes however they see fit. The law is like a standard baseball game; it is not the "game" of "umpire's discretion."

Hart takes no position as to whether the rule of recognition in any legal system must include moral criteria as criteria of legal validity or as constitutional limits on lawmaking authority. On Hart's view, "whatever the king says is law" and "whatever the king ordains for the common good of the subject population is law" are both candidate rules of recognition. So Hart does not go as far, say, as John Locke in holding that lawmaking authority is always and everywhere necessarily subject to moral constraints. But Hart does go further than Austin, and Thomas Hobbes before him, in holding that lawmaking authority is always constituted, and thus limited by a rule, and is never simply a matter of brute power or observable habits of obedience.

So what is the rule of recognition in the United States? It must be something like "whatever has been enacted pursuant to and is consistent with the U.S. Constitution is law, and the Supreme Court has final authority over what is law." This, of course, is not itself a valid law within the United States. Rather, it is a conventional social rule manifest in the behavior, beliefs, and attitudes of participants, especially officials, within the U.S. legal system. Over time, this rule may change. There may come a day when the final authority to say what the law is will rest not with the Supreme Court but, perhaps, with Congress. But if that day arrives, it will arrive not because of some determinate act of valid lawmaking but rather because of changes in the behavior, beliefs, and attitudes of officials and other participants in the U.S. legal system. (This matter is discussed at greater length in Chapter 5 on judicial review. Also discussed there is the difference between extralegal constitutional rules, like Hart's rule of recognition, and constitutional rules that have the status of valid law, like the written U.S. Constitution.) In any event, even though the Supreme Court has final authority over what the law is in the United States, that authority is not unlimited. It is, for Hart, constituted and limited by the rule of recognition from which it derives.

Hart summarizes his view as follows: The law exists always as a union of primary and secondary rules grounded in and unified as a system by a conventional social rule of recognition. The rule of recognition exists only in and through the behaviors, beliefs, and attitudes of those who hold themselves to it as a standard or norm governing their conduct. These are primarily those persons who claim a special authority under the law, the officials within the legal system. Of course, it would rarely make sense to say that a legal system exists if no one subject to it followed the legal rules valid within it. The subject population must generally comply with most or many of the valid legal rules. Where these conditions are satisfied, there is, as a matter of social fact, law. Of course, as an empirical matter, some system of sanctions may be necessary to generate widespread compliance. But no system of sanctions will prove effective unless many citizens are inclined to comply voluntarily with the law independent of any threatened sanctions. So although some system of sanctions may be contingently necessary, sanctions per se are not conceptually necessary to law.

Where there is law, there are legal obligations and rights. The normative authority of the law, its ability to underwrite obligations and rights, derives neither from morality nor from the rational self-interested fear of sanctions. It derives from the validity of the law as law, and this, in turn, derives from the rule of recognition. But why does the rule of recognition have normative authority? The normative authority of the rule of recognition must derive, as with all conventional social rules, simply from its internal acceptance by those, at least the officials within the legal system, who follow it.

At this point, Hart's view may begin to look a bit like Austin's. For it looks like Hart roots the law ultimately and simply in the will of some individual or group self-declared as "official" within the legal system and able to secure the obedience of others to its will. But there is one small difference, and it makes all the difference. Hart roots the law not in the fact of an unconstrained will or power of officials over subjects, but rather in the fact of their will as constrained by a rule. It is this small shift from Austin's view that allows Hart to characterize law as essentially a rule-governed and reason-giving practice, rather than just a complex form of might pretending to make right. As Hart puts it, a gunman unconstrained by rules might "oblige" persons to act in various ways, but only officials acting for reasons given by rules can subject persons to legal "obligations" to act in various ways.

HART ON LAW AND MORALITY

Though there is, for Hart, a necessary conceptual connection between law and rules, there is no such connection between law and morality or moral rules. Whether X is a law is always just a function of applying the rule of recognition, which exists as a matter of social fact and need not incorporate any particular moral content. Of course, there will be many laws the content of which mirrors that of moral rules—the law against murder, for example. But the existence or validity of such laws depends not on their moral content but on their satisfying the validity criteria given by the rule of recognition.

Hart allows that a rule of recognition *might* make moral criteria into criteria of legal validity. It might make being morally sound or correct a necessary or sufficient condition of being legally valid. Indeed, a rule of recognition might include moral criteria among the supreme criteria of legal validity. The rule might be "whatever the king says is law so long as it does not violate the moral rights of his subjects." On this rule, the moral rights of subjects constitute a basic necessary condition of legal validity. But Hart insists that no rule of recognition need incorporate any moral criterion of validity to underwrite a system of valid law. Whether any particular rule of recognition does so is a matter of contingent social fact regarding the conventional social rule evidenced by the behavior, beliefs, and attitudes of the officials within the legal system. There is no necessary or conceptual connection between law and morality.

This view, finally articulated by Hart in the Postscript to the second edition of *The Concept of Law,* has been named *inclusive positivism,* or soft or incorporationist positivism, because it allows for the possibility of a rule of recognition that includes or incorporates moral criteria as criteria of legal validity. It is to be distinguished from hard or *exclusive positivism,* according to which it is conceptually impossible for a rule of recognition to include or incorporate moral criteria as criteria of legal validity. As we shall see, Hart's commitment to inclusive positivism has generated further developments and debate over the content and merits of legal positivism in general. The point to notice here, however, is that Hart allows for contingent connections between law and morality. It is the necessary or conceptual connections that he denies.

Hart recognizes another contingent, but apparently universal, connection between law and morality, at least for humans. To endure for any length of time, a legal system—at least one for humans as we know them—must secure what Hart calls a "minimum natural law content" for at least a nontrivial segment of the population. No legal system can long endure if it does not secure the common good, or at least some core components of it, for at least some members of the population (presumably in addition to the officials). A legal system must provide some protection for the life, body, liberty, and property of at least some members. If it didn't, officials would have to rely totally on coercion or the credible threat of coercion to enforce the law. And no legal system can long endure under such circumstances.

Of course, if human beings were constituted differently, perhaps with hard shells making them invulnerable to attack and with the ability to produce food through photosynthesis, then perhaps a legal system could endure without even this minimum natural law content. But so long as humans are what they are, it appears that this content must be extended to some nontrivial segment of the population in every enduring legal system. Law and morality are connected in this way. However, this connection is thin and contingent. It's thin because legal systems can exist and endure, even though many within the governed population are held as chattel slaves and denied this minimum natural law content. It's contingent because it is a function of contingent facts about human biology and so on, not a function of the essential nature or concept of law itself.

Hart acknowledges one necessary conceptual connection between law and at least one small corner of morality. Justice is a moral virtue, and one aspect of justice is what Hart calls *administrative* or *formal justice*. This is the requirement that like cases be treated alike. This aspect of justice is conceptually tied to law because it is essential to rule-following behavior. It is not possible to engage in rule-following behavior without treating like cases alike under the relevant rule. Because rule-following requires administrative or formal justice, and because law is a system of rules with the rule-following behavior of officials at its foundation, there is a necessary conceptual connection between law and this corner of morality. But this connection does not amount to much. It excludes virtually no substantive injustice, on Hart's view. In both apartheid South Africa and the antebellum United States, the rules were followed and like cases were treated alike, at least so far as the rules went. Of course, the rules were fundamentally unjust. But this is beside the point, on Hart's account. Administrative or formal justice was secured. South Africa and the United States both possessed genuine, though racist and morally defective, legal systems, and those systems imposed on those subject to them genuine legal obligations, at least on Hart's view. What the law is is one thing, what it ought to be is another. Hart affirms this central positivist thesis.

INCLUSIVE AND EXCLUSIVE POSITIVISM

Several lines of criticism have been advanced against Hart's positivism. One in particular has generated a split within the positivist camp. Early on, several critics noted that in familiar legal systems, judges often resolve cases by reference to certain moral principles—principles of fairness, equity, due process, and so on. When this happens, one of two things must be going on, from Hart's positivist perspective.

One possibility is that judges often confront cases in which there is, in fact, no determinate governing law, according to the rule of recognition. With no governing law to apply, they must "make new law" to settle the dispute at hand. They cannot make statutes, of course. They can't literally legislate from the bench. But they can and presumably should resolve the disputes brought before them. And while they must do so according to the law, if there is in fact no existing law to apply, then arguably they must make new law, or at least law for the case they confront. In so doing, a judge may (but need not) appeal to what he or she regards as sound moral principles—not because they are law, but rather because there is no law, and sound moral principles are as good a guide as anything for determining what the law ought to be. In principle, there is no reason why a complex rule of recognition could not authorize judges to make valid law in those cases for which there is no already existing applicable valid law. Judges would then be exercising their official "judicial discretion" whenever they turned to moral principles to resolve a case. In any legal system with a rule of recognition that did not incorporate moral criteria as criteria of legal validity, the exercise of judicial discretion in this way would undoubtedly prove unavoidable and would therefore eventually be authorized itself by the rule of recognition.

The other possibility is that when a judge appeals to a moral principle or principles to resolve a case, he or she does so because the principle(s) are in fact already part of the law according to the rule of recognition. As already noted, Hart allows (this is his inclusive positivism) that moral principles of justice, fairness, equity, and the like may be part of the law if the rule of recognition makes them so—for example, by making moral soundness and relevance criteria of legal validity. In any legal system with such a rule of recognition, judges must appeal to the moral principles so made part of the existing law whenever they bear on the cases before them. Perhaps, then, at least sometimes when judges appeal to moral principles to resolve cases before them, it is because in their legal system the rule of recognition incorporates moral criteria as criteria of legal validity. Each of these alternatives presents problems for the Hartian legal positivist. Consider the first possibility. Whenever this possibility is realized, judges not only make, instead of apply, the law (at least for the cases before them), they also retroactively apply the law they make. But the retroactive application of law is generally thought to constitute a failure or violation of the ideal rule of law. This might seem a minor matter were it to happen only now and again. But judges draw on moral principles quite often when resolving disputes brought before them. And the idea that they are retroactively applying the law they make in all these cases is not a very attractive one, even if the rule of recognition generally authorized them to make law in such cases.

But perhaps whenever we find judges appealing to moral principles to resolve cases before them, we will find that the rule of recognition in their legal system incorporates moral criteria as legal criteria. This would actually fit better with what judges say about their adjudication of such cases—for they say that they discover or discern and then apply already existing law, not that they make new law and then retroactively apply it. Surely Hart formulates his view as a kind of "inclusive positivism" so as to bring under the umbrella of his positivist theory just this sort of adjudication.

But inclusive positivism is not without its own difficulties. First, if a rule of recognition makes some moral principles part of the law by virtue of their moral soundness and relevance, then it may seem unlikely that legal officials will in fact evidence the sort of convergent behavior essential to the existence of the rule of recognition as a conventional social rule in the first place. After all, judges and other legal officials are likely very often to disagree—indeed, they often do disagree—over the soundness and relevance of particular moral principles, especially as those principles are rendered sufficiently concrete so as to ground a legal judgment in a particular case. This is precisely why judges often disagree among themselves over how to resolve a particular case before them. But if judges and other legal officials are bound to disagree over the soundness and relevance of moral principles eligible for validation as law, then those officials are unlikely to behave in anything resembling the relatively uniform manner Hart requires in order to infer the existence of a rule of recognition as a conventional social rule. So it looks like if the governing criteria of legal validity make some moral principles into valid law, then those governing criteria of legal validity cannot be given by the sort of social rule of recognition Hart envisions— certainly not one we could say, from the external point of view, exists as a matter of social fact.

A second difficulty is that the law always presents itself as a genuine and independent practical authority. It purports to give those subject to it self-standing, authoritative reasons for acting. These reasons might be outweighed, of course, by other considerations, all things considered. We might have compelling moral or prudential reasons not to do what the law tells us to do. But the law at least purports to give us, so far as it speaks, authoritative reasons for acting. We need only know what the law is to have an authoritative reason to act in a particular way—namely, legally. This is just what underwrites the law's distinctive advantage as a mechanism for social control.

In any legal system we observe, the law claims normative authority. Suppose the rule of recognition incorporates moral criteria as criteria of legal validity, as inclusive positivism allows. So the rule says, among other things, that to be valid, laws must be fair or substantively just, or at least not too unfair or unjust, or some such thing. Now, given this sort of rule of recognition, everyone must deliberate over the moral merits of any purported law before they can take that law to be valid and thus to provide them with an independent reason to do this or that in any particular circumstance. But then the law is not really authoritative for them simply as law. By itself it makes no practical difference to their reasoning. Everyone must morally deliberate about what to do in any case. That's just what it means to be a moral person. The law provides no independent reason to act this or that way because according to the rule of recognition there is no separate legal reason to so act unless there is also a moral reason to so act. But then the normative authority of the law is not self-standing or independent; indeed, it makes no (or at least very little) practical difference.

Someone keen to defend Hart's inclusive positivism might argue that the moral criteria incorporated as criteria of legal validity into a rule of recognition need not function as the epistemic criteria through which any of us identifies or knows what the law is in our practical deliberations. Citizens or subjects may know what the law is just by reading the paper or listening to what officials say. And officials may know what the law is through forms of reasoning that do not simply collapse into moral reasoning. The rule of recognition is perhaps not mainly a rule for identifying or knowing what the law is. Perhaps it is rather the rule that validates or authenticates the law. In this regard, moral criteria could play an important role without destroying the independent practical authority of the law. Imagine a rule of recognition says, among other things, that unfair laws are invalid, even if properly enacted by the legislature. The legislature passes a law against murder. I need only read the papers to know about the law. And the law gives me a reason not to murder. But suppose the law is written so as to apply to persons who act involuntarily—say, while in their sleep or while having an unforeseeable seizure. So written, the law is manifestly unfair. Its validity is therefore compromised, which will be important to officials as they determine what to do with the law, how to work it into the system of law overall, and so on. But the fact that the unfairness of the law compromises its validity or authenticity under the rule of recognition, with implications for how officials apply and integrate it into the system of law overall, need not necessarily render the law less than authoritative for me or anyone else engaged in practical deliberation over how to act. It may still make a practical difference for me. I have a reason not to murder and that reason is given by the law—period.

Perhaps. But this defense of Hart's inclusive positivism turns on an awfully fine distinction between those criteria through which we know or identify valid law in our practical deliberations and those that in fact validate or authenticate valid law. The distinction is not totally opaque. We may be able to identify or pick out a genuine Picasso from a set of frauds in all sorts of ways. Perhaps we simply have a feel for Picassos. But what makes a genuine Picasso genuine is that it was created by Picasso. And that's true no matter how we identify it as genuine. The question, then, is whether the rule of recognition is best understood as giving only the real criteria of legal validity or authenticity or as giving also the epistemic criteria by which we who are subject to law pick out valid or authentic laws when exercising our practical judgment. If the former, then perhaps Hart's inclusivist positivism can be salvaged against the exclusive positivist objection that if moral criteria count as criteria of legal validity then the legal validity of a law will by itself make no or little difference in the practical reasoning of those subject to it.

At this point I must leave it to the interested reader to further pursue this contest between inclusive and exclusive versions of legal positivism on her own. Space constraints do not permit me to pursue the matter further here.

Convinced that the, to many apparently intractable, conflicts between exclusive and inclusive positivists signal a deeper defect with legal positivism in general, some have turned, to varying degrees, to the natural law tradition for the resources from which to construct a different theory of law altogether. It is to the family of natural law theories that we turn in the next chapter (though we will have occasion there, in the context of discussing Dworkin's criticisms of Hart, to return to the merits of inclusive and exclusive positivism).

In the end, legal positivism today remains organized around the following central claims: First, a general, descriptive theory of law from the external point of view of a nonparticipant observer is possible and philosophically desirable (and morally unobjectionable). Second, such a theory must explain what it is for a law to exist as a valid or genuine law and to possess normative authority simply by virtue of being valid or genuine. Third, the existence or validity of law is always a matter of social fact. In this way, the law constitutes an autonomous or self-standing practical authority. Therefore, fourth, there is no necessary conceptual connection between law and morality, at least when studied from the external point of view.

SELECTED BIBLIOGRAPHY

Sources on Legal Positivism

Austin, John. *The Province of Jurisprudence Determined*. (London, UK: Weidenfeld and Nicolson), 1955.

Coleman, Jules, ed. *Hart's Postscript: Essays on the Postscript of the Concept of Law*. (Oxford, UK: Oxford University Press), 2001.

George, Robert. *The Autonomy of Law: Essays on Legal Positivism*. (Oxford, UK: Oxford University Press), 1995.

Hart, H.L.A. *The Concept of Law*, 2nd ed. (Oxford, UK: Oxford University Press), 1997.

Kelsen, Hans. *The Pure Theory of Law*. (Berkeley, CA: University of California Press), 1968.

Kramer, Matthew. *In Defense of Legal Positivism: Law Without the Trimmings*. (Oxford, UK: Oxford University Press), 1999.

Marmor, Andrei. *Interpretation and Legal Theory*. (Oxford, UK: Oxford University Press), 1992.

Postema, Gerald. *Bentham and the Common Law Tradition*. (Oxford, UK: Oxford University Press), 1986.

Raz, Joseph. *The Authority of Law*. (Oxford, UK: Oxford University Press), 1979.

————. *The Concept of a Legal System: An Introduction to the Theory of Legal Systems*, 2nd ed. (Oxford, UK: Oxford University Press), 1980.

Waluchow, Wil. *Inclusive Positivism*. (Oxford, UK: Oxford University Press), 1994.

————. "The Many Faces of Legal Positivism," *Toronto Law Journal*, vol. 48.3, pp. 387–449, 1998.

3

On Natural Law Theories

LEGAL POSITIVISM AND NATURAL LAW: COMMON AND CONTESTED GROUND

It is today still standard to characterize legal positivism and natural law theory as thesis and antithesis. For example, legal positivism denies, while natural law theory affirms, a necessary conceptual connection between law and morality. But the relationship between legal positivism and natural law theory is probably not quite this simple. One reason for this is that just as there are many legal positivisms, there are also many natural law theories.

In its traditional or classical form, natural law theory predates modern legal positivism and the social scientific and analytic study of law from which it springs. Traditional natural law theories aim to provide normative direction. Most fully exemplified by the work of the medieval monk Thomas Aquinas, they offer a kind of comprehensive moral theory. Law, legal obligations, and so forth are taken up as just some of the many matters necessarily addressed by such a theory. The name "natural law," when applied to traditional or classical natural law theories, derives from the fact that they typically assert that there is inherent in the world or in human nature a single, robust, substantive, universal moral order just waiting to be discovered by reason. There are today contemporary advocates of various traditional or classical natural law theories.

Traditional or classical natural law theories usually proceed from and are addressed to the normative internal point of view. There is

44

therefore no necessary conflict between traditional or classical natural law theories and modern legal positivism, because the latter proceeds from the external point of view and offers only a descriptive and analytic thesis about the nature of law or legal systems. However, there is an apparent conflict between legal positivism and modern natural law theories.

Since its development in the hands of Bentham and Austin, legal positivism has had its critics. They have characterized legal positivism as, variously, conceptually confused, descriptively false, morally pernicious, trivially true (and thus undeserving of the status of a theory of law), or significantly true but fully incorporated within natural law theory itself. One important strand of criticism has centered on the positivist thesis that there is no necessary conceptual connection between law and morality. Modern or contemporary natural law theories typically deny this thesis without taking a stand on whether there is inherent in the world or human nature a single, robust, substantive, universal moral order just waiting to be discovered by reason. In this sense, modern natural law theories appear to conflict directly with legal positivism.

Indeed, proponents of each view have long thought themselves opposed to one another. Bentham and Austin developed legal positivism, in significant part, as a reaction to a kind of natural law theorizing, epitomized by Blackstone's commentaries on English law, which they thought pernicious. Later, during the high-water mark of modern legal positivism, modern natural law theorists, such as Lon Fuller and Ronald Dworkin, began to assert themselves over and against a kind of legal positivist theorizing that had been widespread in Europe prior to World War II, which they thought pernicious. Indeed, shortly after World War II, the German philosopher of law Gustav Radbruch renounced his earlier positivist views in favor of a natural law theory precisely because he thought the widespread teaching of positivist views had led German citizens to assume that if a law was valid, they were in fact obligated to comply regardless of its moral merits. (This, of course, reflects confusion over the positivist thesis, which concerns only legal, not moral, obligations and which allows for the possibility that one might have a moral obligation to violate his or her legal obligations. Hart pointed this out to Radbruch in a famous exchange.)

Both traditional or classical and modern natural law theories foreground key linkages between law and morality. But different natural law theorists insist on different sorts of links and, thus, reject the so-called positivist separation thesis (that there is no necessary conceptual connection between law and morality) in different ways and for different reasons. Aquinas argued that the normative authority of the law depends, in the paradigmatic case, on its being directed at the common good, consistent with the moral law, and issued by one who holds rightful authority. Lon Fuller argued that there can be no system of law, and thus no individual laws, without fidelity to a number of procedural values tied to the systemic function of law. Ronald Dworkin argued that in familiar advanced legal systems, every morally neutral description of the law from the external point of view is really just a moral interpretation of the law proceeding from and addressed to the internal point of view of real or imagined participants. There is common ground here, but it lies more in a shared anti-positivist stance toward legal theory than in any thesis common to all.

THOMAS AQUINAS AND CLASSICAL NATURAL LAW THEORY

Natural law theory finds its first full expression in the work of Thomas Aquinas. Aquinas was himself largely synthesizing themes and distinctions already familiar from Aristotelian, Stoic, and Christian thought. His natural law theory is a comprehensive moral theory. Both it and the theory of law it contains remain objects of interpretive disagreement.

Aquinas's theory of law begins with God. God created the universe and everything in it. And because God is perfect, God did so not willy-nilly, but with a perfectly rational and reasonable plan. Being perfectly rational and reasonable, this plan aims at and instantiates the Good. Only the Good constitutes a final or noninstrumental reason for acting; it is what reason is finally aimed at for its own sake. Aquinas identified God's plan for the universe as the eternal law. The eternal law is the rational and reasonable plan or standards that God wills as binding on the entire universe—both the natural world (you, me, the trees and animals, Earth, galaxies, etc.) and the supernatural world (our souls, the angels, etc.). Although Aquinas held that the eternal law flows from God's will, he did not think that God was free to will any eternal law whatsoever. Rather, the eternal law is necessarily rational and reasonable and perfectly aimed at the Good. Its existence (and thus the universe) may depend on God's willing it, but as an expression of perfect reason (aimed at the Good), the eternal law expresses God's true and rational nature. It does not exactly bind God—for, being perfect, God has no inclination to deviate from perfect reason and thus could not experience the eternal law as binding. But still, God could not have created any other sort of law (or universe).

For Aquinas, God does not stand outside the circle of eternal law. Even though God is the supreme lawmaker and the creator of the universe, God's authority is constituted. It is constituted by God's perfect reason, which is necessarily aimed at the Good. Aquinas, then, was not a voluntarist. The normative authority of the eternal law does not derive exclusively from the unconstrained will and supreme power of God.

The eternal law governs everything in the universe. It therefore binds everything that has a physical or natural existence. In this aspect, it is known as the natural law. The natural law applies to physically existing things without a will (rocks, insects) as well as those with a will (humans). In the former case, the natural law is known to us as the laws of science. In the latter case, it is known as the moral law, because it binds beings who have a will of their own and thus the ability to act contrary to the natural law applicable to them. The atoms making up this page, the tree growing outside my window, or the (nonvoluntary) beating of my heart are all governed by the natural law in the form of empirical scientific laws discoverable through careful description and rational inquiry. My choice as to which words to put on this page, whether to cut the tree growing outside my window, or whether purposefully now to bring my life to an end are all governed by the natural law in the form of a normative moral law, again discoverable through careful observation and rational inquiry. The natural moral law binds, not through the causal workings of the world, but rather through the moral "ought." Conscience, the voice of reason aimed at the Good, is its inner voice.

The eternal law also binds all supernatural elements within the universe—the angels, our souls, and so on. In this aspect, it is known as the divine law. The divine law cannot really be known through careful observation and rational inquiry (what would we observe?). God must reveal it to us. Being generous and cognizant of human limitations and fallibility, God reveals not only the otherwise unknowable divine law governing such matters as the salvation of our souls but also much of the otherwise knowable moral law.

The natural law and the divine law must, of course, be both consistent and coherent. There can be no conflicts. Both belong to the eternal law, itself a perfectly rational and reasonable plan aimed at the Good. The natural and divine law, however, do not together exhaust the eternal law. Human beings possess reason and will, and they are inherently social and necessarily interdependent. They must, therefore, coordinate their conduct and more generally constitute themselves into communities organized as cooperative undertakings. These communities must be rationally and reasonably adapted to various geographic, demographic, economic, historical, and social conditions. Each human community, then, must have its own positive human law, a law that is binding simply because it is "posited" by the proper political authority.

The positive human law of each political community must be consistent and coherent with the natural law and divine law. But the positive human law is not given by the natural or divine law and must be created as a matter of social fact. The positive human law of any given community may be consistent and coherent with the natural and divine law in one of two ways. First, it may be entailed by it. The positive law prohibiting murder may be deduced from the natural law principle prohibiting the purposeful infliction of harm on innocents. Second, it may give concrete or determinate expression to it. The positive law setting the speed limit at 70 miles per hour on the highway may be justified as one of several possible concrete or determinate expressions of the general natural law principle that voluntary conduct ought to be undertaken so as to avoid imposing unreasonable risks on others. Both positive laws just mentioned may be said to follow from the natural law. But neither exists as valid positive human law until positively enacted as a matter of social fact.

Because the natural law aims at the Good, the positive human law of any community must aim at the common good of its members if it is to be consistent and coherent with the natural law. Because the positive law is intended to govern persons as rational social beings with a will of their own, it must be promulgated as a public standard of conduct in clear and understandable terms. And because it is to be authoritative within the community, it must be given by the person or persons possessed of legitimate or rightful authority over the community. Thus, Aquinas concluded, the positive human law is always and necessarily an ordinance of reason directed toward the common good promulgated by one who rightfully has responsibility for the community.

IS AN UNJUST LAW A LAW AT ALL?

Clearly Aquinas posited a necessary conceptual connection between law and morality. But does it follow, as many have supposed, that he was therefore committed to the claim that "an unjust law is no law at all"? And if he was, in what sense is an unjust law no law at all? Is it no law in the sense that it is not valid or genuine as a law? Or is it no law in the sense that it lacks the normative authority normally associated with laws? Or perhaps is it no law in both senses?

Neither Aquinas nor St. Augustine before him ever wrote (in Latin, of course) that "an unjust law is no law at all." Aquinas recognized that in any community, unjust laws are (and unhappily probably always will be) invoked and enforced just like any other laws. He also allowed that there may sometimes be good moral reasons to obey an unjust law—for example, when disobeying the law would do significantly more harm than good by bringing about social chaos. So an unjust law presumably is no law at all not in the sense that it doesn't exist or in the sense that we could have no reason to obey it, but rather in the sense that it lacks something essential to its distinctive normative authority as a law. If this is what Aquinas had in mind, it seems to assert what legal positivists deny—namely, that even unjust laws have the distinctive normative authority of law just in case they are valid or genuine laws. But determining just exactly what Aquinas might have had in mind is no simple matter.

THE STRONG READING

The claim that an unjust or unreasonable law is no law at all is a very strong one. It makes being just a necessary condition of legal validity, and thus the normative authority of law, in all legal systems. Legal positivists have often attributed this strong thesis to Aquinas, only to turn around and ridicule his position as self-contradictory and unhelpful nonsense. After all, unjust laws are regularly enforced. And the legal obligations they impose must have some normative weight; otherwise, they could not be outweighed by other considerations, and those disobeying them would not need to appeal to other considerations (e.g., acting for the sake of justice) to justify their disobedience.

Happily Aquinas did not, or need not be read to, endorse this strong a reading of the claim that an unjust law is no law at all. Nevertheless, it's worth noting that the claim so read is not obviously the self-contradictory and unhelpful nonsense legal positivists sometimes claim. It is not self-contradictory to say that a fake dollar bill is really no dollar bill at all or that a cubic zirconium diamond is not really a diamond. So, why is it self-contradictory to say that an unjust law is really no law at all? The problem with the claim that an unjust law is no law at all is not that it's self-contradictory. The problem is that although a fake dollar is not a real dollar for anyone interested in buying things and a cubic zirconium diamond is not a real diamond for anyone interested in fine jewelry, an unjust law is a real law for anyone concerned with identifying their legal obligations. At the least, an unjust law will be enforced, and its existence would seem to underwrite a reason for action that anyone subject to it must at least consider and weigh, even if other considerations might, in the end, justify disobedience. So, while "an unjust law is no law at all" isn't exactly self-contradictory nonsense, it is perhaps false. Now, a fake law, one I make up in my mind, that really would be no law at all.

This suggests that the claim that an unjust law is really no law at all may be read in a slightly different and weaker way so as to preserve its truth. Suppose you know a judge who is corrupt. It would not be false to say of him, "He is no judge at all." Your point would not be that he is not a real judge for any legal purpose whatsoever. You know he can and does decide cases. Your point would rather be that he is a defective judge, deficient in some important respect. This is the sense at work when a parent screams in rage at a child, "You're no child of mine," or when a patient testifies against a doctor in a malpractice case, "He's no doctor at all, just an incompetent imposter." Of course, this understanding of "an unjust law is no law at all" is plausible precisely because it departs from the strong reading given above. It does not make justice a necessary condition of legal validity; it merely counts injustice as a significant defect or perversion of law. To this thought we will have to return.

But first we should note the weakness of another argument often made by positivists against the strong reading of "an unjust law is no law at all." It is often said that it's nonsense to say that an unjust law is no law at all because unjust laws are routinely recognized as real laws by officials. If officials treat them as real laws, then they must be real laws. It's nonsense to suggest anything else. After all, officials are the experts. They know the criteria of legal validity. But this argument is not very strong. It simply assumes what is at issue. It assumes that officials, presumably in the grips of a conventionalist or positivist conception of law, are correct in their view that an unjust law is a valid or nondefective law. Of course, if you assume a conventionalist or positivist conception of law, then you'll find any natural law theory incorrect. But you can't argue against natural law theory simply by assuming the correctness of a conventionalist or positivist conception of law or legal validity. But if we don't make this assumption, then why is natural law in trouble just because officials talk as if it's false. Perhaps they're mistaken. It's been known to happen. After all, their expertise concerns the content, making, and application of the law, not the conceptual relationship between morality or justice, on the one hand, and the validity and normative authority of law simply as law, on the other.

Notwithstanding the weakness of the foregoing positivist arguments against the strong reading of "an unjust law is no law at all," the strong reading is nevertheless implausible. After all, as already noted, unjust laws seem to be real laws for many, if not all, legal purposes, even if they're also in some sense defective. They seem to underwrite legal obligations and so on. So, if there's anything to be salvaged from the claim that an unjust law is no law at all, it may have to be derived from a weaker reading.

THE WEAK READING

On the weak reading, to say that an unjust law is no law at all is to say that it is in some fundamental sense defective or a perversion, not that it is a fake or counterfeit or not really a law for any legal purpose. A spider unable to spin a web is still a spider, even though it's sufficiently defective or abnormal for us to plausibly say that it's really no spider at all. This is a common enough thought with respect to natural kinds, like spiders, roses, and so on. A rose bush that doesn't bloom is still a rose bush, though we may say to a friend it is not really a rose bush at all. But with natural kinds (spiders and rose bushes), we use nonmoral or nonevaluative criteria to determine whether an instance is defective. Whether the spider spins a web or the rose bush produces flowers is not a question of moral evaluation.

With respect to nonnatural or conventional kinds things are often more complicated. An employee who shows up to work late every other day is defective. We might even say that such an employee is no real employee at all, meaning that she is a defective or nonparadigm instance of the nonnatural kind of "employees." What an employee is, by definition, is someone who works for you when you want her to. Anyone who fails to work when asked is defective as an employee. That's just a fact tied to what we mean by the term *employee*.

Sometimes we appeal to moral or evaluative criteria to determine whether a particular instance of a nonnatural or conventional kind is defective. Such criteria may even figure as the most important in our overall judgments. A lying, cheating, lazy husband may be so defective as to count as no husband at all, whereas one who never signed his marriage certificate may be a genuine husband in all the most important respects. So, with respect to nonnatural or conventional kinds, and law is just such a kind, sometimes we invoke nonmoral or nonevaluative criteria to determine whether an instance is defective (employees are contractually bound to work for their employers; husbands sign marriage certificates), and sometimes we invoke moral or evaluative criteria (employees don't steal from their employers; husbands are honest and hard-working). With respect to some nonnatural or conventional kinds, moral or evaluative criteria seem about equally as important as nonmoral and nonevaluative criteria to any judgment of whether an instance is defective. A haiku must be a certain number of syllables in a certain order to be a haiku, but it also must possess certain aesthetic or moral qualities. Both the formal or nonevaluative and the evaluative criteria must be met.

When we use both moral or evaluative and nonmoral or nonevaluative criteria to determine which alleged instances really belong to a nonnatural conventional kind, as we do with haikus, it may sometimes be the case that an alleged instance satisfies all the nonmoral or nonevaluative criteria but falls well short of the moral or evaluative criteria. A "haiku" may possess seventeen syllables broken into lines of five, seven, and five syllables, respectively, and be about a seasonal topic but still prove fundamentally defective as a haiku because it fails to reorient the reader's attention toward the reality of the everyday in the desired way. We might then say that it is no real haiku at all. And this may well be what Aquinas intended to say about unjust laws. They may satisfy all the nonmoral or nonevaluative criteria for belonging to the nonnatural or conventional "law" but, by virtue of being unjust, fall so far short of the moral or evaluative criteria as to count as radically defective—as "no law at all." If this was Aquinas's view, then perhaps his position was neither self-contradictory nor unhelpful nonsense.

ARGUMENTS FOR THE NECESSARY CONNECTION CLAIMED BY THE WEAK READING

This brings us to the central question. Legal positivists and natural law theorists agree that positive human law is a nonnatural or conventional kind. What they disagree over is whether moral or evaluative criteria apply when it comes to determining whether any alleged instance is really an instance of the kind. Positivists deny this. Natural law theorists assert it. Why should we think that moral or evaluative criteria necessarily figure prominently in any judgment of whether a law is defective simply as an instance of law?

FINNIS'S ARGUMENT

John Finnis suggests one line of argument. Finnis, a natural law theorist committed to something very close to Aquinas's comprehensive moral theory, follows Hart in seeking a philosophically sound description of the central, or paradigm, case of law. Like Hart, Finnis thinks it is philosophically pointless to look for some definition of law in terms of necessary and sufficient conditions. What is needed is a sound and illuminating description of the central case. As Hart recognized, this paradigm case is one within which the normative authority of the law derives not from power or will or force, but from rules and reasons. And in this paradigm case, all or nearly all participants in the legal system—not just officials—internally accept most of the legal rules and thus count them as good reasons for acting one way rather than another. It's possible for a legal system to exist so long as most legal rules, especially the secondary rules, are internally accepted by the officials. But as Hart noted, this is not the paradigm case. In the paradigm case, most citizens (and not just the officials) internally accept most of the legal rules and comply with them for that reason.

But citizens might internally accept and comply with most of the legal rules for any number of reasons. What reasons will they have in the paradigm case? Finnis argues that they'll have good and sufficient—that is, decisive—reasons. But that means they'll have moral reasons, because from the internal normative point of view of persons subject to law, moral reasons usually trump all other reasons. This means that the paradigm case of law or a legal system is necessarily one in which most citizens or subjects have internally accepted most of the legal rules for good moral reasons. Legal systems or individual laws not backed by good moral reasons, then, must be judged defective or nonparadigm instances. At a minimum, this would seem to require that at least Hart's "minimum natural law content" be extended to all those subject to the law in all nondefective or paradigm instances of law.

The trouble with this line of argument is that its central premise is simply asserted, without any supporting argument. It's not obvious what supporting argument is available. The central premise is that the paradigm case of law or a legal system, that which a sound legal theory must describe and explain, is one within which those subject to the law have not only internally accepted the relevant legal rules but have done so for good and sufficient moral reasons. Why is this the paradigm case rather than one within which they merely internally accept the relevant legal rules for whatever reasons or for no particular reasons at all? Why isn't the central case one within which those subject to the law regard the fact that X is a law as a genuine reason to do as X requires? Whether they have good and sufficient moral reasons to do as X requires would seem to be a question relevant to the moral merits of the law or legal system as assessed from the internal point of view, not to its existence as a paradigm or central case as determined from the external point of view.

This is perhaps simply a standoff between Finnis and Hart. Finnis insists on describing the central or paradigm case of law *from the internal point of view* of a participant in the legal system. From that point of view—the point of view of conscience—he may be right that the central case is one within which there are good and sufficient moral reasons to obey the law. But Hart insisted on describing the central or paradigm case *from the external point of view* of a nonparticipant observer. True, Hart referenced the internal point of view of participants. He insisted (against Austin) that it's not possible to give a philosophically sound and illuminating description of law without making such a reference. It is not possible to describe law or a legal system without making reference to the internal acceptance of rules by some participants. But Hart did not venture his description of law *from* that internal point of view, and thus he could insist that it makes no difference why those subject to the law internally accept the relevant rules. All that matters is that they do. Against Hart, Finnis simply asserts the priority of the internal point of view. But this is not sufficient. The internal point of view of individual conscience is surely an important point of view from which to assess law and legal systems. It's surely the point of view from which the moral merits of the law are to be determined. But this is not an argument against Hart's claims regarding the central case being described from the external point of view of the nonparticipant observer.

As we shall see, Ronald Dworkin offers perhaps the best, even if still not decisive, argument for the primacy of the internal point of view within legal theory, and with it a plausible reading of "an unjust law is no law at all." But before turning to Dworkin's views, we must examine a second argument made by natural law theorists for the weak reading of "an unjust law is no law at all." This argument, associated most closely with Lon Fuller, insists on taking seriously the function of law or legal systems in any philosophically adequate description of them.

FULLER'S ARGUMENT

What are legal systems for? What is their function? Is it not to coordinate and govern the conduct of, even to the point of facilitating cooperation between, rational agents? Lon Fuller, a contemporary of Hart, argues that this is indeed what the law is for and that no legal system can perform this function unless it satisfies certain moral or evaluative criteria. A philosophically sound description of the central case of law, then, must posit a necessary conceptual connection between law or legal validity and some moral or evaluative criteria. Legal systems or laws that fail to satisfy these criteria must be described as defective, like a knife that won't cut.

Two questions arise immediately. First, how do we know that this is what the law is for, what its function is? Second, what specific moral or evaluative criteria must a legal system satisfy in order to be described as a nondefective instance of law?

At first glance, determining what the law or a legal system is for would seem to be relatively straightforward. It is characteristic of law or legal systems to issue and enforce rules that claim over citizens or subjects a certain authoritative status. Some laws and some legal systems are, of course, unjust or unreasonable. But that's beside the point. All laws and legal systems at least claim to give citizens or subjects authoritative reasons to act one way rather than another. It is also characteristic of law or legal systems that issuing and enforcing rules in this way tends to improve social coordination and order and thereby facilitate cooperation. So, presumably, it is to achieve this result that legal rules are issued and enforced in their characteristic ways. Because this end result is socially desirable, and because legal systems are pretty clearly conventional social artifacts (made by humans for human purposes), it makes sense to conclude that the purpose or function of legal systems is to secure this desired end result. Legal systems that fail to deliver this desired result must be judged defective. If no legal system can deliver this result without honoring certain moral norms, then any system violating those norms must be described as defective.

This looks like a pretty good argument. The trouble is that there are so many legal systems that fail to meet the necessary moral conditions and thus fail to deliver the desired end result that one wonders whether it is they, rather than those that fulfill the conditions and deliver results, that constitute the central or paradigm case to be described. In a world where there are or have been just as many broken or defective legal systems as there are functioning ones, how can we know which is which without simply assuming what we set out to prove—namely, that the functioning ones really constitute the norm or the paradigm case? How can we know that those that appear broken or defective aren't really the paradigm cases?

We could perhaps simply assume that whenever we want to determine the function of a conventional social artifact like law, we should assume as the context of our determination a world within which human beings flourishing as rational social animals is the norm. Then we would be able to say that even if there are proportionately very few instances, it is the legal systems that fulfill the relevant moral conditions and deliver the desired end results that constitute the norm. Then we'd know the function of law.

But why should we assume a world within which human beings flourish as rational social animals to be the proper context for determining the function of conventional social artifacts like law? If we assume that context, haven't we already given up on describing the law or legal systems from a purely external, nonparticipant observer point of view? After all, from that point of view, misery and suffering and irrational and self-absorbed conduct seem about as common among humans as their flourishing as rational social animals.

Thus, we are back again to an apparently dogmatic assertion by the natural law theorist about the primacy of the internal or evaluative point of view. If we look at the world from the internal moral point of view of individual conscience, then of course the norm is a world within which humans flourish as rational social animals. But that's not a descriptive claim about how the world is. It's a normative claim about how the world ought to be. And if we rely on this claim to set our benchmark for separating the central or paradigm cases of law or legal systems from the defective or deviant ones, then our separation is hardly based on a morally neutral description of the function of law as given from the external point of view. So, Fuller's argument thus far seems to make no advance over Finnis's argument above. Both argue for the weak reading of "an unjust law is no law at all" from the internal evaluative point of view of an interested participant in legal systems.

Perhaps it is time to press on to look at the moral or evaluative criteria invoked by those who defend the weak reading of "an unjust law is no law at all." But first we should pause to recall two unresolved problems. The first concerns the point of view from which the law must be described in order to be described in the most accurate and philosophically illuminating way. Is it the internal or the external perspective (assuming these are fundamentally distinct)? The second concerns the conflict between legal positivism and natural law. Is it apparent or real? If the central theses of natural law theory are all advanced from the internal point of view, then how could there be a conflict with legal positivism, the central theses of which are all advanced from the external point of view?

THE INNER MORALITY OF LAW

Defenders of the weak reading claim a variety of moral or evaluative criteria as essential to the central or paradigm cases of law or legal systems. Some, like Finnis, claim substantive criteria, effectively making Hart's minimum necessary natural law content and much more a necessary condition of a legal system or law being nondefective. Others claim procedural criteria. Fuller, for example, argues that once we understand the function of legal systems, we will see that there is a necessary *inner morality* to law or any legal system. This morality, however, is procedural. Given that law and legal systems function to coordinate and govern the cooperative conduct of rational interdependent beings, there are eight ways in which the law or a legal system can be defective, on Fuller's account. It can fail by (1) failing to issue general rules and simply governing social life in an ad hoc way. It can fail by (2) not publicly promulgating the rules, leaving those subject to them in the dark as to their existence and demands. It can fail by (3) applying the rules retrospectively or (4) changing them very frequently, destroying the ability of persons to plan according to the rules. It can fail by (5) issuing unintelligible rules or (6) contradictory rules or (7) rules requiring impossible conduct. And it can fail by (8) not enforcing the rules in a regular and reliable way.

To be sure, Fuller allows that taken as a whole, these procedural requirements set a sort of regulative ideal to which all legal systems necessarily aspire but need not, indeed cannot, perfectly attain. (e.g., sometimes rules must be changed often, or perhaps even be applied retroactively, and sometimes the generality of rules undermines their intelligibility as guides for conduct in specific cases.) So, all legal systems will prove defective to some degree. But there are defects, and there are defects. Some defects, alone or in combination, are enough to warrant the claim that a particular legal system or law is so defective that it is really no legal system or law at all, that it falls below the minimal moral standard necessarily ingredient in the rule of law and thus reduces to little more than a hodgepodge of ad hoc commands or threats.

The appeal of Fuller's account here is that it severs the natural law position from theistic assumptions essential to Aquinas's classical natural law theory as well as from the controversial substantive moral criteria of law or legal validity essential to Finnis's updated and secularized version of Aquinas's theory. What could be more obvious, Fuller invites us to think, than that ad hoc and unintelligible orders frequently changed and inconsistently and retroactively applied are not law and do not constitute a legal system? It is just not possible to govern human beings as rational social creatures in this way. Ad hoc and unintelligible orders so issued and applied are so defective as law that they really are no law at all; they constitute a legal system only in the way that a broken chain saw constitutes a chain saw. Persons subject only to such orders have no real legal obligations.

This seems correct. But why think that these procedural criteria constitute an "inner morality" of the law, establishing a necessary conceptual connection between law (at least in the central case) and morality. As Hart noted, for many tasks that we undertake, there are better and worse ways of proceeding. If you wish to build a cabinet, you are more likely to succeed if you know and follow the principles of carpentry. If you wish to govern human beings as rational agents, you are more likely to succeed if you know and follow the procedural principles Fuller sets out. But those principles are no more an "inner morality of the law" than the principles of good carpentry are an "inner morality of carpentry." Indeed, if we follow Fuller, Hart maintained, then assassins would do well to master the "inner morality of murder." But this kind of talk just confuses what was already clear—namely, that the idea of law carries within itself certain formal requirements. Hart himself discussed some of these under the notion of administrative or formal justice. If the law is a system of rules, then like cases must be treated alike, the rules must be applied in a consistent fashion, and so on. This much Hart admitted. But such procedural notions are too thin, too substantively empty, to count as "an inner morality of law." After all, it is easy to imagine, and there no doubt have in history been, legal systems that are thoroughly evil yet honor this "inner morality of law."

Against Hart's criticism, Fuller offers two responses. First, he claims that Hart misunderstood the sense in which it is the function of the law to order social life. Hart imagined the law as a kind of social manager, issuing directives to subordinate employees to coordinate and order their conduct to serve the purposes of the manager. If one sees the "inner morality of the law" as rooted in this understanding of law's function, then, sure enough, that "inner morality" will look like no more than the principles of some "techne" or craft, the principles officials should follow if they seek to create social order. Fuller argues that the function of the law is not to manage social life in the sense Hart imagined but rather to organize it so the ends or purposes of all the participants are secured to some meaningful degree. The authority of the law is not the one-way authority of a manager over subordinates (akin to the authority of the carpenter over his wood or the assassin over his victim); rather, it is the authority of officials participating in a relationship of reciprocity with citizens and subjects for the good of all. If the function of the law as a tool of social order is properly understood, Fuller maintains, then it is clear why the procedural criteria of legality constitute an "inner morality of law," whereas the principles of good carpentry or effective killing do not constitute an inner morality of carpentry or killing.

Second, Fuller insists that as an empirical matter, legal systems faithful to his procedural criteria of legality are less likely to work great evils than those that are not faithful. That is, his procedural criteria deliver substantive results, limiting the evil a legal system may work. This, Fuller maintains, is because his procedural criteria require the law to govern persons as rational agents capable of deliberation and choice. In this sense, they constitute an "inner morality of law."

Fuller is surely correct that his procedural criteria require the law to govern persons as rational agents capable of deliberation and choice. But it's not at all clear that legal systems faithful to Fuller's procedural criteria are somehow less likely to work great evils than those not so faithful. Surely, it is possible for legal systems to satisfy Fuller's inner morality of the law to a degree sufficient to count as real legal systems and still work very great evils. Further, though Fuller's procedural criteria ensure that the law governs persons as rational agents capable of choice and deliberation, it's not clear that ad hoc commands or brute force and intimidation govern them as anything other than rational agents capable of choice and deliberation. "Your wallet or your life," I say with a gun to your head. Haven't I given you a choice? Aren't I relying on your rationality as an agent? Is there, then, here an "inner morality" of ad hoc commands or brute force and intimidation?

In the end, Hart argued that while Fuller's procedural criteria may indeed be essential to the idea of law, they do not amount to an "inner morality" of the law. They function simply to ensure that the law remains faithful to its own criteria of legal validity and thus to a purely formal or administrative notion of justice. That is, they must be met if the rule of recognition and all the legal rules it validates are really to be operative as rules. They do not presuppose or entail, then, any view of law other than that of the Hartian legal positivist: law is a complex system of rules and rule-following behavior.

DWORKIN'S THIRD WAY

Perhaps the most influential critique of legal positivism has been that advanced over the years by Ronald Dworkin. In fact, Dworkin has advanced not one, but a series of distinct, even if related, critiques, all leading up to his own theory of law, which he calls "law as integrity."

Dworkin's theory of law is not exactly a natural law theory in the traditional sense. But it is anti-positivist. Dworkin claims a necessary connection between law or legal validity and morality, at least in mature legal systems. He also asserts the impossibility of giving a philosophically complete or adequate description of mature legal systems from the external point of view of the nonparticipant observer. Along the way, he introduces many important ideas and distinctions and presses interesting, if not always successful, arguments.

He characterizes the sum total of his efforts as constituting a third way in the philosophy of law. Dworkin is no fan of classical or traditional natural law theory, even as put by contemporary advocates, but his own views are profitably viewed as a kind of modern natural law theory.

DWORKIN'S CRITICISMS OF HART'S MODEL OF RULES

Dworkin's third way begins with his criticism of what he calls Hart's "model of rules." According to the model of rules, Dworkin claims, the law is a system of rules within which the valid legal rules are determined by the criteria of legal validity embodied in the rule of recognition. Legal rights and obligations are determined, in turn, by the rules. When, according to the rule of recognition, there is no valid law applicable to a dispute, judges or other legal officials must exercise their discretion. In this, they are essentially unconstrained by law. They must, of course, be impartial, respect existing law, and so on, but otherwise judicial or official discretion in so-called hard cases, or cases in which the law has run out, is for Hart what Dworkin calls "strong discretion." It is not the discretion of an architect told to design a two-story American four-square with an open front porch and screened back porch. That is weak discretion constrained or limited by antecedent standards of what is to be done. It is more like the discretion one has in choosing a career or marriage partner. It's simply up to the individual to exercise her best judgment as to how to proceed. When judges exercise their strong discretion in hard cases, they are not, and cannot be, enforcing antecedent legal rights or obligations arising from existing valid legal rules. Instead, they are creating new legal rights or obligations arising from new legal rules, valid by virtue of their (claimed) judicial authority to create them. Judges are more or less free in this undertaking to appeal to a wide range of considerations. They may appeal to moral considerations or to considerations of social utility or policy or economic efficiency or to widely held religious beliefs or to what-have-you. The legal rules, and thus the rights and obligations, they create are then applied retroactively to resolve the hard case that called them to exercise their discretion in the first place. This is Hart's model of rules, Dworkin claims.

This model of rules is neither descriptively accurate nor normatively attractive, in Dworkin's view. It is normatively unattractive because it suggests that judges (who often face hard cases, because easy cases are less likely to be litigated) are often making and retroactively applying new law. But this runs against the grain of not only the rule of law ideal (or the inner morality of law) but also the democratic ideal of a separation of powers according to which the law is made by elected legislators, not judges. Hart's view is descriptively inaccurate, Dworkin contends, because judges neither exercise nor understand themselves as exercising strong discretion in hard cases. Rather, in hard cases, they appeal, and understand and describe themselves as appealing, to legal principles (e.g., the principle that no person should be able to profit from his own wrong). These principles validate the legal rules, rights, and obligations that judges announce and enforce in hard cases. But they are already a part of the law. That's why judges appeal to them.

Hard cases are hard, then, not because there is no valid law determining their outcome. They are hard because the valid law determining their outcome is, in large part, given by legal principles rather than rules, and legal principles determine the outcomes of particular cases in a subtler and more nuanced way than do legal rules. Where the valid law governing a particular case comes in the form of legal principles rather than rules, there is no avoiding judicial judgment. But judicial judgment is not judicial discretion, at least not the strong sort of judicial discretion posited by positivists like Hart.

Like all rules, legal rules work with a certain well-defined and familiar logic. They either apply or they don't. When they apply, they determine a result or yield a judgment in a relatively straightforward way. Rules need not be simple, of course. They may have many exceptions. But the exceptions, like the rules to which they belong, either apply or they do not. It's often difficult to know whether a rule applies. But once one knows that a rule applies, it's usually easy to determine the result. Of course, rules can sometimes appear to conflict. But when they do, the apparent conflict must be resolved either by modifying one of the rules or by determining that one of the rules in fact doesn't apply. A rule may not apply because it contains an exception (perhaps at first unnoticed). Or it may not apply because of some third rule that assigns a certain priority to other rules over it in cases of apparent conflict. In any event, when it comes to rules, real and enduring conflicts are not possible, at least not in a coherent legal system faithful to the rule of law. This is because rules have no weight or force—or, to say the same thing, they all have the same weight and force. It's not possible, then, to resolve a conflict between rules by balancing them one against the other. The only way out is to determine that one of the rules really does not apply at all or to change one of the rules. If one of the rules doesn't really apply at all, then the conflict was merely apparent, not real, all along. If one of the rules is changed, the conflict is eliminated and fails to endure.

So, if there is a rule that plaintiffs have the right to file suit in any county in which they suffer a tortious injury *and* that defendants have a right to be sued only in counties in which they do business, then there is an apparent conflict for any plaintiff injured in County X by a defective product made and sold by Defendant Y only in County Z. In the absence of any legal principles, the only way out of this apparent conflict is either to determine that one of the rules doesn't apply or to change the rules. If both rules in fact apply and there are no legal principles to appeal to, then the legal system is internally inconsistent, and the rule of law is compromised.

Legal principles differ from legal rules. They do not apply in an all-or-nothing way. They shape or influence or ground a determinate result, but they do not determine results mechanically or algorithmically. In general, principles do not contain exceptions. Rather, they are limited by countervailing principles. These often have differential weight and force. Thus, principles can conflict in enduring ways that invite resolution through balancing. When principles conflict, there is no need to modify one of the principles or to seek some metaprinciple that establishes their relative priority. Instead, all that is needed is a judgment as to the relative weight and force of the principles in the case at hand. When principles conflict in a particular case, it is not necessary to determine that one of them really doesn't apply in order to resolve the conflict. Rather, both may apply, but one may outweigh the other or have greater force in the case at hand.

So, if there is a legal principle that persons should not profit from their own wrong *and* a legal principle that intentions expressed in legally valid wills should be honored to the greatest extent possible, then there is competition between principles in any case in which persons set to inherit under the will of another hasten the date of that inheritance by killing the person whose will it is they are set to inherit under. But this competition can be resolved without setting to the side either principle or changing the relevant principles. Rather, both legal principles can remain valid and in play and a judgment can be reached simply by balancing them one against the other to determine which has the greater weight or force in any particular case. Thus, the inclusion in any legal system of these, or any, two competing principles does not render it internally inconsistent or compromise the rule of law so long as the relative weights or force of these principles can be assessed on a case-by-case basis in a reasoned way.

Rules may make reference to principles. For example, the legal rule that unreasonable contracts are void makes implicit reference to a principle of reasonableness. The correct application of such a rule will no doubt require a more complex judgment than the application of a rule voiding contracts not signed by the parties. But a rule that makes reference to a principle is still a rule. It applies in a rulelike way and so on. There is a world of difference between the legal rule that unreasonable contracts are void and a legal principle that contracts should be reasonable.

It is very important to be able to distinguish rules from principles. For example, anyone who watched the confirmation hearings of now Chief Justice John Roberts knows that stare decisis (Latin for "to stand by things decided") is a fundamental principle of law, not a rule. It is the principle requiring judges to respect precedent or past judicial decisions in their reasoning. As Justice Roberts rightly emphasized, stare decisis does not stand for the rule that past precedent must be followed. In particular cases, this principle may be outweighed by other more compelling principles, and good legal judgment will pick out these cases. (This issue was much discussed by Roberts as senators inquired into his thoughts as to whether *Roe v. Wade* constituted a precedent to which he would be bound as a judge.)

Legal rights and obligations can arise out of legal rules, legal principles, or some combination of both. Thus, in a hard case, the judicial task is to examine both the rules and the principles relevant to the case in order to determine the legal rights and obligations of the parties. Legal rights and obligations can appear to conflict, of course. But when they do, it is the job of judges to dissolve the apparent conflict by appealing to the relevant principles and determine the real legal rights and obligations of the parties. It is not the job of judges to exercise strong judicial discretion or to legislate from the bench. Indeed, judges generally ought not be guided in their judgments at all by the sort of forward-looking policy considerations appropriate to legislative judgments, considerations tied to economic efficiency, social utility, and so on. The job of judges is always to look to the existing law to determine the legal rights and obligations of the parties before them, given the facts of the case.

If judges do this, Dworkin claims, they will find that for every hard case they face, there is a single right answer. There is one correct or true legal judgment regarding the legal rights and obligations of the parties before them and thus the proper legal resolution of their dispute. Judges may disagree as to the content of this judgment. They may also make mistakes and miss the mark. But the law is always complete and determinate and awaiting discovery by judicial judgment. And this is what judges necessarily presuppose as they complete their judicial task.

Mature legal systems recognize many legal principles, often simply incorporating moral principles into the law. Every lawyer knows that persons ought not profit from their own wrongdoing; punishment should fit the crime; special relationships (doctor/patient, husband/wife, priest/believer) deserve special protection; persons should take responsibility for the foreseeable consequences of their conduct; and so on all the way to such highly abstract principles as that carved into stone above the U.S. Supreme Court, "Equal Justice Under Law." All these principles are part of the law; so too are the more straightforwardly institutional principles of law, governing such things as the role of precedent or the interpretation of legal documents. Given the full range of legal principles in mature legal systems, it is hard to imagine a dispute beyond the reach of the law's rules and principles taken together. This means that, in principle, there is always, or nearly always, a single right answer waiting to be discovered for every legal dispute. This, in turn, means that judicial discretion is always weak and never strong.

Dworkin is no doubt correct that in mature legal systems, the valid law includes both legal rules and principles. He is also no doubt correct that many legal principles are, in fact, moral principles recognized as law. This looks like a decisive blow to Hart's model of rules. But Hart admitted that Dworkin is right about these things. He admitted that there are mature legal systems (e.g., in England and the United States) within which both rules and principles count as valid law and within which some of the valid legal principles are, in fact, moral principles incorporated into the law. What Hart insisted on, however, is, first, that this is just a contingent fact about some legal systems—it need not be true of all mature legal systems. And, second, wherever moral principles are recognized as valid law, they are so because the governing rule of recognition picks them out as such. In short, Hart adopted the inclusive or soft version of legal positivism as his own and claimed that it can accommodate Dworkin's insights about the legal validity of principles—and in particular moral principles—within mature legal systems. Hart recognized that his turn to inclusive or soft positivism meant giving up the so-called pedigree conception of legal validity, according to which the validity of every particular law is just a function of the social facts surrounding its genesis: Was it promulgated in the right way by the right officials and so on? But Hart insisted that the key positivist point is that the criteria of legal validity in every legal system, whatever they are, are given by a rule of recognition that itself exists simply as a matter of convention or social fact.

However, Hart's inclusive positivism is not immune to attack. Indeed, we have already reviewed (at the end of Chapter 2, in the discussion of inclusive and exclusive positivism) some of the main lines of attack advanced by Dworkin and others—for example, no rule of recognition that incorporates moral criteria as criteria of legal validity could underwrite the sort of convergent official behavior essential to its existence as a social rule or could underwrite the authority the law claims for itself. I do not want to review those arguments here. What I want to highlight is that rather than turning from the inclusive positivism of Hart's postscript to the exclusive positivism thought to be expressed in first edition of *The Concept of Law,* Dworkin argues that all legal principles, including those that look simply like moral principles incorporated directly into the law, belong to the law simply because they are internally accepted as true or correct by officials and others within the legal system. But then, contrary to Hart's view, there are at least some laws or parts of the law—namely, legal principles—that are valid and binding not because they satisfy criteria of legal validity embodied in a conventional rule of recognition, but because they are directly and generally accepted as true or correct from the internal point of view of participants in the legal system.

Dworkin draws the conclusion that Hart cannot sustain the following three theses: (i) wherever there is law, there is, as a matter of conventional social fact, a rule of recognition; (ii) a rule of recognition may include moral criteria as criteria of legal validity; and (iii) the validity of any given law is determined by the rule of recognition and not by whether that law is itself internally accepted by participants in the legal system. If these three theses cannot be sustained, then inclusive or soft positivism is incoherent or unstable. The only options are exclusive positivism or some anti-positivist alternative. Because exclusive positivism entails the thesis that in hard cases judges have strong discretion, Dworkin rejects exclusive positivism. He sets his sights instead on an anti-positivist alternative.

But Dworkin's argument against inclusive or soft positivism is not airtight. It's not obvious, for example, that every rule of recognition that makes moral criteria into criteria of legal validity will engender mainly disagreement and divergent behavior. Some moral criteria may prove less controversial than others. In addition, the rule of recognition may limit the range of relevant moral criteria—say, to those explicitly set out in a constitutional document. Further, there is no reason to suppose that rules of recognition must be different from any other rules when it comes to hard cases. All rules are subject to controversial or borderline cases. That doesn't mean they don't exist as rules as a matter of social fact. The rule of etiquette against interrupting others while speaking is uncertain and controversial in any number of borderline cases. But there is still sufficient convergent behavior to support an inference to the existence of the rule as a matter of social fact. Thus, a rule of recognition with moral criteria for picking out some moral principles as valid legal principles might prove controversial in some borderline cases, but still exist as a rule as a matter of convention and social fact.

Nor is Dworkin's argument against exclusive or hard positivism airtight. It turns on his refusal to accept strong judicial discretion. But if Dworkin's claim is that as a matter of descriptive fact, judges do not have strong discretion, and thus exclusive positivism fails to give an adequate description of law, then he too must explain away many appearances. After all, judges sometimes do act in hard cases as if they have strong discretion. And they sometimes appeal to forward-looking policy considerations to guide them in their exercise of that discretion. Many landmark cases are cases of just this sort. In such hard cases, judges appear to appeal to policy and other extralegal considerations to make new law. They may sometimes say that they are just stating what the law has been all along. But they do so with a wink and a nod, assuming we know the truth.

Alternatively, if Dworkin's claim is essentially that strong discretion is normatively unacceptable, even if it exists as a matter of descriptive fact, then it's not clear what the conflict is with exclusive positivism taken as a descriptive theory of law from the external point of view. Furthermore, though Dworkin is surely correct that strong discretion is in certain respects not ideal, it's not clear that it is normatively unacceptable. As Hart noted, if there really is no law governing a hard case, then the litigants have no legal rights or obligations dispositive of the case, and the retroactive application of the new judge-made law to their case cannot violate their existing legal rights. Indeed, it cannot even violate their legitimate expectations, because without legal rights dispositive of the case, they could form no legitimate expectations about how it would be legally resolved. A retroactive application of law is, of course, retroactive and thus not ideal. But it's not obviously unfair where there really are no dispositive legal rights or obligations in play. And it may be better than not resolving the dispute at all or resolving it in some other way. As to whether it is the business of the judiciary to make law, the fact is that all sorts of officials other than legislators make law, from regulators and administrators to political executives. And judges are particularly well suited to make law for particular kinds of cases, because they're closest to the facts.

Dworkin's early criticisms of Hart are vulnerable at other points as well. For example, whereas Dworkin's distinction between rules and principles is clear enough in some easy cases, it's much less clear in others. Indeed, arguably there is no bright line that divides rules from principles in terms of their logical operation. Rather, there is just a continuum, depending on how important it is to retain flexibility in judgment, cultivate and protect well-defined expectations, and so on.

LAW AS INTEGRITY

Perhaps suspicious that he had not scored a decisive victory over Hart, and legal positivists in general, Dworkin advanced an alternative line of attack subsequent to his attack on the model of rules. It is not discontinuous with that earlier attack, but it is distinctive.

Focusing on judicial reasoning and judgment, Dworkin maintains that when judges—usually appellate court judges—reach divergent judgments about how to resolve a case, they typically do so because they disagree over what the law governing the case in fact is. But these disagreements are not about what is written in the statute books or in past judicial decisions or constitutional documents. They are theoretical disagreements ultimately over the grounds of law. It's as if judges disagree over what the rule of recognition in fact is.

Dworkin claims that Hart and other earlier theorists of law missed this fact of deep theoretical disagreement in law because they suffered from what he calls "the semantic sting." They assumed that if judges sometimes disagree over what the law is in particular cases, then they must, if their disagreements are to be intelligible at all, be talking about the same thing, namely, law. Otherwise, their disagreements would turn out to be pointless or unintelligible, like a disagreement over which bank is closer to a particular location when one person means a river bank and the other means a financial institution. Assuming that judges must all mean the same thing by *law* (otherwise their disagreements about what the law is in particular cases would be unintelligible and without a point), Hart and earlier theorists set themselves the task of delivering that meaning. They offer a semantic account of law—or at least so says Dworkin.

But Dworkin is just wrong here. Although Hart titled his book *The Concept of Law,* he nowhere undertook in that book to give a semantic account of the meaning of *law* as such. Rather, he sought to give a philosophically illuminating description of what he believed to be the central or paradigm case of a legal system and thus of legal obligations and related phenomena. Happily, for Dworkin, his claims regarding the semantic sting are, notwithstanding the pithiness of the phrase, tangential to his main point. His main point is that when judges disagree over what the law is in particular cases, it is often—perhaps almost always—because they disagree at the theoretical level about the grounds of law. They disagree over how much weight precedent should have or the extent to which the law is constrained by considerations of fairness or justice or how statutes should be interpreted, whether by the literal meaning of the terms used, the drafter's intent, standards of reasonableness, or some other criterion. These disagreements are intelligible and have a point. They are just the sort of disagreements about what the law is that fully competent judges confront every day.

These theoretical disagreements about the grounds of law are like familiar disagreements over whether it is good or required manners to remove one's hat upon entering a church or hold doors open for women. We disagree in these cases because we have different understandings of the point and purpose of manners. We interpret the social practice called manners in different ways. What a conservative, religious, old-time male chauvinist means by manners is not what an egalitarian, atheist socialist means by manners. Yet, when they disagree about the etiquette of hats in churches or holding doors for women, they are not like two ships passing in the night, each talking about a different thing. Rather, their disagreement is intelligible and subject to reasoned argument. It is, Dworkin maintains, an interpretive disagreement. Such disagreements are common within mature social practices, like manners. They arise once the "interpretive attitude" takes hold among those engaged in the practice.

The interpretive attitude is the reflective, evaluative attitude taken by those who begin to wonder about the point or purpose of a particular social practice from their internal point of view. If you think the point and purpose of manners is to show deference to traditional power relations, then you'll think one thing about hats in churches and opening doors for women. If you think it is to give social embodiment to a presumption of equal respect for all, then you'll think something else. Disagreements about hats in churches or opening doors for women, then, are sometimes really deep theoretical or interpretive disagreements about the point or purpose of the social practice called manners. When they become commonplace within the practice—that is, when the practice itself becomes one within which individuals are called upon to exercise their own best judgment as to what the practice itself requires—the practice itself becomes an interpretive practice. Law, Dworkin argues, is an interpretive practice, at least in mature legal systems.

Suppose Hart was correct that law is, at least initially, a complex system of rules and rule-following behavior. So long as participants remain free of the interpretive attitude, all is well. We can accept Hart's description. But suppose that at a certain point, some participants begin to wonder whether they've really understood the point or purpose of their rule-following behavior. Perhaps two rules conflict in a way not anticipated, and it's unclear how to resolve the conflict, or perhaps some new unanticipated case arises not covered by existing rules. In such cases, it's only natural to reflect on the point or purpose of the rule-following behavior, or the social practice, at hand. Otherwise, one has no compass to guide the way to a solution. Participants drawn to reflect on the point or purpose of their social practice and rule-following behavior are likely, at some point, to begin to arrive at different judgments. They'll interpret the practice in different ways. As those differences take shape, become entrenched, and inform debate and judgment, the practice itself will shift from being a more or less unreflective and uncritical rule-following practice to a reflective and critical interpretive practice. In the United States, England, and other familiar mature legal systems, the law is just such an interpretive practice. It is this that previous theorists, especially Hart, ignored or missed, according to Dworkin. And because the law is an interpretive practice, it can neither be described simply as a system of rules or a matter of rule-following behavior nor have its function simply declared as a matter of descriptive fact. Dworking regards the kinds of claims made by Finnis and Fuller in defense of the weak reading of "an unjust law is no law at all" as interpretive, and therefore partly evaluative, rather than purely descriptive claims.

Indeed, because the law is an interpretive practice, it cannot even be described, at least not fully and completely, from the external point of view of a nonparticipant observer. Within an interpretive practice, the point, purpose, meaning, and content of the practice is contested by participants from their diverse internal points of view. Any attempt by a nonparticipant observer to describe the practice fully and completely will necessarily take sides between the various views participants have of the practice itself from their diverse internal points of view. It is not possible to provide from the outside, from the external point of view of the nonparticipant observer, a neutral description of what the practice really and completely is. Every "description" of what the practice really and completely is necessarily endorses just one of the many contested interpretations of the practice competing with others from the diverse internal points of view of interested participants.

Thus, Dworkin concludes, the positivist aspiration for a philosophically sound and illuminating description of law from the external point of view is hopeless, at least for mature legal systems within which the interpretive attitude has taken hold. Such legal systems can only be interpreted; they cannot be described, at least not in a complete and morally or evaluatively neutral way. And that means there can be no general theory of law, at least no theory of interest, for all legal systems or for law as such. A philosophy of law is always the philosophy of a particular legal system.

Dworkin concedes that for any interpretive practice, including law, those engaged in it must at least agree that they are interpreting the same social practice, even as they offer competing interpretations of that practice. You and I can intelligently disagree over whether an Andy Warhol print or film is art, but only if we have some shared understanding of the social practice called *art*. We need not mean the same thing by *art*. We need not be able to agree on a semantic definition. But the central or paradigm cases of what we each call *art* must overlap to some significant degree. If you insist that every leaf on every tree, your handwriting, all television commercials and all street maps are art but that nothing housed in any art museum is really art, and I insist that only objects in art museums are art, then you and

I do not have a sufficiently shared understanding of the social practice called *art* to have an intelligent and purposeful disagreement about the artistic merit of Andy Warhol prints or films. We cannot have an interpretive disagreement, because we are not participants in a shared practice called *art*. But so long as we share some paradigm or central cases, we can each take very different views about the point or purpose of *art*, and thus about whether Andy Warhol's prints or films count as real art.

So, interpretive disagreements, and thus interpretive practices, presuppose a preinterpretive consensus of some sort. If law is an interpretive practice, then officials and citizens must share some preinterpretive consensus over certain central or paradigm cases of what counts as law. At least, they must if their disagreements are to be intelligible as disagreements over the grounds of law. They must agree, for example, that the Constitution and the Clean Air Act are law, or that the Tennessee criminal code and the decisions of federal courts are law, and so on. They must have some shared paradigm or central cases. These need not be fixed or beyond revision. After all, officials and others may come to realize that what they thought was law is not. Nor need these cases be great in number. They need only be sufficient to sustain intelligent, interpretive disagreement between citizens and officials.

Interpretive disagreements arise because participants in the social practice have taken a critical and evaluative stance from their internal points of view toward the preinterpretive consensus. Parties to an interpretive disagreement will offer different theories as to what the practice is really about, what it really requires, and why. A good theory must both fit and justify the practice to a great enough extent and in a sufficiently compelling way to underwrite a determinate judgment as to what the practice really requires for the case at hand. The best theory will do so better than any of its rivals. The best theory expresses what the practice is really about and thereby underwrites determinate judgments about what the practice really requires in the case at hand.

These two requirements, fit and justification, reflect the complex nature of interpretation or interpretive judgment, or what Dworkin calls *constructive interpretation*. Constructive interpretation stands midway between, and joins together, description and evaluation. An interpretation that fails to fit its object at all is descriptively deficient. An interpretation that fits its object but fails to reveal the value of that object is normatively or evaluatively deficient. A good interpretation both fits and justifies the object of interpretation, and it does so better than all rival interpretations. It makes sense of the object of interpretation, showing it in its best light as an exemplar of its kind.

Thus, if art is an interpretive social practice, then a good interpretative theory of art will fit enough of what we take to be art to count as an interpretation of the practice. It will also justify that practice and our evaluative judgments about it, casting the practice in its best evaluative light. A theory of art that did not fit or that fit very little of what we typically take to be art (at the level of preinterpretive consensus) would be less plausible than one that fit more neatly. Similarly, a theory that called into question most of our practice of and evaluative judgments about art, a theory that shows nearly all of what we thought to be good art was really pointless rubbish, would be less plausible as an interpretive claim of what the practice is really about than one that cast our practice and evaluative judgments in better light. Of course, it's always possible that we'll find ourselves interpreting a social practice so incoherent and without value that no interpretation, or no interpretation that urges us to continue it in any positive way, will both fit and justify the practice to a sufficient degree to merit serious consideration. In that case, the best interpretation may be one according to which the practice doesn't really mean anything at all, should be abandoned, and requires nothing in the case at hand.

When we find ourselves engaged in an interpretive practice, we cannot determine what the practice requires in any particular case without coming to a prior interpretive judgment as to what the practice itself really is or is about. We can come to a reasoned judgment as to whether Andy Warhol's prints or films are art only after we've come, whether consciously or not, to some view as to what art really is or is about. Of course, our view as to what art really is or is about may shift over time as we come to see more clearly its implications for particular cases. We may be driven at first by our theory of art to judge Warhol's prints or films as art. But later, after being driven by our theory to many similar and less plausible judgments, we may come to question the theory itself. We should then undertake to interpret the social practice anew.

So, how does all this apply to law? On Dworkin's view, officials and other participants in advanced legal systems routinely and inevitably take an interpretive stance toward what they all call *law* at the level of preinterpretive consensus. They then come to have different theories or conceptions of what the law really is or is about and why. Each regards his or her own theory of law as fitting and justifying the social practice of law better than the alternative theories affirmed by others. Thus, they see their own theory as constituting a reasoned basis for rendering determinate judgments about what the law really is or what it requires in particular cases. Thus, when judges disagree in particular cases about what the law is, it's often because they affirm different interpretive theories of law. Dworkin examines three such theories. Each has, he concedes, a plausible claim to fit and justify the law. But, according to Dworkin, the third—what he calls the theory of law as integrity—fits and justifies our interpretive social practice of law better than the rest. It, then, ought to guide us in our judgments as to what the law is, both in general and in particular cases.

Dworkin recognizes that he cannot prove in any sort of final way that his own law as integrity is the best interpretive theory of law. All he can do is offer arguments and challenge the interpretive theories affirmed by others. Each person has to make up his or her own mind as to which theory is best. That's just the nature of an interpretive practice. Interpretation is, in Dworkin's own words, a deeply Protestant affair—Protestant in the sense that final authority lies with the individual conscience of each believer.

Here we can return briefly to the natural law slogan that "an unjust law is no law at all." On Dworkin's view, this slogan is best understood as a claim made at the interpretive level. The Nazi legal system or the legal system of apartheid South Africa may have possessed enough similarity to those paradigm instances of legal systems that constitute the preinterpretive consensus we share with others (presupposed by our interpretive disagreements with them over law) that we could agree that they both constitute "law" or a "legal system" for the purposes of debating their status or merits as law or legal systems. But if from our own inescapable interpretive point of view we think serving justice to be among the most fundamental purposes of law, then both "legal systems" may be so defective as exemplars of what they aspire to be that within them what appears to be law is really no law at all, or what appears to be a legal system really is not. The interpretive judgment that Nazi law is no law at all is structurally no different from the interpretive judgment that an Andy Warhol print is not really art at all, assuming that the claim is made to someone with whom we shared a sufficient preinterpretive consensus to sustain a reasoned interpretive disagreement over the status of a Warhol print as art.

Of the three theories or interpretations of law Dworkin discusses, the first, which he associates with Hart and legal positivism, he calls *conventionalism*. Conventionalists maintain that the point and purpose of the law is to regulate coercive state action in light of past political decisions so as to render social life predictable, to protect expectations, and so on in order to make possible rational planning by those subject to the law. Given this point and purpose, conventionalists maintain that the law should be as clearly and explicitly tied as possible, in conventional and empirically observable ways, to past political decisions. In this way, it will best serve its point or purpose. This means relying on straightforward empirical criteria of legal validity (e.g., bills passed by Congress and signed by the president are law) and shunning inherently controversial moral criteria of legal validity. The strength of the conventionalist view is that it takes seriously past official acts as a basis for existing law and thus for legal rights and obligations. This both fits central or paradigm aspects of what we call law and is something we can see the value of. The weakness of the conventionalist view is that it renders moral considerations completely irrelevant to any judgment about what the law is in any particular case. This, Dworkin argues, doesn't really fit our practice, because judges often invoke moral considerations when deciding what the law is. Nor does it cast our legal practice in its best light, because it suggests that some of the cases we most celebrate— *Brown v. Board of Education,* for example—were wrongly decided (because they relied so heavily on moral principles and argument rather than law conventionally established by past political acts).

The second theory Dworkin examines he calls *pragmatism* and associates with legal realism (discussed in Chapter 4). Pragmatists maintain that the point and purpose of the law is to serve as a tool for bringing about some desired social goal, increased utility or economic efficiency, or some similar forward-looking goal. Given this purpose, whether the law should regulate coercive state action in light of past political decisions depends on whether doing so is likely to advance the relevant social goal. As far as social order and protecting expectations goes, all the law need do is appear, for the most part, to govern coercive state action in accord with past political decisions. It need not really do so; appearances are enough. Thus, judges and other officials ought never really feel constrained by past political decisions, even though they may often have reason to pretend to feel so constrained. They should really feel free always to make or change the law if so doing is the surest path to desired social goals. That's what the law is for. The strength of the pragmatist conception of law is its forward-looking openness to a wide range of considerations bearing on existing law and thus on legal rights and obligations in particular cases. Its weakness is its tendency to exclude fundamental moral considerations and thus to treat legal rights and obligations as if they were no more than tools, revisable at will and thus mere fictions. Pragmatism does not "take rights seriously."

The third theory or conception of law Dworkin examines is his own—law as integrity. He associates it with natural law theory, recast now as an interpretive theory of law. On this view, the point and purpose of law is to regulate coercive state action in light of past political decisions so as to constitute through the law a community within which coercive state action is never just force or power but is instead always morally legitimate when assessed from the internal point of view of those subject to it. To accomplish this, the law aims to constitute a community able to speak with and from one coherent and morally principled voice, or with and from integrity, as Dworkin puts it. Within a community committed to ruling its members through law subject to a morally principled integrity, Dworkin maintains, the obligation to obey the law has at least prima facie moral force. Coercive state action to enforce the law is, then, at least prima facie morally legitimate. Constituting such a community, on Dworkin's view, is both what we've been trying imperfectly to do through law for the past two centuries and what we should be trying to do ever more perfectly in the coming decades and centuries.

Given this understanding of the point and purpose of law, what the law is in any given case is best determined not simply by some conventional rule (of recognition) related to past political decisions taken as social facts. Rather, it is determined by the best interpretation of past political decisions as the acts of a community committed to realizing itself through law as a morally principled community with integrity. The best interpretation, of course, is that which best fits and justifies those past political acts as the acts of such a community. This interpretation then determines the law, the legal rights, and the legal obligations in the case at hand. From the point of view of any judge committed to law as integrity, then, there is for every legal dispute a single right answer. There is no room for strong judicial discretion.

Thus, law as integrity fuses the backward-looking strength of conventionalism with the forward-looking appeal of pragmatism, all while avoiding, Dworkin thinks, the weaknesses of each. It is, he insists, the best interpretation of our own legal practice. If we want to know what law is, or what the law in a particular case is, we ought to begin our thinking from the point of view defined by law as integrity. It expresses the real nature of law. Of course, it's not a pure description given from the external point of view. It's an interpretation defended by Dworkin from his own internal point of view as an interested participant in the legal system of the United States (and, less directly, England, where he has worked for many years).

Dworkin's theory of law is interpretive at two levels. Because law is an interpretive social practice, it cannot simply be described but must be interpreted. Law as integrity is Dworkin's preferred interpretation of law. But law as integrity posits that what the law is in any given case is itself a function of interpretive judgment. Judges committed to law as integrity must interpret past political decisions to arrive at a judgment as to what the law is in the cases that come before them. This second level of interpretation, one not present within either conventionalism or pragmatism, Dworkin describes as the Herculean task of judging.

There are, then, on Dworkin's view, two necessary connections between law and morality. First, once the interpretive attitude has taken hold, it's not possible simply to describe law as a social practice. It must be interpreted, and that is in part an evaluative task. Second, from within the best interpretation of law—namely, law as integrity—what the law is in any given case is itself a function of interpretive judgment. All legal judgment is interpretive; judicial reasoning is always interpretive. This doesn't mean the law is just what the judges say it is. Quite the contrary, on Dworkin's view. Dworkin insists that there is always a single right answer to every, or very nearly every, legal question. Judges, when reasoning correctly, discover that answer. In any case, they always aim at it. Although they may have the last word, finality is not the same thing as infallibility. On this point, Hart and Dworkin are agreed.

Dworkin describes the judge committed to law as integrity as an author writing in a chain novel. In a chain novel, an author writes a chapter then delivers it to another author, who must continue the novel with a new chapter, making it the best he can. He then delivers it to yet another new author who does the same and so on. Each author acquires a text that must be continued in the best possible way. No author (except the first) is free to start a new novel. Each must continue the one in progress. But each must do so in a way that makes of it the best novel it can be. This calls on interpretive judgment. Each will seek a way of continuing the novel through his own chapter that both fits what was written before and makes of the new novel as a whole, including his contribution, the best novel it can be. Judges do much the same thing when they decide particular cases. Delivered to them are lots of previously written chapters, statutes, past court decisions, legal principles, even significant events in the political history of their society. They must then make their own addition to this material, an addition that both fits and perfects it. That is how they arrive at their judgment as to what the law is in the cases before them. Of course, this is hard work. And so Dworkin names a judge who carries it out perfectly in every case Hercules.

DIFFICULTIES WITH DWORKIN

Whether Dworkin's Hercules is, like the Greek version, just a myth is a question we shall take up in earnest in the next chapter (on legal realisms). But here one difficulty must be raised, because it touches on the plausibility of Hercules as an ideal judge, as well as on Dworkin's larger argument for law as integrity as the best interpretation of our (the United States, the United Kingdom, etc.) legal practice. Both Hercules and Dworkin (when he interprets our own legal practice) engage in constructive interpretive reasoning and judgment. And on Dworkin's view, the basic structure of constructive interpretive reasoning and judgment is given by two fundamental axes—one of fit, the other of justification. But these can obviously pull in different directions. Hercules may find that a judgment ending legalized segregation in *Brown v. Board of Education* would not fit past decisions very well, even if it would better perfect and justify the law, than would a decision not to end segregation. Which is more important? Fit or justification? Dworkin gives no answer. He does clearly endorse the decision reached in *Brown*, which suggests that in that case the justification criterion weighs more heavily. But how is that to be known or determined? Dworkin emphasizes that the two interpretive criteria, fit and justification, are not commensurable. There is no exchange rate between them, no way of knowing how to reach a reasoned judgment when one interpretation fits better while another justifies better. But then, how is a reasoned interpretive judgment possible in hard cases, which are presumably hard precisely because fit and justification considerations pull in different directions?

Dworkin attempts to get around this problem when it comes to interpreting law as a social practice. There he claims that law as integrity both fits and justifies better than its rivals, conventionalism and pragmatism. Assuming he is correct and that there are no other plausible rival interpretations of law as a social practice (and this he does not set out to prove, but rather just assumes from the historical record, which is dominated by positivism, realism, and natural law theory), then we can at least see how his judgment in favor of law as integrity is determined in a reasoned way. But when it comes to adjudicating cases, at least hard cases, judges are likely rarely to find that one interpretation of past political decisions both fits and justifies better than all its rival alternatives. But how is a reasoned determinate judgment possible? Could even one possessed of Herculean intellect arrive at a reasoned and determinate judgment as to what the law in fact is in such a case?

These difficulties with Dworkin's idea of constructive interpretation are not the only difficulties with his theory of law as integrity. For example, Dworkin insists that for Hercules or any real judge modeling herself on Hercules, there is a single right answer for every, or nearly every, legal dispute. But this so-called single right answer thesis, which runs through Dworkin's earlier and later work, depends on there being a single right answer to all or nearly all moral questions, because the law is complete and determinate only through its incorporation of morality in the form of legal principles. This means that Dworkin owes us what other philosophers have been unable to deliver for centuries—namely, a compelling account of morality or moral reason as complete and determinate. It also means Dworkin owes us an account of how the law incorporates enough of morality to constitute itself as complete and determinate without simply becoming morality by another name. Are judges free to draw on any and all of morality to arrive at the single right answer in a hard case? If so, what is the difference between law and morality? Dworkin rightly insists that there is a difference—that there is a difference between what the law is and what, as a purely moral matter, it ought to be. But the basis for this distinction is not entirely clear. It lies, on Dworkin's account, in a distinction between two different kinds of integrity at which the law might aim. On the one hand there is inclusive integrity. It takes into account all values of political morality. This is the integrity that determines what the law is. On the other hand, there is pure integrity. It takes into account only the value of justice. This is the integrity that determines what the law ought to be. As judges and other officials reflect on and work to close the gap between what the law is and what it ought to be, they work the law pure.

Another difficulty with Dworkin's argument for law as integrity as the best interpretation of our shared legal practice is that it simply presupposes that one interpretation of law is better than another if it can show the obligation to obey the law to be a prima facie moral obligation and thus can morally legitimate coercive state enforcement of the law. But why should we presuppose this? Even if we accept that every interpretation of the law necessarily proceeds from the internal evaluative point of view, why should we weigh the moral value of our having a moral obligation to obey the law or of the legitimacy of coercive state action more heavily than other moral values associated with law, for example, the moral value of predictability in social life?

Finally, Dworkin seems to concede to Hart what he (Dworkin) claims to deny—namely, the possibility of a significant descriptive theory of law. Dworkin admits that interpretive disagreements always arise against a background of a preinterpretive consensus concerning various presupposed paradigms or central cases. We cannot disagree about the nature of any legal system or even law in general unless our judgments already converge to some significant degree. But why, then, Hart may rightly ask, is it not a valuable philosophical project to give an illuminating description of that preinterpretive consensus from the external point of view of a nonparticipant observer? Rather than showing such a project impossible, Dworkin seems to have shown its necessity. Dworkin maintains that there are no philosophically interesting questions to ask about law at the level of the preinterpretive consensus. But surely Hart's work is, and raises questions that are, philosophically interesting.

Both Hartian legal positivism and natural law theories account for the validity and normative authority of the law in a way that draws a sharp line between law and mere power or politics. Whether there is a necessary conceptual relationship between law and morality, Hartian positivists and natural law theorists agree that law, on the one hand, and power and politics, on the other, are distinctive social phenomena. We turn next to the relationship among law and power and politics and to a family of views, all connected in some way to legal realism, according to which the law is always simply power and politics by another name.

SELECTED BIBLIOGRAPHY

On Natural Law Theories

Aquinas, Thomas. *On Law, Morality, and Politics.* (Indianapolis, IN: Hackett Publishing), 1988.

Blackstone, William. *Commentaries on the Law of England.* (Chicago, IL: University of Chicago Press), 1979.

Dworkin, Ronald. *Taking Rights Seriously.* (Cambridge, MA: Harvard University Press), 1977.

———. *Matters of Principle.* (Cambridge, MA: Harvard University Press), 1985.

———. *Law's Empire.* (Cambridge, MA: Harvard University Press), 1986.

Finnis, John. *Natural Law and Natural Rights.* (Oxford, UK: Oxford University Press), 1980.

Fuller, Lon. *The Inner Morality of Law.* (New Haven, CT: Yale University Press), 1964.

George, Robert. *Natural Law Theory: Contemporary Essays.* Oxford University Press, 1992.

Murphy, Mark. *Natural Law and Practical Rationality.* (Cambridge, UK: Cambridge University Press), 2001.

Soper, Philip. *A Theory of Law.* (Cambridge, MA: Harvard University Press), 1984.

Weinreb, Lloyd. *Natural Law and Justice.* (Cambridge, MA: Harvard University Press), 1987.

4

On Legal Realism
and Its Progeny

L egal positivism has dominated the philosophy of law in the United
States, England, and much of Europe since the nineteenth century
(except in the Catholic countries, including Spain and Italy, where
the natural law tradition remains robust). Legal positivism developed
against a generally positivist orientation in the nineteenth century and
was associated with the emerging social sciences. The rough idea of
this orientation was that human behavior, like the rest of the natural
world, was governed by discoverable empirical laws, the identification and understanding of which would pave the way for the first
truly rational, enlightened, and enduring reform of social life. Once
the empirical laws governing social life were understood, social institutions might finally be mastered and put to good and effective
instrumental use. Legal positivism applied this positivist orientation
to the social practices and institutions commonly thought of under
the heading of "law."

Oddly, in the United States, legal positivism's initial influence
produced a kind of formalist approach to the study of law, exemplified best by the work of Christopher Langdell, dean of the Harvard
Law School. On this approach, existing social practices and institutions called *law* were assumed to embody a kind of ideal law just
waiting to be discovered and articulated. This legal formalism culmi-
nated in the early twentieth-century effort by the American Law
Institute to produce formal "restatements" of the ideal legal doctrines

that were waiting just beneath the surface of everyday legal discourse and practice to be unearthed. The ALI produced restatements, taxonomically and logically organized, of various traditional areas of law: contract, tort, property, and so on.

Legal realism emerged as an anti-formalist and empirically oriented response to and rejection of the legal formalism of Dean Langdell and the ALI, as well as of the "mechanical jurisprudence" or "science of law" with which both became associated. In many ways, this legal realism better captured the positivist, empirically oriented, reformist spirit of legal positivism than any earlier tradition of American legal thought. It began around the start of the twentieth century and ended as a distinct movement around the time of World War II. Some of its chief theorists were Oliver Wendell Holmes, Karl Llewellyn, Felix Cohen, Jerome Frank, and Underhill Moore. Though it no longer exists as a well-defined movement, many of its central claims have been accepted by and mainstreamed in the philosophy of law, which it continues to influence. Indeed, some of the most visible late twentieth-century movements and developments in the philosophy of law derive in large measure from legal realism. These include critical legal studies, law and economics, and even feminist jurisprudence and critical race theory. In many ways, these are all the progeny of legal realism.

LANGDELL AND LEGAL FORMALISM

While dean of Harvard Law School, Langdell instituted a wide number of changes that revolutionized legal education. The most important, for present purposes, is the case method of study. Langdell thought that within each traditional doctrinal area of law—torts, property, contracts, and so on—there lurked just beneath the surface of the decided cases well-defined legal rules and principles that, once identified, might be systematically and taxonomically organized so as to reveal a complete, logically coherent, and determinate legal order. With this order in hand, lawyers and judges might then be able to arrive with certainty at objectively correct legal judgments. The practice of law might be made more regular and reliable and its study more scientific.

Langdell's method required students to study a wide range of cases in each substantive area of law, with the aim of distilling the latent rules and principles. These they were then to organize into a coherent body of doctrine, something like a scientific theory of each substantive area of law. To facilitate this method, Langdell developed the casebook. Law school textbooks soon followed the pattern of "Cases on Tort" or "Cases on Contracts." Of course, Langdell recognized that students were not likely to discover the rules and principles latent within actually decided cases without some prompting. Therefore, he encouraged law professors to use the so-called Socratic method of questioning. This method soon dominated legal education and was made famous by the book and movie *The Paper Chase*.

Though Langdell's orientation toward law was much influenced by legal positivism's aspiration to understand the deep structure of legal practice and institutions, it was ultimately a kind of idealism. Langdell did not set out empirically to discover the scientific laws governing legal practice and institutions, whatever they might be. Rather, he assumed, prior to any empirical inquiry, that there was—there must be—lurking beneath the surface of the law a formal structure of ideas that was rational, complete, determinate, and so on, just waiting to be discovered. His case method of inquiry aimed to reveal this structure in relatively fine-grained detail. Legal reasoning and judicial judgment were to be determined by this structure.

Langdell thought that the law contained both rules and principles and that there was, for every legal question, a single right answer waiting to be discovered. But he also thought the law was given only by the positive acts of those with the legal authority to make law—legislators, judges, and so on. He thought that legal reasoning was essentially deductive, algorithmic, or, to use the pejorative term introduced by his critics, "mechanical." The science of jurisprudence involved extracting the rules and principles from the positive acts of legislators, judges, and so on and then deducing from those rules concrete results for any determinate set of facts presented by a particular case.

LEGAL REALISM

Legal realism initially arose as a reaction against Langdellian formalism. Interestingly, just as the latter was addressed primarily to students and practitioners of law, so too was the former. Unlike legal positivism and natural law theory, however, legal realism was not developed mainly by philosophers of law.

The early legal realists maintained that as a matter of empirical fact, judges do not decide cases based solely on the legal rules or principles that Langdell claimed were immanent within the traditional substantive areas of law. Such rules and principles were typically too abstract to yield, by themselves, a single right answer to any concrete legal dispute. They might limit the range of possible answers, but they always allowed many possible answers. In deciding cases, then, judges necessarily rely on their intuitions or hunches about the fairest or most socially beneficial way to resolve the cases before them as an instance of a general fact pattern of social significance. Legal rules and principles are relevant, but mostly as a sort of loose constraint. They do not, in fact cannot, determine uniquely correct results, mechanically or otherwise.

According to the legal realists, when presented with a case, judges first discern the general fact pattern presented. They then identify it as an instance of a particular type of case. In doing this, they rely not on Langdell's formalist legal categories, but rather on categories tied to pressing social concerns. For example, a case might be identified as an instance of the class of cases associated with harms caused by defective products, or business deals broken due to changing market conditions, or the pressure to break the link between ownership and control of productive assets so as to facilitate their most efficient use, and so on. Judges then rely on their own intuitions or hunches about how to resolve the case before them as understood in this way. These intuitions or hunches are the product of, and can be fully explained by reference only to, observable psychological and sociological forces. The rules and principles Langdell thought latent within the formal structure of the law are invoked by judges only after having reached a decision on other grounds and only to rationalize or legitimate that decision. Given the inherent indeterminacy of the legal rules and principles, judges are almost always able to rationalize or legitimize a decision they reach on other grounds.

Of course, legal realists did not claim that judges do all this self-consciously. Judges may think they're applying legal rules and principles in a mechanical way. What legal realists claimed is that this is what judges in fact do, whether they realize it or not.

For the legal realists, then, the law was not some "brooding omnipresence" in the sky waiting to be discovered (as Oliver Wendell Holmes characterized the formalist conception of law), and adjudicative legal reasoning is not and could never be algorithmic or the "mechanical" application of some legal rule to a set of facts.

Rather, *the law is what particular judges do,* or will do, in particular cases as they respond to general fact patterns or case types, driven by pressing social concerns and a range of moral and policy considerations, as well as psychological and sociological forces. For the legal realist the study of law as it really is must involve more than the distillation of abstract rules and principles from decided cases organized into ideal types. It also has to involve the study of the wide range of considerations that in fact influence judges to decide cases as they do. Any realistic approach to law will emphasize this.

The early legal realists were generally successful in making this point. After legal realism, the casebooks first introduced by Langdell were revised to include materials on the sorts of considerations emphasized by legal realists. These casebooks were renamed. What was "Cases on Torts" became "Cases *and Materials* on Torts." They were also reorganized around chapters devoted to relevant fact patterns—manufacturer defects in consumer products, detrimental reliance on a commercial promise, and so on—rather than to abstract legal doctrines.

Legal realists advanced two general claims. Each remains of interest today, yet both have been misunderstood by critics. The first is that the law is often indeterminate and that judges, accordingly, must and do often draw on extralegal considerations to resolve the disputes before them. The second is that the best answer to the question "What is (the) law?" is "Whatever judges or other relevant officials do." Underlying both these claims is a healthy skepticism about the ability of legal rules and principles, or valid law in general, to yield determinate answers when the legal rights and obligations of parties are in dispute. Of course, if the valid law rarely yields such answers, then the law functions as little more than a substitute for more overt forms of politics and power when such disputes are, in fact, legally settled. Contemporary realists differ with respect to their skepticism regarding legal determinacy in that some are more skeptical than others. But all affirm some version of the indeterminacy thesis and thus share some skepticism about the rule-of-law ideal.

THE REALISTS' INDETERMINACY THESIS

Like legal positivists, legal realists regard properly enacted statutes, past judicial decisions, and other conventionally authoritative legal texts and events as sources of valid law and sound bases of legal judgment. But they argue that these rarely, by themselves, determine what the law is in particular cases. One reason for this is that in any particular case, judges must rely on general principles of legal reasoning to reason from these sources of valid law to a decision. But on almost any set of facts, the general principles of legal reasoning— principles of legal interpretation, precedent (or stare decisis), burden of proof, presumption, standards of evidence and review, and so on— will typically permit a wide range of inferences from the valid law. Thus, whether the plaintiff or defendant wins is rarely just a function of the valid law applied according to general principles of legal reasoning. It's rather a function of something like a fairly strong judicial discretion.

In certain respects, Hart appeared to say things very much like what the legal realists say. But this appearance is misleading. The realists are more radical. Hart said that in any legal system, there will sometimes be "gaps" in the law, cases for which the existing valid law and principles of legal reasoning fail to determine a uniquely correct legal result. These gaps aren't just a function of the inability of lawmakers to anticipate every possible case. They exist sometimes because language, and thus the language of law, is unavoidably "open-textured." A rule like "no vehicles in the park" might or might not apply to roller skates or to a sculpture of a motorcycle. Rules or principle requiring "reasonable" behavior or imposing standards of "reasonableness" will be similarly indeterminate at the margins. Of course, often the meaning of terms for particular cases is clear enough. But just as often, judges must simply exercise their discretion to interpret the relevant language and thus resolve the dispute before them.

Legal realists recognize this open-textured aspect of language and its import for legal reasoning. But they go beyond Hart to argue for further and more substantial causes of indeterminacy in the law. They emphasize that even when the relevant language is clear enough, judges find themselves able to arrive, through valid legal reasoning, at several possible legal judgments. Indeed, the realists argue, this is why so many cases get litigated, especially at the appellate level (where issues of fact are usually not eligible for review): the law is very often indeterminate until a judge actually decides one way rather than another.

Even apparently straightforward cases are less determinate than they appear. Consider a statute with clear, unambiguous language supported by substantial evidence of the legislature's intent. Judges must still decide whether to interpret and apply the statute literally and strictly, in the absence of any evidence that the legislature intended otherwise, or to interpret and apply it liberally and reasonably, so as to give effect to what the legislature would and should have intended had it contemplated the case at hand. There are legal principles of statutory interpretation supporting both approaches. Thus, sometimes even when the law appears most determinate, it is still relatively indeterminate.

The same sort of thing happens when judges reason from previously decided cases or past precedents. According to the common law doctrine of precedent, or stare decisis, lower courts are bound by the cases previously decided by higher courts in their own jurisdiction, are to recognize as weighty considerations cases previously decided by equal courts in their own jurisdiction, and are to take due notice of cases previously decided in other jurisdictions. But the past decisions of other courts constrain lower courts in one of these three ways only if they are sufficiently similar to be "on point." Because no two cases are ever identical (they can't be) and because every case is similar in some respect or other to other cases, judges must exercise their discretion to determine whether any particular past decision is "on point." This introduces into the law substantial indeterminacy.

A similar point may be made when it comes to identifying what legal rule or principle a past decision judged "on point" stands for. One principle of legal reasoning makes the legal rule or principle invoked in a precedent case binding in the present case. But is it the rule or principle exactly as formulated in the previously decided case or as it should or could have been formulated that is binding? The answer is that it can be either. Another principle makes the rationale or pattern of reasoning in the precedent case, rather than its rule or principle, binding. But, again, is it the rationale or reasoning as given or as it could or should have been given? Yet another rule makes only the result reached in a precedent case binding; everything else is to be given due consideration. Obviously, judges can all agree that in some present case a particular past decision is a precedent, yet all reach very different legal judgments in the present case. The legal doctrine of stare decisis is a source of some determinacy and a great deal of indeterminacy within the law. The fact that in many cases there are multiple judicial opinions just muddies the water even further, for there are different principles for how to assign weight to concurring and dissenting opinions, and so on.

The result is that even when judges find themselves with no shortage of legally valid and applicable statutes or precedent cases,

ON LEGAL REALISM AND ITS PROGENY

they will find themselves free to arrive, through valid legal reasoning, at several apparently legally correct results. This means that very often judges must ultimately be driven to the results they reach by extralegal considerations. Indeed, such considerations must very often determine what judges regard as the relevant facts in the cases before them. For if the law is indeterminate, then judges cannot rely on the law to separate the legally relevant from the legally irrelevant facts. But they must apply the law to some set of facts. So they must rely on extralegal considerations (their sense of pressing social concerns, for example) to arrive at their sense of what the relevant facts are.

Judges are to apply the already existing law, or so the saying goes. But the reality is, the realists argue, that judges are guided at every step by extralegal or nonlegal considerations. Such considerations determine which facts count as legally relevant and then how the already existing valid law is to be applied and thus what result is to be reached. The "already existing valid law" is then invoked to legitimate or rationalize the decision reached on extralegal or nonlegal grounds. This law functions as a constraint, but only a weak constraint, on judges and other officials.

We can distinguish between two kinds of indeterminacy asserted by legal realists (and later by their progeny within critical legal studies). The first might be called *justificatory indeterminacy*. The claim here is that in many cases, the valid law and established principles of legal reasoning do not exclusively justify a single right answer or legally correct result. The second might be called *explanatory* or *causal indeterminacy*. Here the claim is that the valid law and established principles of legal reasoning do not, by themselves, explain or cause judges to give the answers they do or reach the results they reach. These are distinct notions. For example, the valid law and principles of legal reasoning might justify a uniquely correct result, but a judge might be caused to reach the result she reaches by a bribe or stupidity. Legal realists typically assert both kinds of indeterminacy, but they ground their claim regarding explanatory or causal indeterminacy in a claim about justificatory indeterminacy. They do not argue for the widespread corruption or incompetence of judges. That would be unrealistic. Rather, the point is that the law cannot always cause judges to decide as they do, because it cannot justify uniquely correct legal results in many cases. It's important to note, though, that even if the law could justify uniquely correct legal results in all cases, it might still fail to cause or explain the results judges in fact do reach. And those interested in what judges do rather than what they should do will probably be interested in what causes or what explains the results judges do, in fact, reach. Legal realists do not claim that the law is fully indeterminate. They recognize sources of valid law and legal rules, and they allow that when conjoined with principles of legal reasoning, these will sometimes—perhaps often—prove sufficient to justify a single right answer or legally correct result. Not every case is a hard case; there are easy ones. The point is that there are lots of hard cases. These hard cases are not just a function of the open texture of language. In these hard cases the law is whatever the judge says it is.

THE PREDICTIVE THEORY OF LAW

The early legal realists argued that the best answer to the question "What is (the) law?" is "Whatever the relevant legal officials say it is or do." Were this a claim about the concept of law, in Hart's sense, it would be silly, even incoherent. Surely, when a judge asks himself, "What is the law here?" he cannot be asking, "What is it that I'm going to say or do?" That's nonsensical. No matter what he said or did, it would be law. But then there would be no point in asking, "What is the law here?"

Happily, the legal realists' claim is not conceptual. It is advanced not from the point of view of the philosopher, but rather from lawyers, judges, legal officials, and other participants in any legal system with a practical need to determine how to act and thus to know, as contextual information, how others are likely to act. The realists' claim is essentially a kind of shorthand for one or another explanatory causal claim. From the point of view of someone with a practical need to know how a judge or other legal official will act in a legal dispute, appeals to valid legal rules and principles of legal reasoning are of limited value, due to the indeterminacy of the law. What is needed is insight into the true extralegal causes or explanations of judicial decisions and official legal actions. The claim that the law is whatever the judge says it is or does is just a shorthand reminder to look for these extralegal causes or explanations.

Contemporary legal realists advance just the sort of naturalistic, social scientific study of law that Kelsen tried to exclude from a properly analytic jurisprudence. They approach the law and judicial conduct as effects realized by natural causes discoverable through empirical observation and scientific reasoning. In response to our practical need to know how judges and other legal officials will act, they offer empirically informed predictions.

In general, they point to two kinds of causes of law and judicial decisions. Some point to individual, and often quite variable, causal forces, usually psychological in nature. So, for example, Jerome Frank argued that a complete causal account of law and judicial decisions must make substantial reference to unconscious anxieties and desires, often of a Freudian sort. Now, this view depends, of course, on the ability of Freudian psychoanalytic theory to deliver an empirically meaningful causal explanation of behavior, and few today have much confidence on this front. But suppose Frank's supposition could be made good. We would then be left with a most disquieting picture of law and judicial decisions. Behind law's appearance of rules, reasons, and normative authority lies the reality of unconscious and irrational or prerational anxieties and desires, brute psychological forces operating in ad hoc ways on different individuals.

Other legal realists point to more general and less idiosyncratic sociological causes of law and judicial decisions—professional training, economic class, ideological commitments, social position, and so on. In a hard case where the law is indeterminate, forces of this sort ultimately determine what the judge will say or do. They will lead her to particular extralegal considerations of, for example, social utility, fairness, conventional morality, or a conservative preference for the status quo, and these will, in turn, lead her to an intuition or hunch about how the case ought to be resolved. If that resolution can be defended from the already existing valid law and principles of legal reasoning, then the matter is resolved. All that remains is the drafting of the rationalization intended to legitimate the result as an application of the law.

Once the core claims of legal realism are properly set out, they seem relatively straightforward and noncontroversial. Indeed, in many ways, these claims have been largely integrated into contemporary work in the philosophy of law and jurisprudence. They also inform a great deal of contemporary empirical work on law done in political science and legal studies departments. But, nevertheless, legal realism has given rise to more controversial positions still actively debated today. So, we turn now to its progeny.

We'll look briefly at three positions, or position families. The first is associated with what is known as the critical legal studies movement, or CLS. Here the key position concerns the indeterminacy of the law. Starting in the 1970s, CLS theorists began to argue that the legal realists had underestimated the indeterminacy of the law. On their view, already existing valid law and principles of legal reasoning do not function as even a weak constraint on what judges can do. The law is just politics by another name, pure and simple.

The second set of claims concern the search for the best sociologically informed causal explanation of the law and judicial decisions. In the latter half of the twentieth century, many legal scholars began paying close attention to the ways in which class, gender, and race function as sociological forces causally responsible for the content and development of law. Others focused more narrowly on traditional economic causal explanations of the law and judicial decisions. They argued that the law is best described and explained in terms of economic rationality and considerations of economic efficiency. Naturally enough, many of those working on either of these fronts saw their work as a preliminary to needed legal reforms, whether aimed at the elimination of economic, gender, or racial oppression or at improving the law's contribution to economic efficiency. This brings us to the third set of claims—claims of a normative sort regarding the proper aims of legal reform.

THE CRITS

Critical legal studies (CLS) grew out of a conference in the 1970s that sought to bring together the New Left politics of the 1960s, legal realism's emphasis on indeterminacy in law and its instrumentalist stance toward law, and European social theory (mainly structuralism and poststructuralism). CLS began as a radical critique of law under conditions of modern capitalism, but over time, it became a more radical critique of the very idea of law itself.

CLS is organized around two theses. The first is that legal systems are even more indeterminate than legal realists had realized and thus even less capable of subordinating the exercise of coercive political power to any system of legal rules or reasons. The second is that legal systems are best understood, in both their content and their operations, as ideological systems of legitimation, a way of hiding the reality of power and force behind pretty legal words and mystifying legal rituals. Together, these theses underwrite the proposition that law is always and everywhere mainly the politics of power by another name.

Like legal realism, CLS understands the content and structure of the law to derive largely from extralegal or nonlegal sources. And like legal realism, it seeks honesty about this fact. But unlike legal realists, who sought to reveal the reality of law so as to more effectively put it in the service of morally reputable political commitments (generally utilitarian and progressive), the crits (as those working within CLS came to be known)—at least the more radical of them—argued that the law could never be put to good use in the service of enduring deep political, social, or economic change. Because the law was inherently indeterminate, it was inherently unstable and therefore unreliable as a tool for lasting social change. Legal rights might be first introduced as progressive or emancipatory legal reforms (e.g., the legal rights associated with contract law or, more recently, the legal right to vote). But eventually and ironically they become just another tool through which those with power accomplish and legitimate their oppression and manipulation of those without. For CLS, then, the point of demystifying the law and exposing its true ideological nature was to encourage extralegal or nonlegal means to social reform and a transition to a "postlegal" social order.

THEIR INDETERMINACY THESES

By the 1960s, few legal philosophers thought that mature legal systems possessed sufficient internal resources (valid laws and principles of legal reasoning) to justify a single determinate answer to every legal question. The existence of so-called hard cases was taken for granted, not in the limited Hartian sense tied to the open texture of language but in the broader sense urged by legal realists. But no one at that time thought that all, or even most, cases were hard cases. Indeed, the existence of hard cases was regarded as a problem to manage, if not to solve. (Hence, Dworkin began arguing that there really are no hard cases.) By the 1980s, though, many crits were arguing in the other direction, claiming there were many more hard cases than had been realized.

The crits advanced two lines of argument. The first granted Dworkin's premise that the law included many moral principles, especially including principles of liberal political morality (regarding freedom, equality, privacy, etc.). But this argument then claimed that these principles were themselves inconsistent, incoherent, or unstable. Thus, rather than rendering the law more determinate, they just exacerbated the justificatory indeterminacy that legal realists had already revealed. Liberal political morality valued both individual self-interest and the collective or common good; saw the individual as ultimately free and responsible but also as socially constituted; favored legal rules on the ground that they protected expectations and ensured predictability, while recognizing the need for more flexible standards to ensure that substantive justice could be done on a case-by-case basis; insisted on a neutral state but favored secular modernist humanistic ways of life and conceptions of the good; committed itself to the political and legal equality of all citizens, but also to their freedom and thus all sorts of inequalities arising from its exercise; and so on. Liberal political morality was shot through with binary oppositions, both sides of which were valued. This, in itself, need not be a problem, provided there is a stable hierarchy to the relevant values. But the crits argued that these oppositions were unstable, always subject to reversal. If liberal political morality was inconsistent, incoherent, or unstable, then giving judges and legal officials free rein to appeal to it in their legal judgments and actions, as Dworkin did, could only make the law more, rather than less, indeterminate.

This is not the place to set out the content or to assess the merits—including the consistency, coherence, or stability—of liberal political morality (the generic political morality shared by all those who favor constitutional democracy with certain familiar basic rights and liberties and a minimum social safety net). But one point must be made. Dworkin made it in his reply to the crits: It is easy to confuse competing principles and commitments with inconsistent, incoherent, or unstable principles and commitments. But they are not the same. Liberal political morality may contain principles of or commitments to both the freedom and equality of persons. These principles or commitments may compete, because the more freedom individuals are given, the more unequal they may find themselves in power, possessions, reputation, and so on. But it doesn't follow that liberal principles of or commitments to both the freedom and equality of persons are inconsistent, incoherent, or unstable. It follows only that they must be balanced, weighed, adjusted, and so on, one against the other. Or, to put it another way, our commitments to freedom and equality are not commitments to absolute freedom or equality as if those were the only relevant values. They're commitments to some measure of freedom or equality, appropriate in light of all the other things we are correctly committed to. And this measure is something we may always be in the process of discovering. Thus, crits eager to demonstrate the radical justificatory indeterminacy of the law by pointing to the inconsistency, incoherence, or instability of liberal political morality must do a lot more than point out obvious tensions between liberal commitments to freedom and equality, self and community, predictability and substantive justice in their most abstract and decontextualized form—for in that form, they're not really liberal political values at all.

The second CLS line of argument for the radical justificatory indeterminacy of the law appeals to the structure of language, and even thought, itself. The argument here, drawn from poststructuralist linguistic and social theory, is that the very possibility of language, thought, and cognitive meaning depends on there being a multiplicity of meanings for any particular utterance or statement. This is fundamentally because language, thought, and cognitive meaning are made possible only through a mental process of differentiation—sounds, symbols, concepts, experiences, and so on, all endlessly differentiated one from another so as to give each some content. But this process of differentiation is ongoing and without any fixed or stable center. There is no initially "given" content in terms of which all differentiations are made or grounded. Rather, everything is in flux. And so the content or meaning, the place within the system of differences, of any given sound, symbol, concept, experience, and so on, is never finally fixed or determined. In fact, a sound, symbol, concept, experience, and so on *can mean something* (through differentiation) *only if it can mean more than one thing* (because the process of differentiation has no given foundation or stable center). Extending this claim to the language, concepts, and so on of the law, some crits argue that every attempt to arrive at a uniquely correct determinate legal judgment could be destabilized or undone by revealing that it depends on fixing or taking as given the meaning of some term or concept or rule the meaning of which was essentially and unavoidably multiple, plural, and fluid. These crits use "deconstructive" strategies of critical reading to "trash" legal judgments and arguments privileged as "correct" within the conventional order of legal reasoning.

Again, this is not the place to set out the content or to assess the merits of poststructuralist linguistic and social theory. But one point seems clear enough: If the crits are right about the nature of language, thought, and meaning, then it is hard to see how purposeful human conduct, including social reform, is possible at all. If every thought or utterance is both more and less than it seems, if every assertion dissolves into an endless proliferation of meanings, it's hard to see how any rational, intelligent political progress is to be made. To make such progress, ends must be established, means to those ends assessed and chosen, and so on. Insofar as the stated aim of CLS is to demystify and delegitimize the law so as to clear the way for extralegal or nonlegal paths to a more progressive and morally acceptable social order, this would seem to be a problem.

But if these arguments for the radical justificatory indeterminacy of the law are not compelling, what reason is there for thinking that the law is more indeterminate than already claimed by legal realism? One possibility concerns the nature of rules. Rules do not apply themselves. Accordingly, their content is never finally fixed and determinate. Take the counting rule apparently at work in the sequence "2, 4, 6, 8, 10, 12, ..." It appears that 14 comes next and that the rule is "count by 2's." But it's possible that 15 comes next and the rule is "count by 2's until 12 and then by 3's." Or 14 may come next, but the rule may be "count by 2's until 100 and then by 10's." It's not hard to imagine other possibilities. The same point may be advanced with respect to legal rules. The law may appear to be certain and determinate as a system of legal rules, but in fact the rules themselves are, like the counting rule just examined, indeterminate to a high degree.

But this isn't a very compelling argument. Within any mature legal system, the valid legal rules are interrelated and nested, each having implications for many others. Taken apart from its larger legal context, any given rule may be logically indeterminate in certain respects. But once returned to its natural legal context, other rules exclude many logically possible understandings of the rule. Further, there is almost universal agreement that the law typically includes not just rules but also principles. And these principles can render the rules more determinate. Finally, the larger legal context to which valid legal rules and principles belong is informed by shared understandings and is organized around shared purposes, which also help determine the scope and limit of any rule.

In the end, CLS offers little reason to affirm anything more than the rather limited, and to almost all lawyers and judges common-sensical, justificatory indeterminacy thesis advanced by legal realists.

Dworkin rejected this thesis, of course. He maintained that for every legal question or hard case, there is a single right answer. This uniquely correct legal result is given by the valid law and the legal reasons it underwrites and is discoverable through an interpretive or constructive legal judgment. But, as Dworkin acknowledged, in any hard case, perfectly competent judges may reasonably disagree over what the right answer or correct legal result is. Of course, it does not follow that there is no objectively right answer or correct legal result in these cases.

But suppose a hard case makes its way to the U.S. Supreme Court. There are nine justices. They reasonably disagree over what the right answer or correct legal result is. They agree there is one, but they can't agree on what it is. How do they decide the case? Well, they vote. But this just reintroduces indeterminacy back into the law, at least indeterminacy of the limited sort asserted by legal realists. From the point of view of those subject to the law wanting to plan their lives and thus be able to predict how the Court will act, the fact that each judge aims at and thinks she or he has the single right answer or correct legal result in every hard case is beside the point. What is important is that judges often reasonably disagree over what that answer or result is, and when they do, they count votes. But there is no reason to think that the legal position best justified is always the position favored by the majority. Voting is a crapshoot, as they say. So, the law in such a case—the law in any sense other than the "brooding omnipresence in the sky"—is whatever a majority on the Court happens to say it is; the already existing valid law and principles of legal reasoning function as only a weak constraint. That the Court might be wrong in some sense is irrelevant, at least for those concerned practically with planning their lives. (It may be relevant for lawyers and judges with the authority and opportunity to overturn or revise the erroneous decision at a later date.) So Dworkin offered no good argument against the legal realist thesis that for those with a practical need to know what the law is so they can plan their lives, there are good reasons to look to extralegal forces as the true causes of legal decisions. If legal decisions are often not uniquely justified by the law, then they must be brought about by something other than the justificatory force of the law.

This brings us to a final point about CLS and the indeterminacy of the law. Even if the CLS arguments for the radical justificatory indeterminacy of the law fail, their claims about causal indeterminacy in the law still need to be examined. Causal indeterminacy can exist, even if there is always a single right answer to every legal question as a matter of justification. It may be that as an empirical matter, judges are simply unmoved by the force of legal arguments. Judges may, in fact, be causally moved to make the decisions they make only, or mainly, by other extralegal or nonlegal considerations. They may even be so moved to make the very same decisions they'd make if they were to be moved only by the force of legal arguments. The point is that even if the law were more determinate as a matter of rational justification than many in CLS have claimed, judicial and other official decisions could in fact still be largely caused by something other than the law—even by the sociological and ideological forces of capitalism, patriarchy, and racism.

Interesting questions arise here. How could we prove causal indeterminacy in the law, especially if judges and officials routinely do and say only what is justified by the law? And if we could prove causal indeterminacy, why should we care about it, especially, again, if judges and officials routinely do and say only what is justified by the law? And if causal indeterminacy is true, what happens when the relevant extralegal or nonlegal causes drive a judge to an answer or result that is wrong or incorrect when assessed against what is justified under the law? These and related questions all remain on the table.

LAW AND ECONOMICS

The law and economics movement uses the concepts, methods, and principles of microeconomics to describe, explain, and critically assess the law. As a development or movement within legal philosophy, it gained visibility in the 1970s, with Richard Posner's *The Economic Analysis of Law*. But its roots go deeper. They run not just to the early 1960s, when Guido Calabresi, Ronald Coase, and others did pioneering work on the relationship between law and economics, but also to the classical legal realists, many of whom argued that economic considerations inevitably did and ought to shape the law, especially judicial decisions. Indeed, it is not a stretch to characterize the law and economics movement as a direct descendant of legal realism, though some bristle at this because classical legal realism is often seen as progressive. This movement sought to put the law in the service of aggregate utility and thus the common good, rather than of the abstract rules (often advantageous to elites) thought by formalists to express the deep or ideal structure of the law. The contemporary law and economics movement is generally seen as being more conservative. It appears to subordinate or reduce all values to economic efficiency, leaving the law little more than a servant to or extension of a free market ethic.

Several law and economics theses have been advanced. One is straightforwardly descriptive: some or all of the law is said to be best or most illuminatingly described exclusively or primarily in terms of economic efficiency. The law of tort, for example, is best understood as an institutional attempt to minimize the costs of accidents overall for society, including the cost of preventing accidents. A second thesis is straightforwardly normative: some or all of the law is said to be properly criticized and assessed exclusively or primarily in terms of economic efficiency. Wherever the law fails to promote or realize economic efficiency, it should be reformed. If strict liability rules are more economically efficient than fault liability rules in the law governing auto accident law, then strict liability rules ought to be adopted. Other theses claim that considerations of economic efficiency are the key to making accurate predictions of future legal developments or to explaining why certain legal practices arise, persist, or decline or even to giving the best interpretation of various legal systems.

The normative thesis is today probably the most widely discussed. But taken as a thesis about the primary or overriding aim of law, it is not compelling. Economic efficiency is no doubt an important value, one very relevant to the critical evaluation and reform of the law. But it is not likely the only or supreme value.

ECONOMIC EFFICIENCY

Economic efficiency is a property of transactions or relations between persons. It is related to, but not the same as, aggregate or total utility. Indeed, it is meant to function as a proxy for aggregate utility. The aggregate utility associated with any state of affairs is the sum total of the utility enjoyed by each person (or animal, if it experiences utility) implicated in or impacted by that state of affairs.

To talk about utility is to talk about value. Because the most basic values are intrinsic values, utility is generally defined in terms of some intrinsic value (instrumental value depends on intrinsic value; a dollar has value only because you can use it to get something you value intrinsically). Some philosophers argue that utility is pleasure or agreeable consciousness. Others argue that it is having one's preferences satisfied or desires met. Still others argue for other understandings of utility. How we define or understand utility is not important here. What is important is that a great deal of late nineteenth- and early twentieth-century economic thinking, including that done by legal realists, was utilitarian in spirit. And according to utilitarianism, one state of affairs is better than another just because it contains or yields more total utility or value. Thus, whenever we have a choice, we should choose that course of action that will yield the greatest total or aggregate utility, at least if we want to do what is morally right. Economic transactions and relations, then—indeed the economy as a whole and the legal regime that structures it—should be arranged so that over time, they maximize aggregate utility, or at least tend in that direction.

But if economies and legal systems ought to tend to maximize aggregate utility, then we must be able to add up the utility enjoyed by all those implicated in or impacted by any given economy or legal system with respect to which we have some choice to make. Here we confront the problem of interpersonal utility comparisons. To sum or aggregate individual utilities, we have to have some way of valuing them along a single metric or yardstick. Otherwise, we'll find ourselves adding apples and oranges, as the saying goes.

Suppose Sally says she enjoys five units of utility. Suzy says she does, too. We're tempted to add five and five and say that together Sally and Suzy enjoy ten units of utility. But unless we have some way of knowing that what Sally calls five units of utility is the same as what Suzy calls five units of utility, we cannot really sum their utilities together as ten. Maybe what Sally calls five units is really equal to what Suzy calls three units. How would we know? We'd have to look in their respective heads, but that's not possible. Of course, we can *say* Sally and Suzy together enjoy ten units of utility, but without some way of comparing Sally's five units to Suzy's five units, we'd just be mouthing the word "ten" without knowing what we meant by it. Do we mean ten units using Sally's metric, or Suzy's, or some third alternative, or what? This is the problem with interpersonal utility comparisons. It's a problem not just for utilitarians, who think the morally right thing to do whenever we have a choice is to choose that state of affairs that maximizes aggregate utility. It's a problem for anyone who thinks it's at least always worth considering the aggregate utility associated with various options available to them when they confront a choice.

It's tempting to point to money as the common metric here. If Sally is willing to pay X to have Y and Suzy is willing to pay X + Z, then Suzy must value Y more to the tune of Z, and thus it must yield for her more utility equivalent in amount to Z. Unfortunately, this won't work. Whether we think of utility in terms of pleasure or preference satisfaction or whatever, the amount Sally or Suzy is willing to pay for something will be a function of how much money either has and what else either would like to use that money for. We can use money to arrive at some sense of how each person values various items for herself relative to the other. (If Sally is willing to pay more for a Mustang than for a Buick, then evidently she values the Mustang more.) But we'll still be without any basis for commensurating the rankings we arrive at for both Sally and Suzy. Supposing that each has the same amount of money won't solve the problem. It might enable Sally and Suzy to arrive at a fair distribution of the goods available to them, because they each start with equal bargaining or purchasing power. But there's still no guarantee that the utility Sally derives for every ten dollars spent is the same as the utility Suzy derives. We can assume that it is, if we want. But then we must recognize that we're making an assumption.

Happily, there is a way around the problem of interpersonal utility comparisons. It is the modern idea of economic efficiency, the germ of which was developed by the late nineteenth century economist Vilfredo Pareto. Pareto's basic idea was that if a transaction or relation makes all those it affects better off, or at least no worse off by their own lights, then we have good reason to believe that it increases aggregate utility. True, we can't know by how much, because we can't add the individual utilities. But because they're all presumably positive integers, the sum must also be positive and thus represent an aggregate utility gain. A transaction or relation that makes at least one person better off and no one worse off by their own lights is said, then, to be Pareto superior to its status quo ante. Any state of affairs from which no Pareto superior change is possible is said to be Pareto optimal. From any given state of affairs, it may be possible to make many different Pareto superior changes, each leading to a different Pareto optimal state of affairs. The total set of such possible Pareto optimal states of affairs marks the limit of our ability to act rationally so as to improve aggregate utility from any given status quo. We can call it the efficiency frontier. It's possible, of course, that some non-Pareto optimal states of affairs (those within which some regard themselves as worse off by their own lights) may actually represent gains in aggregate utility over any or all Pareto optimal states of affairs (the set of which constitutes the efficiency frontier). But without being able to do interpersonal utility comparisons, we have no way of reliably picking them out.

If the law and judicial decisions are really determined to a large extent, as many legal realists assert, by extralegal or nonlegal considerations of economic efficiency, then we ought to be able empirically to observe a pattern of Pareto superior legal developments up to the point of Pareto optimality. And if the law really ought normatively to serve the utilitarian end of maximizing aggregate utility, then it should be reformed to facilitate or produce Pareto superior transactions and relations up to, but not beyond, a point of Pareto optimality. The law may promote Paretian economic efficiency in at least three ways: (i) by distributing legal rights and entitlements to those who value them most; (ii) by redistributing, through law, the costs and benefits of some transaction or relation so as to render it efficient on the Pareto criteria; or (iii) by sustaining an open and transparent market with low transaction costs and few incentives for strategic holdout behavior, so that persons can voluntarily exchange legal rights and entitlements until they arrive at a Pareto optimal state of affairs.

As it turns out, unhappily, the Pareto criteria of economic efficiency have limited application in the real world of law and economics. This is because most transactions or relations between persons carry transaction costs or generate adverse third-party effects. Suppose you want to sell your legal right to a 1962 ragtop, two-door Impala (a cherry sled, as they say), and I want to trade my legal right to some sum of money in my bank account for your cool ride. Before any transaction can take place between us, we'll need to find each other. That may involve one or both of us spending time or money on advertising or making inquiries. Then we'll need to arrive at an agreement, and that will mean bargaining, which takes time and energy and perhaps even money, as I'll likely want my mechanic to inspect your car. These are all transaction costs. When transaction costs are high, individuals may not enter into transactions or relations that would otherwise leave them better off by their own lights. And then there are adverse third-party effects. Suppose I purchase your 1962 Impala and then spend all my time working on or playing with it, neglecting my family obligations. My wife and children suffer. That is an adverse third-party effect of the transaction. But it's not one either you or I took into account when determining that we were each better off making the deal we made. But if neither of us took this cost into account, how can we be sure that our deal actually improved aggregate utility? Perhaps the suffering of my wife and children is large enough that it cancels whatever utility you and I gain from our transaction. After all, by their lights, our deal left them worse off than they were before.

Because the Pareto criteria of economic efficiency are of limited real-world value, most economists today rely on the Kaldor-Hicks criterion of economic efficiency. On this criterion, a transaction or relation is economically efficient (and thus presumptively an aggregate utility gain) only if those who gain by their own lights could, in principle, draw from their gain to compensate anyone who thinks herself made worse off so as to produce the result that the transaction or relation leaves no one worse off, and still makes at least one person better off, by their own lights. It's not necessary that those who gain actually compensate those who lose; it's only necessary that in principle they could do so in a manner or to a degree that leaves everyone at least no worse off than they were before and at least one person better off. If my wife and children would be indifferent to my neglect of them in favor of my car if they received a thousand dollar payment and if you would have been happy to have sold the car to me for a thousand dollars less than you did, then you could, in principle, compensate my wife and children for their loss so that they're made indifferent between the status quo ante and the new status quo, leaving you and I each still better off by our own lights. Our transaction, then, is Kaldor-Hicks efficient, a presumptive gain in aggregate utility.

Within the law and economics movement, most analyses proceed in terms of Kaldor-Hicks efficiency. But this is not entirely unproblematic. The Kaldor-Hicks criterion is itself problematic at the level of application. The problem is that two different states of affairs may be reciprocally Kaldor-Hicks efficient. (i.e., it may be Kaldor-Hicks efficient to move from state of affairs A to B, but then also Kaldor-Hicks efficient to move from B back to A. This is known as the Scitovsky paradox.) But it's not possible for two different states of affairs to each have more aggregate utility than the other, which means the Kaldor-Hicks criterion isn't always reliable as a proxy for aggregate utility.

Economists continue to develop more refined criteria of economic efficiency. The underlying idea remains the same, however.

Economic efficiency is a proxy for aggregate utility. It is, as the saying goes, about the size of the pie.

THE DESCRIPTIVE THESIS

It is clearly possible, superficially, to describe many areas of the law in terms of economic efficiency. But the extent to which the law is well described in such terms is difficult to determine. Take the law governing accidents. Accidents involve unintended harms arising out of conduct engaged in for its benefits. The law governing accidents usually takes the form of liability rules. Those who cause such harms are liable to those who suffer them under certain specified conditions. This is, no doubt, a more efficient way for the law to proceed than for it to prevent people from engaging in any beneficial conduct that might risk harm to others, unless they get the permission of those put at risk, or for the law to simply ignore all harms resulting from accidents. So we might say as a descriptive matter, that it is economically efficient to have a system of liability rules governing accidents. It leaves everyone better off, or at least no worse off than they would be under alternative feasible legal arrangements.

But it's hard to see how we could say much more than this. There are lots of different liability rules we might use in a system of accident law. We can vary in all sorts of ways the conditions under which people are liable for the unintended harms their conduct visits on others. If we really want to determine whether a given system of accident law is economically efficient, we need to examine the content and effects of its rules in close detail. But the information required to carry out such a study will in almost all cases prove overwhelmingly complex and often simply unavailable. The expected costs associated with any particular rule will be a function not just of the degrees and probabilities of harm from accidents covered by the rule, but also of such things as the costs of the care required to avoid liability and of administering and enforcing the rule across society. Even if we could get all this information, how would we ever be able to determine whether the state of affairs determined by any given rule was economically efficient when compared with all its viable alternatives?

A great deal has been written about the economic efficiency of many different areas of law, tort, contract, and so on. But in the end, the descriptive thesis advanced by law and economics looks like it becomes less and less compelling as the picture of law to which it is applied is made more and more complete, realistic, and fine-grained. The jury is still out, though. More refined conceptions of economic efficiency and more full-blown and carefully refined studies may vindicate the descriptive thesis after all. And it's surely true that considerations of economic efficiency will at least figure into, even if they don't exhaust, any complete and adequate description of the law.

Early on in the law and economics movement, some theorists argued that the law was not only best described mainly or primarily in terms of economic efficiency but also that considerations of economic efficiency best explained why the law was what it was. Somehow economic efficiency figured prominently in, and perhaps dominated, the causal story of the law. Either judges and other officials sought directly to promote economic efficiency or, through some causal mechanism, their essentially self-interested or ideologically driven choices regularly, if indirectly, generated economic efficiency gains.

There are at least two problems with this explanatory or causal thesis. First, it presupposes the descriptive thesis, which we've just seen appears to be only superficially plausible. Second, it's unclear how it could ever be empirically verified. Accordingly, attention in recent years has shifted away from the descriptive and explanatory theses toward a normative thesis about the relationship between law and economic efficiency.

THE NORMATIVE THESIS

Some argue that no matter how the law as it presently stands is best described, or what caused it to be what it is, surely it ought to be made more economically efficient whenever possible. Thus, the law should be evaluated to assess its present economic merits and reformed whenever there is a viable Kaldor-Hicks reform available.

But even if we thought economic efficiency was the most important virtue a legal system or domain of law could possess, if we cannot presently determine the truth of the descriptive thesis because we lack the necessary information, how are we to intelligently reform the law to improve economic efficiency? And even if the necessary information was, in principle, available, the costs of gathering it (complex information not just about the status quo and the proposed reform, but also about viable alternative reforms) would likely sometimes be so great that any gains from a justified legal reform would be swamped by the costs of justifying that reform. The costs of the necessary analysis would cancel any expected benefits from the reforms it recommends. So, we know in advance that it will sometimes be economically inefficient to perform the necessary analysis. But when? We can't know without knowing the potential gains from viable possible reforms. And we can't know that without doing the analysis.

Of course, if we were confident that over the long haul we'd generate more gains from some implemented reform than we would suffer costs from wasted analyses, we might proceed in any event. But what would it take to be confident about this? We may think the benefits of a proposed legal reform are pretty clear as we imagine how citizens acting out of rational self-interest will act once officials implement it in a regular and reliable way. But we also need to think about how the officials who make and implement the reform will act. If, for the sake of projecting the benefits of a proposed reform, we assume that citizens will all act out of rational self-interest, then why would we assume anything different about the legal officials making and implementing the reform? Why assume that their behavior in making and implementing the reforms will be subject to different causal mechanisms than the behavior of citizens? But if what legal officials will do when making and implementing a proposed reform is to be projected as a function of their rational self-interest, then they may not do what we initially supposed they would do, and we may need to revise our sense of what citizens will do in light of this new expectation regarding official behavior.

But suppose we could know, with some significant degree of confidence, that a proposed reform would increase economic efficiency. This is surely possible in some cases. Shouldn't we make any and every such reform?

It is still not at all clear why economic efficiency should be taken as the only or most important normative priority for the first virtue of legal systems, ours or anyone else's. For utilitarians, there may be good reasons to insist that legal reforms always be efficient relative to their status quo ante. But even for utilitarians, there are no good reasons to insist that legal reforms be either Pareto optimal or Kaldor-Hicks efficient. Neither necessarily guarantees a gain in aggregate utility over the status quo ante. It's possible to arrive at a Pareto optimal point through a non–Pareto superior change. In such a case, there's no reason to think that aggregate utility was necessarily increased. It's also possible for two states of affairs to be Kaldor-Hicks efficient with respect to each other. So a Kaldor-Hicks efficient legal reform may not entail an increase in aggregate utility. Thus, there are no good utilitarian reasons to make Pareto optimality or Kaldor-Hicks efficiency the sole or supreme moral aim of the law. And it's doubtful that there are any good nonutilitarian reasons for doing so. Considerations of fairness or consent or respect for autonomy are not likely to justify privileging Pareto optimality or Kaldor-Hicks efficiency as the sole or overriding aim of the law. Thus, the case for grounding legal criticism and reform exclusively in considerations of economic efficiency is weak. Still, considerations of economic efficiency may (and probably should) play a subordinate role in legal criticism and reform

As Dworkin and others rightly argue, economic efficiency is but one of the values, and certainly not the foundational or most important value, relevant to the moral assessment and reform of the law. The values of justice, fairness, freedom, equality, solidarity, care, and so on are also each independently relevant to the moral assessment and reform of the law. None are fully subordinate or reducible to economic efficiency.

When pushed its hardest, the law and economics movement threatens to collapse into a sort of legal formalism—one that supposes a priori that there is and should be in the law an economic rationality; one just waiting to be extracted and formally articulated; one that would, if we could only lay our hands on it, ground a proper legal science. This is especially ironic given that most in the law and economics movement think of the legal realists as their ancestors, and the realists were most concerned with rejecting just such legal formalisms.

FEMINIST JURISPRUDENCE

It may seem odd to discuss feminist jurisprudence in a chapter devoted mainly to legal realism. But like legal realism, feminist jurisprudence aims to reveal the true causes of the law so as to demystify it and allow for its more effective instrumental use toward morally sound goals. The early legal realists may not have been feminists. But many feminists working in contemporary philosophy of law take for granted claims first established by the legal realists.

Feminist jurisprudence is an immense and varied domain within the philosophy of law. It has been and remains theoretically diverse and rich and politically and methodologically open. This is not least because feminist legal theorists have often allied themselves with and drawn on the work of those pursuing other emancipatory political agendas. Thus, one can find within feminist philosophy of law substantial strands of inquiry, discourse, and advocacy drawing on legal realism, CLS, race theory, queer theory, psychoanalytic theory, game and rational choice theory, and so on.

Characteristic of feminist jurisprudence are two claims—one descriptive and explanatory, the other normative. The descriptive and explanatory claim is that the systemic patriarchal oppression of women is fundamentally realized through law. It is so realized through the substantive content of a rationally determinate legal order that oppresses (and legitimizes the oppression of) women, or through the actions of judges and other legal officials causally moved, not by a rationally determinate legal order, but rather by other extralegal or nonlegal forces, especially patriarchy as a sociological and ideological force, or through some combination of both legal and extralegal forces. In any case, the systemic patriarchal oppression of women is largely accomplished by the contingent linking – through and in law – of biological sex to gender and gendered norms in such a way that the former seems to provide a naturalistic justification for the latter. Some of the most interesting and illuminating work in feminist jurisprudence has been done in the service of this descriptive and explanatory thesis. Feminist studies of the practice and development of employment law, rape law, contract law, property law, and so on have all shed valuable light on the ways in which the forces of patriarchy, and the sex-gender system in particular, shape the content and practice of law.

The normative claim is that the ending of patriarchal oppression and the emancipation of women must rank at or near the top of the list of aims in terms of which the law is properly criticized and reformed. Apart from these claims, however, there is little general consensus within feminist jurisprudence. Positions vary with respect to whether the law oppresses women mainly through its substantive content or through extralegal and nonlegal forces operating on judges and other legal officials; whether women and men share all the same fundamental interests; whether those interests are rooted in a biologically or psychologically given human nature; the extent to which they are malleable regardless of their genesis; the proper relationship of the law to those interests; whether it is possible to end patriarchy fully without radical transformation of modern liberal legal orders; and so on.

However, we can distinguish broadly between two camps. The more moderate rejects any claims about the indeterminacy of the law more robust than those taken from legal realism and already mainstreamed into legal thought. This camp thinks it is the content or substance of the law through which women have been, and to some extent still are, oppressed, not the very rule of law itself. The more radical camp affirms one or another more robust indeterminacy thesis of the sort associated with critical legal studies. It thinks that women have been and will continue to be oppressed so long as the rule of law is sustained, for the law inevitably functions as a tool through which those with power (i.e., men) accomplish and legitimize their oppression of those without (i.e., women).

The moderate camp divides itself into two distinct groups. In general, all in the moderate camp regard the abolition of patriarchy as a substantially completed task, the full completion of which is possible under the rule of law. But some think it is possible under the rule of law without significant change to the basic structure of modern liberal legal doctrines and practice. They insist there are some areas of law still in need of reform (e.g., rape law, employment law, marriage law), but they regard the needed reforms as relatively straightforward and simply a matter of content. Other moderate feminists argue that more significant changes to the basic structure of modern liberal legal doctrines and practice are needed. For example, they might challenge the ideal of equal rights, arguing that without special rights for women distinct from those afforded men (e.g., a battered women's syndrome defense in some homicides or special rights in employment), it will not be possible to eradicate patriarchy completely. Or they might argue that the government must have the authority to intervene in domains traditionally defined as private under the law (e.g., regulating the use by adults of adult pornography in the privacy of the home or physical contact between husbands and wives). These sorts of reforms are about both the structure and the content of the law and are controversial for that reason, with some moderate feminists arguing they are unnecessary or undesirable.

The more radical feminist camp argues, first, that patriarchy continues to exist in a rather robust and pervasive way, not yet having been substantially defeated, and, second, that this rather robust patriarchy depends on and is at least partially constituted through both the substantive content of the law and the rule or nature of law more generally. Because this camp regards the systemic oppression of women as still pervasive, they are prepared to countenance far more radical challenges to the legal status quo to bring about the end of patriarchy. They may reject key concepts and categories basic to modern liberal legal doctrine and practice as just so many instruments and manifestations of patriarchy—for example, legal reasoning, due process, legal rights (and not just equal rights), procedural fairness, state neutrality, individual responsibility, autonomy, the distinction between the public and the private, justice through and under the law, objectivity, impartiality, adversarial trials, the role of rules in moral and legal judgment, and so on, including the rule-of-law ideal itself. They may also offer as substitutes for, rather than supplements to, these traditional doctrines and practices alternatives said to be morally preferable, such as care, mediation, particularism, negotiated settlement, collective responsibility, solidarity, subjectivity, rule of persons, partiality, and so on.

It would be easy and appropriate to devote an entire chapter to feminist jurisprudence. But as noted in my introductory chapter, it is not possible in a book of this sort to cover in depth every topic that merits coverage. Therefore, readers interested in feminist legal theory, or critical race theory, or queer legal theory, or other recent developments aimed at revealing the reality and true causes of the law so as to facilitate a more progressive reform of it, are encouraged to consult the bibliography for further reading.

SELECTED BIBLIOGRAPHY

On Legal Realism and Its Progeny

Altman, Andrew. *Critical Legal Studies: A Liberal Critique.* (Princeton, NJ: Princeton University Press), 1990.

Duxbury, Neil. *Patterns of American Jurisprudence.* (Oxford, UK: Oxford University Press), 1997.

Feldman, Stephen. *American Legal Thought: From Premodernism to Postmodernism.* (Oxford, UK: Oxford University Press), 2000.

Fisher, William; Horowitz, Morton; and Reed, Thomas eds. *American Legal Realism.* (Oxford, UK: Oxford University Press), 1993.

Frank, Jerome. *Law and the Modern Mind*. (Magnolia, MA: Peter Smith Publishers), 1985.

Frug, Mary Jo. *Postmodern Legal Feminism*. (New York, NY: Routledge), 1992.

Kairys, David, ed. *The Politics of Law: A Progressive Critique*. (New York, NY: Pantheon Books), 1982.

Kelman, Mark. *A Guide to Critical Legal Studies*. (Cambridge, MA: Harvard University Press), 1987.

Leiter, Brian. "American Legal Realism," *The Blackwell Guide to Philosophy of Law and Legal Theory*, W. Golding and W. Edmundson, eds. (Oxford, UK: Blackwell Publishing), 2005.

Llewellyn, Karl. *The Bramble Bush*. (Dobbs Ferry, NY: Oceana Press), 1930.

MacKinnon, Catherine. *Feminism Unmodified: Discourses on Life and Law*. (Cambridge, MA: Harvard University Press), 1987.

Minow, Martha. *Making All the Difference*. (Cambridge, MA: Harvard University Press), 1990.

Polinsky, A. *An Introduction to Law and Economics*, 2nd ed. (Boston, MA: Little Brown), 1989.

Posner, Richard. *Economic Analysis of Law*, 5th ed. (Boston, MA: Little Brown), 1998.

Smith, Patricia. *Feminist Jurisprudence*. (Oxford, UK: Oxford University Press), 1993.

Unger, Roberto. *The Critical Legal Studies Movement*. (Cambridge, MA: Harvard University Press), 1986.

5

On Constitutionalism, Democracy, and Judicial Review

Legal realists, natural law theorists, and legal positivists all agree that judges must or do sometimes exercise their moral and political judgment when resolving particular cases. Positivists may think this should happen only when the law, as given by conventional sources, has run out. Realists may think it happens a lot of the time, whether or not judges admit it. Natural law theorists may think it should happen all the time. But they all agree that judges must or do sometimes exercise their moral and political judgment when making a legal judgment. This raises worries, of course, about the extent to which the rule-of-law (rather than the rule of man) ideal can be realized or sustained in any political community.

This problem takes on special urgency when the legal questions that judges address are constitutional or fundamental, the political community is a democracy, and the judges are not elected. For then it looks like what the law is, at its most basic level, is a function of the moral and political commitments of unelected judges rather than either their more narrowly legal judgment or the moral and political commitments of the voters or the people in general. And that seems downright undemocratic. Surely, in a democracy, if what the law is at its most basic level is to be a function of moral and political, rather

[handwritten: problem w/ judges directing moral + political of judgment — not democratic]

than narrowly legal, judgment, then it ought to be the judgment of the voters or people in general, rather than a handful of unelected judges. Or so it is commonly said, at least in the United States, where debate over judicial review is long-standing, robust, and heated. Judicial review refers most generally to the power or authority of judges to review legislation and executive acts and to declare them legally invalid if they are found to suffer from one or another fatal defect, including constitutional defects, as a matter of law. In this most general sense, judicial review is noncontroversial. Judges must say what the law is, and in so doing, they must apply criteria of legal validity. In a constitutional system, these will be, at rock bottom, constitutional criteria. If Congress or the president fails to make a valid law, say by failing to hold the necessary vote or to affix the necessary signature, then judges must refuse to recognize the alleged law as valid.

Judicial review is or becomes controversial, however, when the defect alleged to render the law invalid is something other than a noncontroversial procedural defect in the manner or form of enactment, when it is a matter of controversial substantive constitutional criteria of legal validity over which persons, and thus branches of government, may or do reasonably disagree. Still, most judges, lawyers, and philosophers of law today accept some measure of even this more controversial exercise of judicial review—for example, judicial invalidation of statutorily prescribed punishments thought to violate the Eighth Amendment's prohibition on "cruel and unusual" punishments.

Yet there have been and remain dissenting voices. Justice John Gibson in *Eakin v. Raub* (1825) argued that the Court should enforce all laws duly enacted, even those it judges unconstitutional. Something very close to Gibson's view prevails today in Great Britain, where the court does not have the power to invalidate legislation it deems inconsistent with the British constitution (though it can now trigger review by the European Court by declaring a law unconstitutional on human rights grounds). Jeremy Waldron has championed something like this view in the United States in recent years.

Besides Waldron and a few others, however, most legal officials and philosophers of law in the United States today accept some measure of substantive judicial review. But some still share the view expressed by James Thayer late in the nineteenth century. He argued that the Court should defer to the judgments of the other branches of government as to the constitutionality of their actions (laws passed or executive orders issued), unless their judgments are so clearly incorrect that there could be no rational debate over the matter. Thayer sought to limit the Court's exercise of substantive judicial review as much as possible. Whatever the merits of his view, it has not dominated judicial practice in the United States, though there are still substantive areas of the law in which the Court continues to take something like Thayer's approach to judicial review. In most cases, however, judges usually understand themselves to be bound to exercising their own best judgment as to what the law is, not to abdicating that responsibility to others. And so constitutional adjudication is today rarely as restrained as Thayer argued it should be.

Those who today argue for judicial restraint in the United States rarely have Thayer's position in mind. (The terms *judicial restraint* and *judicial activism* are not particularly helpful. At the very least, the court can be restrained or active on at least two fronts: (i) with respect to the number and range of cases over which it exercises judicial review; and (ii) with respect to its deference toward the constitutional judgments of the other branches when it exercises judicial review. The terms are often used as pejoratives. For example, you describe a judge as "activist" if she reaches a result you don't like.) They instead usually mean to argue either for a cautious judicial concern with the likely acceptance and effects of constitutional rulings (as when the Court decided not to take up the issue of miscegenation laws in the 1950s so soon after and amid the social unrest generated by its desegregation decision in *Brown v. Board of Education*) or for a particular theory of constitutional interpretation, say, originalism. Nevertheless, something like Thayer's view has shaped judicial practice elsewhere. In some countries—New Zealand, for example—judicial review is restrained by the principle that the court should always interpret legislative or executive acts so as to render them constitutional and thus enforceable, rather than invalidating them as unconstitutional. This is a way of implementing judicial deference to the nonjudicial branches of government.

Judicial review becomes more controversial the more judges actively exercise their own independent or nondeferential judgment as to the constitutionality of legislative and executive acts, as they do in the United States, frustrating the apparent will of democratically elected officials acting in full compliance with the constitutional requirements governing the procedural form and enactment of legislation. In the book that launched the contemporary debate over judicial review, Alexander Bickel described judicial review as antidemocratic, because it "thwarts the will of the representatives of the actual people here and now." This is the so-called countermajoritarian difficulty raised by judicial review. The countermajoritarian difficulty is made more difficult when the Court draws on controversial substantive values or principles not literally expressed in the Constitution to ground its constitutional judgment.

It becomes yet still more difficult when the Court claims for its constitutional judgments, as it does today, final authority over all branches of government, and indeed over the body politic as a whole. The active exercise of independent or nondeferential judicial review is compatible with the other branches of government exercising their own judgment as to the constitutionality of their acts and how to proceed in the face of a judicial determination that an act is unconstitutional. In his second inaugural address, Abraham Lincoln argued for a strong version of this view, known as departmentalism: each branch of government is co-equal, and thus no branch of government must necessarily submit to the constitutional judgments of any other, not even to the judgments of the judicial branch. More recently, some critics of current practice have advocated a weaker version of this view, known as weak judicial review: judicial judgments regarding the constitutionality of legislative or executive acts are binding on all branches unless and until they are overturned by a procedurally valid act of those other branches. Recently, there have been bills introduced into Congress to establish weak judicial review as a legislative matter through Congress's authority to regulate the courts.

Such bills have been introduced because, as we have it today in the United States, judicial review is neither of Lincoln's departmentalist nor of the weak judicial review sort. What we have today is what we might call strong judicial review. It is the conjunction of the active exercise of independent or nondeferential judicial review with the assertion of complete judicial supremacy over the other branches of government with respect to constitutional issues. Strong judicial review is a relatively recent development in American legal practice, emerging bit by bit in fits and starts over the past two centuries and almost always against some not insignificant resistance.

Strong judicial review is, however, still constrained by the fact that the written constitution authorizes the Supreme Court to act only when faced with a "case or controversy." It cannot issue binding advisory constitutional opinions whenever its sees fit. So, strong judicial review as we have it today could be made still stronger. There are countries—France, for example—within which the constitutional court has general jurisdiction and may issue constitutional opinions whenever it thinks it necessary or useful to do so, in something like the manner that state attorney generals issue legal opinions in the United States, without any particular case or controversy before them.

Strong judicial review is undeniably controversial, in both public and academic circles. Whether the issue is gay marriage or the ability of cities and states to use the power of eminent domain to take private property or the resolution of the 2000 presidential election, the cry against so-called activist judges who "legislate from the bench" or "rewrite the Constitution" has become familiar background noise in public political debate. But it is not just background noise. It is often also a call to action. Legislators, citizens, and other political actors increasingly try to influence, maneuver around, effectively overturn, or take political advantage of Supreme Court rulings. Indeed, the Supreme Court has become an increasingly important site of political action and contest during the past century.

Whatever its power, given current practices, the Court is clearly just one institutional actor in a vastly more complex political process within which all sorts of political actors, both institutional and non-institutional, strategically interact. The political activities surrounding both the legal recognition of gay marriage and judicial appointments to the Supreme Court provide recent and visible examples of how controversial and contested, as well as how fully nested and incomplete, is the power of the Supreme Court. Whatever the merits of strong judicial review, it is just one element of what we might call *constitutional politics*. This is an important point to bear in mind as one considers claims to the effect that the United States has been or is being transformed from a constitutional democracy into a sort of elitist jurocracy.

Public debate regarding judicial review usually generates more heat than light. Slogans are tossed about without any real or deep philosophical inquiry into the issues at hand. That is too bad, because the issue of judicial review in a constitutional democracy is among the most philosophically complex and interesting issues discussed today by legal theorists, philosophers of law, and political philosophers in general. It is complex and interesting because it requires us to wrestle with three very fundamental questions, each of which cuts across our previous discussions of legal positivism, natural law theory, and legal realism. These questions are: What is a constitution? What is a democracy or, more to the point, a constitutional democracy subject to the rule of law? And, is judicial review, either in its present form or in some revised form, at least consistent with, if not required by, the ideal of a constitutional democracy subject to the rule of law?

To understand and evaluate the practice of judicial review, we need to answer these three questions. If the ideal of a constitutional democracy under the rule of law is feasible and attractive, and if strong judicial review as currently practiced is inconsistent with it, then we have a problem. How to solve the problem will depend on whether weaker forms of judicial review are consistent with the ideal.

WHAT IS A CONSTITUTION?

Every political community governed by law has a constitution. In the most fundamental sense, a constitution is that which constitutes a body politic. The constitution of a body politic committed to the rule of law must constitute the authority of legal offices and specify when and how they may exercise that authority on behalf of the body politic and much else. It integrates the members of the political community into an institutional and legal structure within and through which it is possible to legislate, adjudicate, enforce, regulate, and so on.

The constitution of a body politic committed to the rule of law may be written or unwritten. The United States has a written constitution. The United Kingdom does not. Constitutions may be democratic or nondemocratic. The United States has a (highly but not purely) democratic constitution. Oman does not. Whether written or unwritten, democratic or nondemocratic, the constitution is, in some sense, basic within the legal system it constitutes. It is basic not because it deals only with the most important matters, and not because ordinary laws within the legal system cannot deal with such important matters as how laws are made or how cases are adjudicated. It is basic because within the legal system, the legal authority of officials and the legal validity of ordinary laws are predicated on their fidelity to it.

Constitutions are thus always more firmly entrenched than the ordinary laws subject to them. It's always formally harder to amend or revise the constitution than it is to pass or change an ordinary law. Constitutions need not be immune to legal amendment or revision. The U.S. Constitution provides for its own amendment in Article V. In this sense, constitutions can be like ordinary laws. But they are always more firmly entrenched within the legal system. Sometimes a constitution or constitutional provision may be fully entrenched and thus immune to revision, either for a period of time or permanently.

Because constitutions place some elements of the legal system beyond the immediate reach of present actors seeking reform, they function as a kind of constraint on day-to-day political processes, including democratic processes. But this need not make them inherently antidemocratic. For one thing, constitutions always require interpretation and thus cannot fully escape the judgments of present-day actors. Still, even a constitution only relatively entrenched—say, one allowing for formal amendment and requiring a good deal of interpretation—may come to seem antidemocratic if it is thought to entail something like strong judicial review vesting the court, rather than the people, with final and full authority over its meaning.

No constitution is perfect, of course. And thus in any constitutional system, there will likely always be dissenters pressing for constitutional reform. But in general, everyone does better with a legal system governed by a relatively stable, even if suboptimal, set of basic or constitutional legal rules than they would with a system within which any and all legal rules, including basic procedural rules, are easily challenged, changed, and so on. It is their relative entrenchment (relative to ordinary laws) that makes constitutions so valuable. Because they are relatively entrenched, constitutions secure the possibility of coordinated and cooperative conduct over time through law. They signal to actors both inside and outside the body politic that certain political–legal conditions are likely to remain stable. These need not be limited to procedural matters. For example, the framers of the U.S. Constitution determined that it would be highly advantageous to entrench a provision ensuring that present contracts and debts will be honored by future generations, because without such an entrenched provision, interest rates would likely quickly become prohibitive. Because of the benefits secured by constitutional stability, dissenters will often accept what they regard as a suboptimal constitution, seeking to correct or improve it only through constitutionally valid means.

So far, so good. But now we must introduce a wrinkle. There are two senses in which we may speak of a constitution. There is, first, the constitution as the fundamental or supreme law within a legal system. It exists as law. The U.S. Constitution, the written document as interpreted, has this status. So too does the unwritten British constitution (even though the British courts lack the power to invalidate legislation on constitutional grounds). In any constitutional system of law, there is a legal constitution in this sense. But then there is also the constitution in a second sense, what we might call the *political constitution*. This is the constitution understood as the extralegal norms or social practices in terms of which citizens and officials ultimately validate all law within their system, including their legal constitution as the fundamental and supreme law within it (recall Hart's rule of recognition or Kelsen's *grundnorm*, neither of which is itself a valid law). In the United States, the written constitution as interpreted is the legal constitution, the fundamental and supreme law within the system. But it is so because we, citizens and officials, adhere to a political constitution that picks it out as such. That political constitution also includes norms and expectations governing the interpretation of the written constitution, the practice of judicial review, and the relationship between the different branches of government and between government and the people in general.

In a sense, then, in every constitutional legal system, there are two constitutions, although each instantiates a different sense of the term. One exists as law within the legal system: in the United States, the written constitution and the judicial decisions interpreting it. The other exists as a necessary condition to the legal system and is given by or through the normative political practices of citizens and officials: in the United States, something like the rule of recognition manifest in the behavior of officials and citizens, behavior largely organized around the practice of strong judicial review. Both constitutions are necessary to a constitutional legal order. Each is distinct from the other, though the two stand in a relationship of mutual interdependence. The U.S. Constitution, the basic and supreme law within the U.S. legal system, might be changed (e.g., pursuant to the Article V provisions governing constitutional amendment) without any accompanying change to the political constitution. Conversely, the political constitution (e.g., expectations and norms regarding the authority of the Court to determine the meaning of the Constitution for all the branches of government or regarding acceptable approaches to interpreting the Constitution) may change without any significant change to the Constitution as law. But although the two constitutions are, in principle, distinct and may change independent of one another, more generally there is a kind of dynamic interplay between the two: changes in one yield changes to the other. For example, changes to the political constitution may yield changes to the legal constitution.

Indeed, for some critics of judicial review as presently practiced in the United States, this is precisely what has happened over the past two hundred years. On the view of these critics, the political constitution governing the authority and meaning of the legal constitution have steadily changed. The written constitution does not itself legally establish or address judicial review in any obvious way. The current practice of strong judicial review arose, in fits and starts, over the past two hundred years. (It's often said that Justice John Marshall established judicial review in *Marbury v. Madison* [1803]. But not even the most sympathetic and expansive reading of that decision will yield anything like the current practice of judicial review.) This practice slowly developed into its present form as the judiciary, and especially the Supreme Court, increasingly asserted itself and its authority over the content and demands of the legal constitution. Over time, citizens and officials accepted, or at least acquiesced to, this shift in practice, bringing about a shift in the political constitution. Eventually, this shift secured for the Court what it claimed for itself—namely, final political authority to determine for all branches of government the content and demands of the legal constitution. Once possessed of this authority, the Court could do what it could not have done one or two hundred years ago, perhaps even fifty years ago. It could declare that *as a matter of law,* the Constitution confers on the Court the authority it had been claiming and exercising as a matter of political fact. Strong judicial review, then, emerges as a legal doctrine authoritatively tied to the legal constitution. Of course, once strong judicial review is seen as given to the Court *as a matter of law,* then the Court can legally determine the meaning of those constitutional provisions governing its own jurisdiction—the "cases and controversies" constraint, for example.

For many critics of judicial review as presently practiced, then, slow but steady changes to the political constitution eventually enabled the Court to make at least one fundamental change to the legal constitution. On the view of these critics, the Court has managed, over time, effectively to do an end run around the Article V provisions governing constitutional amendment and to amend the legal constitution through sheer judicial assertiveness, securing the authority exercised under strong judicial review as a matter of constitutional law. These critics are to be found on both sides of the traditional right–left political divide. Those on the right go on to complain that through its exercise of strong judicial review, the Court has managed to amend the Constitution so as to confer a constitutional right to individual privacy, or to prohibit legislative encroachment on abortion in the first trimester or on consensual homosexual sex. Those on the left cite instead the judicial invalidation of various forms of progressive legislation or the resolution of close presidential elections on what they take to be highly suspect constitutional grounds. What both sets of critics agree on is that reasonable disagreements over fundamental constitutional law should not be resolved finally and for the entire body politic by a handful of unelected judicial officials not politically accountable to the people. The legal constitution belongs, they claim, to the people; the people make the legal constitution, at least in a constitutional democracy.

WHAT IS CONSTITUTIONAL DEMOCRACY?

In a democracy, citizen members are politically free and equal and have final authority over the structure of their body politic. Of course, they cannot exercise this authority save through some institutional arrangement. That arrangement is given by their constitution. There are many possible democratic constitutions. But all will vest all competent adult citizens with the most basic official authority in a democracy—the right to vote. The authority of citizen members in general, then, is mediated by the collective authority of voters. Of course, in most democracies, voters do not or only rarely rule directly. Typically, they delegate their authority to elected representatives. These representatives may be elected on a one person, one vote, majority rules, winner takes all basis, or they may be elected on some other basis, say, by a system of proportional representation. Whatever the electoral process, it must be justified by reference to the ideal of voters standing in as proxy for citizens sharing as free equals in the final authority over the structure of their body politic. Once elected, legislators and other officials will legislate on behalf of the citizens who elected them or of the people more generally. When they find themselves unable to agree, they too will typically settle matters by voting. Again, voting may be by one person, one vote, majority rules or by some other voting procedure, perhaps a supermajority requirement or a bare majority subject to some right to a veto by a minority. Whatever the decision procedure followed by elected representatives, it must remain faithful to the fundamental democratic ideal of citizens generally sharing as free equals in final authority over the structure of their body politic. That is not the only relevant ideal, of course, but it is a fundamental one.

Beyond this, it becomes difficult to say just exactly what a democracy is as a matter of institutional or constitutional design. There are several good reasons for this. One is that the ideal of citizens sharing as free equals in the final authority over the structure of their body politic is a highly abstract ideal in need of further interpretation. Another is that no particular democratic decision procedure or institutional arrangement is likely to follow uniquely from any particular interpretation of the ideal, and different sorts of arguments may be given for different candidate arrangements. Yet another is that when it comes to selecting democratic decision procedures or designing institutions, empirical differences between societies often make a difference. A democratic decision procedure or institutional arrangement justified in a highly homogenous society with a long history of social trust may be unjustified in a highly heterogenous society with no such history.

So, democracy cannot be easily identified with any particular well-defined institutional or constitutional arrangement, though it surely cannot be identified with any arrangement at all. What else can we say about constitutional democracies? Well, one thing is that whatever else a democracy is, at least any democracy worth having, it is not a system of domination or oppression through which the common good is regularly sacrificed to the good of some, even a majority. A democracy may make use of majoritarian decision procedures, but not as a vehicle for regularly enabling some to dominate or oppress others. To put the point another way, a democracy, or at least any worth having, will be broadly republican in character, committed to government "of the people, by the people, and for the people." Although there are many institutional or constitutional arrangements capable of securing this feature of any democracy worth having, there are also some arrangements inconsistent with it, even arrangements that grant all competent adults the right to vote.

In addition, we can say that whatever else a democracy is, it is not merely a tool for resolving disagreements by counting uninformed votes cast without any meaningful deliberation. Democracy, or any democracy worth having, requires that voters have significant access to relevant information and meaningful opportunities for deliberation.

We can also say that whatever else a democracy is, it is not merely a mechanism for voters to select among options determined by others. Voters, and ideally citizens in general, must have final authority over more than just the outcomes of political processes. They must also have final authority over what makes or doesn't make it onto the political agenda, and this applies to both issues and candidates. That citizens vote for representatives who then vote for political outcomes is not sufficient to render a polity a democracy (for this happens in many nondemocratic states). Citizens must also have the authority and ability to nominate or run themselves as candidates for elected office, as well as to place items on the political agenda either directly or through their elected representatives. The political process must be ultimately responsive to citizens at both ends— agenda setting and outcome determination. Again, many institutional or constitutional arrangements will likely prove consistent with this aim. But not all will.

Finally, we can say that whatever else a democracy is, at least any worth having, it is a polity subject to the rule of law. The people may have final authority over their body politic, but they rule as and through voters and other officials possessed of and constrained by legally constituted authority. There is more than one way to arrange institutions or design a constitution faithful to the rule of law. But there are also many ways to miss the mark.

To sum, then, a constitutional democracy is a polity within which members share a political commitment to their status as free and equal co-authors of their body politic and thus a constitution and institutional order within which the competent adults among them govern both the political agenda and political outcomes through their office as voter or elected official, with access to good information and opportunities for meaningful deliberation, with broadly republican aims, and subject to the rule of law. Their legal constitution must secure such an order.

But so too must their political constitution, the norms and shared expectations manifest in and constitutive of the shared political prac- tice within and through which they validate their legal constitution as law. A constitutional democracy requires not only a legal constitution democratic in character, but also a political constitution equally democratic in character. The legal constitution must find its validity as law by reference to criteria, whether given by a rule of recognition or otherwise manifest in the normative behavior of members in gen- eral, faithful to their self-understanding as free and equal co-authors of their body politic. These criteria ought to be broadly democratic in character. So when reasonable disagreements arise over their content or implications—and this is just what most disagreements over constitutional law are, disagreements over the content or implications of the criteria of legal validity applied at the level of constitutional law— presumably they ought finally to be resolved in a manner faithful to fundamental democratic ideals. It's here that worries over strong judicial review first emerge. A body politic within which citizens and officials generally acquiesce to unelected judges resolving all conflicts over criteria of constitutional legal validity in a final and binding way arguably lacks a democratic political constitution. It may still possess a democratic legal constitution, but as a matter of political fact, it has entrusted that legal constitution to a small number of unelected judges. A body politic within which those judges legally have final and binding authority to resolve all such disagreements for all branches of government and the body politic as a whole is arguably one without a democratic legal constitution, or at least with a flawed one.

This is the context within which the problem of judicial review arises for constitutional democracies subject to the rule of law. The problem is complex. We cannot endeavor to discuss all the relevant issues. So we shall move in stages, discussing just three. First, does constitutional democracy subject to the rule of law require judicial review in anything like its present form? Second, if it does not require it, does it at least permit it? And third, if it does permit it, how should the court interpret the constitution when it does so?

IS JUDICIAL REVIEW NECESSARY
TO CONSTITUTIONAL DEMOCRACY?

The most common reason given for judicial review is the need to secure against democratic encroachment those constitutional rights essential to ensuring that democracy does not collapse into a "tyranny of the majority" intent on running roughshod over the common good or the basic rights and interests of a minority. But while constitutional rights, whether enshrined in a written constitution or not, are surely essential to any democracy worth having, it does not follow that anything like strong judicial review is necessary to the preservation of constitutional rights. Indeed, if we look beyond the United States, it is pretty clear that constitutional democracies can persist and preserve constitutional rights without strong judicial

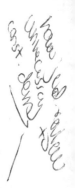

review or anything like it. Indeed, the framers of the U.S. Constitution pretty clearly thought that well-designed democratic institutions, coupled with a diversity of interests cutting across different groups, would be sufficient to preserve constitutional democracy and the constitutional rights necessary to it without anything like strong judicial review. Of course, it may still be that something like strong judicial review will prove necessary under some specific historical conditions or in some specific states. In any case, the fact that it is unnecessary to constitutional democracy doesn't show that it is inconsistent with it. The point here is that general worries about tyrannies of the majority cannot justify the practice as a necessary component of every constitutional democracy worth having.

But if strong judicial review isn't necessary to preserve constitutional democracy against a tyranny of the majority, might it at least be sufficient to do so? That seems unlikely. Even with the power of strong judicial review, the court must ultimately depend on its ability to continue to persuade others, including officials in the other branches of government, to acquiesce to its judgments. As a formal matter, it is, at least under the U.S. Constitution, "the weakest branch." This may make the practice of strong judicial review less of a threat than it may at first seem. But it also makes it an implausible bulwark against a tyranny of the majority, especially a majority bent on running roughshod over constitutional rights or constitutional democracy itself. If there is any bulwark to be had here, it must be achieved, and happily is achieved in many states, in other ways. Strong judicial review might be an ingredient in a broader network of institutional checks and balances, but its ability to stand as a wall against a determined majority ought not be overestimated.

That is perhaps a good thing. When there have been determined majorities in the United States, they have more often than not been progressive. Many of the most celebrated progressive victories in the history of the United States have been won through the legislative process, often only after overcoming judicial attempts to block the path forward on controversial constitutional grounds. In the early decades of the twentieth century, during the so-called Lochner era, the Court regularly invalidated progressive legislation aimed at setting minimum wages, workplace safety requirements, limits on the hours worked per day in particular industries, and so on, all on the grounds that such laws conflicted with a right to "freedom of contract" alleged to be ingredient in the Constitution. While a bit of a distortion, the common line is that it took Franklin Roosevelt's "court packing" plan to convince the Court to stop invalidating such progressive and widely supported legislation and to allow the democratic process to unfold. Those who defend judicial review as inherently progressive usually cite the civil rights cases, gender equity cases, or reproductive or sexual freedom cases. But in all these cases, legislation at various levels was slowly but steadily moving in a progressive direction.

None of this is to say that determined majorities cannot be wrong or act in ways that threaten constitutional rights. It's just to say that the empirical evidence suggests that the Court may have contributed less to the preservation or expansion of constitutional rights in the United States than is usually supposed. With respect to both desegregation and gay rights, progress was being made steadily through legislative and executive and private sector actions prior to the much celebrated judicial actions in *Brown v. Board of Education* and *Lawrence v. Texas*. And there is some evidence to suggest that these judicial decisions did not do as much to advance the cause as is usually supposed. The same thing might be said about *Roe v. Wade* and women's reproductive rights. Prior to *Roe*, legislation was moving in most states, slowly but steadily, in a progressive direction. *Roe* polarized the country and transformed the issue of abortion from one that is democratically deliberated and settled legislatively to one settled by the courts. Since *Roe,* there has been no further gain to and arguably a steady erosion of women's reproductive freedom. So, it's not clear that strong judicial review or anything like it is particularly conducive to preserving or expanding constitutional rights over and against a tyranny of the majority.

Strong judicial review may even prove corrosive of constitutional rights over the long haul. Constitutional rights depend ultimately on the willing support of the vast majority of officials and politically active citizens. In the absence of that support, neither the Court nor the government more generally will likely be able to sustain them without a degree of oppressive coercion inconsistent with the general ideal of a free and open democratic society. Because strong judicial review assigns to the Court final responsibility for the preservation of constitutional rights against the legislative and executive branches, it invites those branches, and indeed citizens more generally, to give less consideration to constitutional rights when exercising their official powers. Constitutional rights become mainly a judicial concern rather than a broadly political concern. This may invite a steady legislative or a more generally civic abdication of responsibility for constitutional rights that cannot be good for a constitutional democracy.

Probably neither strong judicial review nor anything like it can be defended as necessary or sufficient to constitutional democracy or the constitutional rights it requires. Worries about tyrannies of the majority are, while real, usually overstated. (Indeed, in most constitutional democracies, it is a tyranny of a minority that poses the bigger threat.) In any case, there are many ways in which they can be met through effective institutional design. So, if strong judicial review or something like it is to be defended, then it must be as simply consistent with our ideal of a constitutional democracy.

IS JUDICIAL REVIEW CONSISTENT WITH CONSTITUTIONAL DEMOCRACY?

The case against strong judicial review has been well put by Jeremy Waldron, Mark Tushnet, Larry Kramer, and others. They argue that constitutional issues typically arise because there is reasonable disagreement over what the legal constitution requires or means. The roots of such disagreements very often reach into the political constitution. Different interpretations or understandings of our shared political practice and fundamental ideals give rise to different judgments regarding the meaning or requirements of the legal constitution. It should come as no surprise, then, that the justices on the Court often find themselves unable, through argument, to resolve their disagreements and must finally turn to counting votes. Counting votes is just what we'd expect in a democracy. But why should the votes of only nine unelected officials be final and binding for all. Shouldn't the voters or the people in general have the last word? There is nothing wrong with allowing the Court to resolve the constitutional issues that come before it; it must. But there is something wrong, something undemocratic, about giving the Court the final binding word on the meaning of the legal constitution when even the highest-ranking legal officials find themselves driven by their deeper political disagreements to intractable reasonable disagreement over its meaning.

Giving the Court the final binding word in such cases cannot be defended by reference to some special legal expertise possessed by judges. These cases arise either because there is no constitutional law on point or because there is reasonable disagreement among the legal experts as to what it is, disagreement ultimately rooted in disagreement over the content and requirements of the political constitution. So serious constitutional issues present themselves as essentially political, not legal, in nature. Judges have no special expertise in political matters. Indeed, presumably, it is citizens or voters who possess the relevant expertise in a democracy committed to citizens sharing as free equals in final authority over the structure and actions of their body politic.

One might argue that strong judicial review is perhaps faithful to this democratic ideal insofar as federal judges, including Supreme Court judges, must be appointed, and can be impeached, by elected officials. In any case, the people can always overturn their rulings through an Article V amendment. But this is probably not sufficient to establish the democratic credentials of strong judicial review. The fact is that judges are less accountable to the electorate than are any other officials, yet they are empowered to resolve the most fundamental questions for the body politic. Further, Article V constitutional amendments are difficult to secure and then become themselves objects for constitutional adjudication via strong judicial review.

PROCEDURALIST DEFENSES

Perhaps, insofar as the Court endeavors to enforce against a present majority a decision reached and entrenched by a past majority, there is nothing inherently antidemocratic about judicial review after all. At any given moment in time in a democracy, the majority may wish not only to pass a law but also to entrench it or immunize it against easy revision by making it constitutional law. Of course, for such an entrenched piece of constitutional law to survive and play the role assigned it by the majority, it cannot simply be entrusted to future majorities. The whole point is to tie their hands to some degree. And so, at any given moment in time, the people will have a reason to accept some form of judicial review, even a relatively strong form, so long as it is exercised with the aim of enforcing against future majorities the democratic will of a current majority committed to entrenching a certain law as constitutional law. But this means that at any given moment in time, the people will have reason to accept judicial review, even a fairly strong form of judicial review, as a constraint on their present majorities, so long as the constraints were entrenched as constitutional law by a past majority. Thus, there is nothing inherently countermajoritarian about judicial review. It simply favors the constitutional lawmaking of past majorities over the ordinary lawmaking of present majorities. It therefore helps to secure the will of "we the people." This is roughly the argument advanced by Bruce Ackerman for the consistency of judicial review with constitutional democracy.

Ackerman distinguishes ordinary politics from constitutional politics. In the latter, citizens are politically engaged to a heightened degree. If they then intend either explicitly (as when they formally amend the Constitution) or implicitly (as, perhaps, during the New Deal) to entrench some law or laws over and against future majorities within the day-to-day run of ordinary politics, then those laws should be treated as constitutional and enforced by the Court against any future majority within the day-to-day run of ordinary politics. Of course, a future majority may, through its own constitutional politics, overturn the entrenched results of a past majority's constitutional politics. And to a present majority engaged to a heightened degree in a sustained constitutional politics, the Court should yield. But so long as the Court restricts itself to enforcing against present majorities within ordinary politics the entrenched results of past majorities' constitutional politics, there is nothing antidemocratic or countermajoritarian about it at all. Indeed, Ackerman maintains, such a system of "dualist democracy" is just what the framers intended.

On Ackerman's view, there are only a handful of periods of genuine constitutional politics in the United States: the period surrounding the drafting and ratification of the Constitution and the Bill of Rights, the period surrounding the Civil War and the Reconstruction amendments, and the period surrounding the New Deal. The periods surrounding extending the right to vote to women and the Civil Rights Movement of the mid-twentieth century are presumably also candidates. These were all heightened and sustained periods of constitutional politics aimed at entrenching results over and against shifting majorities in ordinary politics. That the New Deal, for example, did not result in any formal amendments under Article V is beside the point.

So far, so good. But Ackerman's view is not without its difficulties. First, what about all those constitutional amendments formally passed without any such heightened and sustained periods of constitutional politics (say, the Sixteenth, Seventeenth, and Twenty-Third

129

amendments)? Should the Court enforce them against a hostile present majority within ordinary politics? And how are we to distinguish constitutional from ordinary politics in any event?

For that matter, why should we think that the founding was a period of heightened political participation by citizens in general? By some estimates, no more than 25 percent of the eligible adult males participated in the elections to select delegates to the ratifying conventions. And they constituted just a small fraction of the members of the body politic. In many states, ratification was secured by very narrow margins and only through suspect means (bribes etc.). So although there was surely an intent to entrench a constitution, the idea that it was as a descriptive matter the intent of "we the people" is probably a fiction.

Furthermore, why should the Court enforce the will of any majority if it is contrary to the moral core of the democratic ideal? Ackerman takes an essentially positivist stance toward democratic lawmaking. The authority of the law derives simply from the will of the people—in a democracy, the majority—who posit it. But is it plausible to read the democratic ideal in this way? Doesn't the democratic ideal carry some substantive content, for example, that certain basic interests of all citizens are to be secured or that the state is to show all citizens "equal concern and respect" or something to that effect?

This is no small problem for Ackerman. On his essentially positivist understanding of the law, including constitutional law, the normative authority of the written constitution for later generations depends on the active willing by a majority of citizens during the ratification process. In the absence of such willing, which is a real historical possibility as noted above, its normative authority could be given only by the moral principles in favor of the Constitution itself. This is probably how the framers themselves understood the Constitution and their ratification of it, since they were drawing on a tradition of natural law and natural rights and no doubt intended talk of "we the people" to be understood in that sense. So Ackerman faces something of a dilemma. If he sticks with his positivist reading of our dualist democracy, then it's not clear that the ratified Constitution has the normative authority we all agree it has. If he rejects that reading in favor of a natural law reading, then it's not clear that judicial review should be limited to enforcing the expressed will of past majorities engaged in constitutional lawmaking against present majorities engaged in ordinary lawmaking.

In any event, on Ackerman's view, for the Court to claim *legally* that its authority under strong judicial review is a constitutional authority immune to revision by a present majority within the ordinary run of democratic politics, there would have to have been some past period of heightened political activity during which a past majority entrenched strong judicial review as a matter of constitutional law. But there has never been any such period. Strong judicial review was not posited in the original Constitution (assuming that was such a period of heightened political activity), and there has since been no heightened and sustained period of constitutional politics within which a majority undertook legally to entrench strong judicial review against shifting future majorities within ordinary politics. Rather, strong judicial review emerged in fits and starts and to some degree under cover of night, without anything more than passive, often oblivious, acquiescence from most citizens and officials. Thus, on Ackerman's view, the Court's assertion of strong judicial review cannot be defended as a matter of enforcing the people's constitution against the run of ordinary day-to-day politics.

But on what grounds then can it be defended as consistent with constitutional democracy? It would appear to be a simple political assertion of judicial power. Were it noncontroversial and widely accepted upon due deliberation as such, perhaps then it could be affirmed as consistent with constitutional democracy. But it clearly is not. Those who deliberate divide deeply over the issue. And those who acquiesce do so largely out of ignorance or lack of interest. Were it required by the best moral understanding of the ideals of constitutional democracy, then perhaps it could be affirmed as consistent with constitutional democracy. But then Ackerman would have to abandon his positivist reading of our dualist democracy.

In the end, the most Ackerman's argument can establish is that constitutionalism with some form of judicial review under which the Court enforces the legal constitution against present political majorities is consistent with our ideal of constitutional democracy. But that leaves the key question unaddressed. If the nine justices on the Court reasonably disagree over the legal meaning or requirements of some past act of constitutional lawmaking by "we the people," and if their disagreement is itself rooted in deeper disagreements over political morality, then shouldn't "we the people" retain final binding authority to resolve the disagreement over the legal meaning or requirements of what we did at some past point in time?

John Hart Ely defends judicial review as consistent with constitutional democracy so long as it is exercised only as a last resort to preserve and perfect the procedural elements of constitutional democracy, rather than to determine substantively the outcome of issues properly settled by democratic processes. The Court may review and overturn legislation arising out of democratic procedures that turn out, upon inspection, to be effectively closed to certain constituencies (so-called discrete and insular minorities) or to be corrosive of the democratic process itself, as with excessive or discriminatory voter registration restrictions. But it ought not review or overturn wrongheaded or unjust laws so long as they arise out of democratic processes not themselves procedurally suspect. And the Court may interpret the legal constitution so as to preserve or perfect it as the institutional blueprint for a procedurally viable constitutional democracy. The role of the Court, then, is to preserve and perfect democratic procedures, not to overturn the democratically expressed substantive judgments of the people or their elected representatives.

But it is often not easy and may sometimes not be possible to identify the essential ingredients in democratic procedures without taking substantive positions on controversial issues of, say, economic justice or social policy. For example, some feminists would argue that a legal and large trade in traditional (patriarchal) pornography creates a general political climate within which women's voices cannot be heard or taken seriously in political debate, since women will routinely be cast by men, even if only subconsciously, primarily as objects of sexual desire rather than fellow citizens whose views should be accorded equal weight with those held by men. But then the laws legalizing pornography should be subject to judicial review and invalidation by the Court. Presumably, however, Ely means to reject just this sort of substitution of judicial for legislative judgments over contested substantive issues of social policy. That is why he limits the role of the Court to preserving and perfecting democratic procedures. A legal and large trade in patriarchal pornography may, in fact, be something that ought to be eliminated in a constitutional democracy committed to treating all members as free and equal co-authors of the body politic's structures and actions. But, on Ely's view, it should be eliminated through democratic political processes, not judicial review. Unhappily, this just begs the question, for many citizens think that so long as such pornography exists as an ubiquitous cultural force, democratic decision procedures cannot really exist.

Robert Dahl argues that constitutional democracies should secure three sorts of basic rights or interests for all members as a matter of justice. But only rights or interests of the first two sorts are eligible for judicial enforcement. The third must be secured through ordinary democratic politics. Were the Court to have the power to secure rights or interests of the third sort, the polity would no longer be a constitutional *democracy*.

The first sort of right or interest is constitutive of or ingredient in any recognizably democratic political process. There is no democratic process without, for example, the right to vote, to share information and thus to speak in public, and to do so without risking physical attack, and so on. When the Court enforces these rights or secures these interests, it does so in the name, and not at the expense, of constitutional democracy.

The second sort of right or interest is not literally ingredient in any recognizably democratic political process, but it is necessary or highly conducive to the proper functioning of any such process. Democratic processes are seriously compromised if individuals do not enjoy a basic education, a minimal standard of material well-being, access to good information, the ability to register easily to vote, and so on. So, again, when the Court enforces these rights or secures these interests, it acts in the name, and not at the expense, of constitutional democracy.

The third sort of right or interest is essential not to well-functioning democratic processes but to the complete realization of the substantive moral content of the democratic ideal, the ideal of citizens as free and equal co-authors of their body politic. For example, an economy organized under rules faithful to a conception of distributive justice more egalitarian than that embodied by our present rules may be (or better, undoubtedly is) required by the substantive moral content of the democratic ideal. But it is not necessary to well-functioning democratic procedures (though some limits on the role of money in politics may be). Similarly, the substantive moral content at the heart of the democratic ideal may justify extending the legal right to marry to homosexual couples. But, again, it seems fairly clear that democratic procedures can function pretty well without the legal recognition of gay marriage. Thus, were the Court to enforce or secure a more egalitarian conception of economic justice or a marriage law recognizing gay marriage, it would be acting at the expense of, even if also in some sense in the name of, constitutional democracy. This, Dahl maintains, it ought not do, at least if judicial review is to remain at least consistent with the ideal of constitutional democracy itself. Matters or issues tied to this third sort of right or interest are for the people or voters alone to resolve through ordinary political processes.

Ian Shapiro offers another variation on the theme. On his view, whatever else a democracy is, it is not a system of domination. Democracy builds on the republican ideal of nondomination. Democratic decision procedures are intended to ensure that power relations within society remain always contested, always revisable, always shifting. In this way, they function as a bulwark against tyranny, whether by a majority or a minority. Judicial review is fully consistent with constitutional democracy, so long as it is exercised with the aim of securing and enforcing those rights and rules necessary to keep the democratic political process open to and competitive between a wide range of interest groups and constituencies.

Ely, Dahl, and Shapiro each defend judicial review by trying to place it solely in the service of the apparently noncontroversial procedural component of the ideal of constitutional democracy, isolated and cleaved off from its more controversial substantive components. The idea is that judicial review, even strong judicial review, is at least consistent with constitutional democracy so long as it serves only the democratic process itself, leaving citizens and their elected representatives to resolve their substantive disagreements through that process. This is the charm of proceduralist defenses in general; it is likely also the Achilles heel. Many attempts to isolate and cleave off a noncontroversial procedural component of the democratic ideal seem inevitably to collapse under the weight of reasonable disagreement over more substantive aspects of the ideal. Indeed, what else could explain the reasonable judicial disagreement over the meaning or requirement of the allegedly noncontroversial procedural components? It follows that in exercising its authority over the legal constitution so as to preserve and protect it as the procedural basis of a constitutional democracy, the Court will often be resolving substantive political disagreements over which the people themselves ought to have the last word.

Consider: Is one person, one vote, majority rule an acceptable democratic decision procedure within a racially divided, though increasingly geographically integrated, polity? What if it leads to minority candidates routinely losing over and against majority candidates? Is race-based gerrymandering of electoral districts then permissible? Or is a system of proportional representation required? Can we determine the meaning or requirement of our legal constitution with respect to these matters without taking a stand on deeper and more controversial issues with respect to the substantive content of the democratic ideal presumably at the heart of our political constitution? If not, then what may have first appeared to be merely a matter of the judiciary preserving and perfecting the noncontroversial procedural components of a constitutional democracy is really a matter of its selecting and enforcing a particular view of or orientation to political morality over which citizens and other officials reasonably disagree. But that seems inconsistent, rather than consistent, with the ideal of constitutional democracy.

SUBSTANTIVE DEFENSES

Dworkin argues that when we commit to constitutional democracy, we commit to a particular substantive moral ideal, not just to democratic decision procedures—at least this is the best interpretation of our political act of committing to constitutional democracy. The ideal to which we commit is constitutive insofar as it is through our commitment to it that we constitute ourselves as a particular kind of body politic or moral community. On Dworkin's view, this ideal is not best understood in terms of the individual or collective liberty of members. It is rather best understood in terms of "equal concern and respect." In a constitutional democracy, equality is the "sovereign virtue."

The moral foundation of a constitutional democracy, then, is not a commitment to individual or collective liberty, though a constitutional democracy will properly make room for each. It is rather a commitment to treating all members of the body politic as equals, showing them all equal concern and respect, at least with respect to the design and conduct of the body politic as a whole. This does not mean ignoring differences between members or treating all equally. Rather, it means acknowledging that every member has the same basic moral claim on or status within the body politic. The good of every member matters and matters equally. Taking this seriously will sometimes mean treating different members differently. To treat a person *as* an equal, one must sometimes treat that person differently from others.

If we thought it possible for the government or some set of officials to know reliably the good of every member of the body politic, then we might think it okay for the state or its officials to act toward citizen members in something like the way parents act toward their children. A good parent cares equally for and, let us suppose, reliably knows a great deal about the good of each of her children. Accordingly, she will be able to show equal concern and respect for her children by taking concrete, effective steps toward leading each to his or her good. A constitutional democracy is different insofar as the citizen members will reasonably disagree over what is good for them as individuals or in association with others (and thus as a body politic). Neither the government nor any set of officials can be trusted reliably to know the good of every member. Thus, in a constitutional democracy, citizens cannot show their commitment to equal concern and respect by authorizing their government or its officials to take, in paternalist or parentalist fashion, concrete and effective steps toward advancing their good as individuals. Instead, citizens will show their commitment to equal concern and respect by requiring their government to ensure a more or less equal distribution of basic resources and by authorizing it to act only after having given equal consideration to the good of each member as he or she understands it. This will require government through democratic decision procedures of some sort. Such procedures enable members to make known and to shape political outcomes in light of their own views about their own good. That is the point of democratic decision procedures.

The point of democratic decision procedures is not, however, to enable any particular majority to put the body politic into the exclusive service of any one or another determinate and controversial conception of the good over which citizens usually reasonably disagree. The body politic belongs to all members as free equals and must show all equal concern and respect to all. Therefore, it ought to remain neutral between the controversial conceptions of the good over which members care the most and divide most deeply. After all, what reason would anyone have, as a free equal, for affirming his membership in a polity that might run roughshod over that which he cared about most deeply any time enough others reasonably disagreed with him? You may have a reason as a free equal to affirm membership in, and thus to accept the electoral outcomes of, a constitutional democracy authorized to act in a wide range of domains where you share with others an interest in collective action (arranging for your common defense, or for the production, distribution, and consumption of goods and services, etc.) but share no consensus on how to move forward. But what reason could you have to affirm membership in such a polity if it was authorized to act on electoral outcomes with respect to ends you reasonably rejected and in which you had no interest at all? Further, what reason could you have if the ends in question were ones you reasonably rejected for the deepest of moral, religious, or philosophical reasons tied to your sense of the meaning and purpose of life, the highest good for humans, and so on? Since you, as a free equal, could have no such reason, to treat you with equal concern and respect, a constitutional democracy must limit democratic decision procedures to the pursuit of ends you, in some sense, share with other members of the body politic, or at least ends neutral with respect to the reasonable conceptions of the good or moral, religious and philosophical doctrines over which you and your fellow citizens so deeply divide. This, roughly, is Dworkin's ideal of state neutrality.

Our commitment to state neutrality is signaled by several important constitutional provisions—think, for example, of the rights protecting freedom of religion. On Dworkin's view, our commitment to state neutrality fits and justifies our political past. Thus, when the Court interprets the legal constitution so as to find and enforce against the body politic as a whole a commitment to state neutrality, it acts in the name, and not at the expense, of the substantive moral ideal of constitutional democracy that really captures and expresses our shared political constitution.

Dworkin applies a similar line of reasoning when it comes to democratic outcomes touching on issues over which there is racial (or similar sorts) of division. If democratic decision procedures are to remain faithful to our substantive political commitment to showing all members of the polity equal concern and respect, then citizens must not be allowed to vote in such a manner as to negate the equal consideration to which others are entitled within the democratic process. For example, racists must not be allowed to vote their belief that the state ought not give equal consideration to the good of those in a racially disfavored group. This belief does not concern their own good; rather, it concerns their preferences regarding the good of others—namely, that the good of some others should not be given any consideration or weight in collective decisions. But this is inconsistent with equal concern and respect for all, and so this belief or preference must be screened out of any democratic decision procedure faithful to that ideal.

Our commitment to nondiscrimination is signaled by several important constitutional provisions—not least the Reconstruction amendments. A commitment to nondiscrimination, on Dworkin's view, fits and justifies our political past. Thus, when the Court interprets the legal constitution so as to find and enforce a commitment to nondiscrimination against the body politic as a whole, it acts in the name, and not at the expense, of the substantive moral ideal of constitutional democracy that really captures and expresses our shared political constitution.

In general, on Dworkin's view, when government officials or citizens are prevented from acting in ways inconsistent with the substantive ideal of equal concern and respect, there is no democratic loss, no affront to the ideal of constitutional democracy. It's true that when they are so limited, there may be some loss of individual liberty for some individuals. But there will likely also be a gain in individual liberty for some other individuals. Summing up these losses and gains is likely an impossible task. (Do judicial invalidations of racially discriminatory laws statistically increase or decrease individual liberty summed across the whole population? How would we tally up a gain in one kind of liberty against a loss in another kind?) So it's not clear that the imposition of such constraints constitutes an affront to individual liberty overall. And in any case, individual liberty is not the sovereign virtue of our constitutional democracy, at least not on the best interpretation of it. Equal concern and respect is. — *sovereign virtue - Dworkin*

It's also true that when officials or citizens are so limited by the Court, there is a loss to the collective or political liberty of citizens as a whole, as they are prevented from doing with their body politic whatever they want. But this loss is justified, because no exercise of their collective liberty could morally bind all as members of a shared democratic community if it was inconsistent with the ideal of equal concern and respect. This ideal must be honored if the laws that citizens or their representatives make are to have normative authority simply as laws, binding all together in a moral community of principle. Particular laws may always have normative authority by virtue of their moral content, of course. For example, the law against murder has normative authority because murder is morally wrong. But if a law is to have some normative authority simply by virtue of its being posited as a law and apart from its moral content, then, on Dworkin's view, it must at least be consistent with the ideal of equal concern and respect. This is essential to the associative obligations citizens have to obey the law within a community of principle. Because laws passed by legislative or electoral majorities may sometimes be inconsistent with this ideal, these

*not ~~constrain~~ antidemocratic. Instead, consistent w/
moral code of const. dem.*

laws are properly subject to review and invalidation. Limiting legislative or electoral majorities in this way is not antidemocratic. Rather, it's consistent with the moral core of democracy. Because the legal constitution may be applied or interpreted in ways inconsistent with this ideal of equal concern and respect, the judicial interpretation and enforcement of the legal constitution so as to preserve its consistency with this ideal is also not antidemocratic.

Dworkin acknowledges that the foregoing argument does not justify strong judicial review over and against other institutional mechanisms for ensuring that legislative and electoral majorities honor the principle of equal concern and respect. But he also argues that we now have strong judicial review as a matter of historical fact, and because it is at least consistent with the ideal of constitutional democracy, the only real question is how it ought to be exercised, not whether we ought to have it. But this is perhaps inadequate. On Dworkin's own interpretive approach to the philosophy of law, historical facts settle very little. The question is always "What is the best interpretation of the historical facts?" And so Dworkin must vindicate strong judicial review not merely as one of several institutional alternatives consistent with the best interpretation of constitutional democracy, but rather as essential to it.

One way to vindicate strong judicial review would be to claim that judges have some special expertise when it comes to interpreting the principle of equal concern and respect and to evaluating legislation in light of this principle. But given the broadly moral nature of this principle, why should we think judges have any special expertise with respect to it? After all, as Dworkin notes, judges can and do make mistakes with respect to both the meaning of the principle of equal concern and respect and its import for particular pieces of legislation. Of course, legislators and citizens generally make such mistakes, too. But unless judges make fewer or less egregious mistakes, it is not clear why we should favor strong judicial review over some other institutional mechanism that assigns elected representatives or the people themselves final authority for reviewing legislation to determine whether it is consistent with the principle of equal concern and respect. Strong judicial review may not be antidemocratic, but it may still be less democratic than a number of alternative institutional mechanisms for enforcing against the body politic its constitutive moral commitments. Indeed, Dworkin's arguments seem to lead more directly to weak judicial review, for then the more democratic branches of government have the last word with respect to the substantive content of our constitutional commitment to equal concern and respect.

The fact is that the principle of equal concern and respect is itself a highly abstract principle in need of interpretation, and reasonable people can disagree over what it means and requires in particular cases. Indeed, arguably, the vast majority of substantive constitutional issues faced by the Court in recent years arises out of just such disagreements: What does it mean to show equal concern and respect to all members of the polity? Must we allow or prohibit abortion? Gay marriage? Equal pay for equal work? Affirmative action? Race-based gerrymandering of electoral districts? If these are matters over which people committed to equal concern and respect reasonably disagree, then why should nine unelected judges, rather than the electorate or their representatives, settle them? Furthermore, though Dworkin wants to limit the Court's authority under judicial review to matters of principle—in particular the principle of equal concern and respect—many matters of policy seem inseparable from such principled concerns. Should the Court have the authority to set aside a tax or environmental law on the grounds that it will harm the least-advantaged in society while benefiting the most advantaged? Isn't such a law inconsistent with a principled commitment to equal concern and respect?

This brings us to another problem with Dworkin's defense of judicial review. Dworkin argues that democracy means more than majority rule and thus is not compromised simply by the fact that sometimes majorities aren't able to do what they want. Strong judicial review is therefore not antidemocratic. But Dworkin fails to notice that when judges reasonably disagree over the constitutionality of legislation, when they disagree over the meaning of the principle of equal concern and respect or its import for a particular case, they settle their disagreements by voting, and *majority rules*. So, Dworkin has not offered us a way around the finality of majoritarian decision procedures. Rather, he's simply taken some issues away from the broadly inclusive majoritarian processes of general elections or legislative processes and turned their final resolution over to the less inclusive majoritarian process of judicial voting. But how is that democratic? How is it consistent with equal concern and respect for all citizens confronted with the fundamental political fact of both deep disagreement and the need to find some way to live together?

One final difficulty with Dworkin's view merits mention. Dworkin's defense of judicial review presupposes that the moral core of constitutional democracy is a commitment to equal concern and respect. We need not reject this view of constitutional democracy (I think something like it must be right) to see that others might, and in fact sometimes do, reasonably reject it in favor of some other not unreasonable alternative. But if the moral core of our constitutional democracy is itself a matter over which citizens and legal officials, including judges, may and sometimes do reasonably disagree, then surely drafting the Supreme Court into the exclusive service of one of the rival conceptions of that core and giving it the authority to impose that conception on the body politic as a whole hardly seems democratic.

Christopher Eisgruber argues that turning many contested political issues over to the Court is, in fact, democratic because the Court represents the people as a whole, whereas elected officials represent only the voters. As officially constituted by law, voters are a subset of the people in general. The people must necessarily rule themselves through voters. But voters ought not be completely trusted to represent and rule the people themselves. Some check is needed to ensure that they remain faithful to the terms of trust under which they receive their official authority to represent the people. But this check cannot come from the legislative or executive branches because they are already exclusively responsive to voters. What is needed, then, is a judicial branch *not responsive to voters* but committed to *representing the people themselves* more generally. Whether strong judicial review is democratic turns, first, on the degree to which the Court has fulfilled its assigned role in representing the people themselves (rather than, say, the wealthy or privileged) and, second, on whether it might have fulfilled its role even more completely through some other institutional practice, perhaps a weaker form of judicial review.

The first matter is an empirical question to be settled by examining the Court's track record. Although the Court's record is mixed, Eisgruber maintains that it has, in fact, represented the people to some significant degree. The second matter is empirical and comparative. We need to know whether the Court's actual track record might be improved upon by adopting some other approach to judicial review. But absent historical cases to compare, this requires something like a massive social experiment, something we cannot practically do. In any case, Eisgruber argues that there are good reasons to think that the Court as we have it has contributed substantially to our ability to claim for ourselves a history of progressively realizing or perfecting government by and for the people themselves. One reason for this, he argues, drawing on Dworkin's theory of legal and constitutional reasoning, is that the Court is especially well suited to adjudicating legal issues that turn on basic principles of political morality.

Eisgruber defends strong judicial review as a way of allowing the voice and constitutive commitments of people themselves to have final authority, through the Supreme Court, over the most fundamental constitutional issues. The trouble is that there is no one voice or constitutive commitment belonging to the people themselves. They are divided. And if they are divided, shouldn't constitutional issues be decided in such a way as to subject them in the end to a majoritarian decision procedure within which the people are broadly included? Why should the Supreme Court get to decide whether we the people need proportional representation or gay marriage or publicly financed elections in order to fulfill our democratic self-understandings? Shouldn't we decide? In any event, why think the Court representative of the people? Surely justices look a lot more like one another in background and orientation than they do the average citizen.

We can assume that any morally defensible conception of democracy will ground itself in constitutive moral ideals such as that of equal concern and respect, or the inviolability of persons, or some list of constitutional rights as natural rights, or a conception of the virtuous polity, or some such. The trouble is that in any free and open democracy members will reasonably disagree over the constitutive moral ideal at the heart of their democratic institutions and practices. They may divide over the ideal itself—some affirming one, others affirming another—or they may divide over the meaning or implications of a single ideal commonly affirmed. In either case, there is no democratic way around such reasonable disagreements except through voting. As Jeremy Waldron puts it, the only question is "Who votes?". In a democracy, surely the answer must come as close to "the people themselves" as institutionally possible.

STUCK WITH THE STATUS QUO?

In the end, Waldron argues, whenever there is deep disagreement and a need to move forward together, there is no justification for anything other than majority rule operative across as inclusive a section of the polity as is institutionally feasible. If the majority favors the primacy of individual constitutional rights, or a principle of equal concern and respect, or some conception of a virtuous polity, then they should be able to enforce it against the polity. What democratic justification could there be for subordinating their will to that of a minority? As we've seen, empirical worries about tyrannies of the majority are not well founded. Indeed, tyrannies of a minority are more common in history. In any case, strong judicial review doesn't get around the problem of a tyranny of the majority, for a majority of five justices can dominate or oppress the other four (and perhaps go on to oppress many citizens, constituting a tyranny of a minority).

But perhaps, against Waldron, strong judicial review can be defended as consistent with constitutional democracy after all. Even with its present authority under strong judicial review, the Court is but one institution nested in a much larger network of institutions. It controls neither the purse nor the police and military. It seems doubtful, then, that the Court could effect any substantial constitutional change without the broad support of the people, even if only begrudging support. Widespread active political resistance from the people is a force the Court probably could not overcome. Further, the people themselves influence what the Court does in a variety of indirect ways. As already noted, they influence who gets appointed to the Court. But they also shape the public discourse within which judicial decisions are discussed and evaluated. They push various cases and issues until they reach the Supreme Court. Judicial rulings cannot be enforced without the cooperation of the people. The people can also amend their constitution, at least in the United States. The Court, the other branches of government, and the people in general, then, might be seen as being in a sort of complex extended democratic conversation, with each communicating to and influencing the other. Thus, strong judicial review may be consistent with, and may even contribute to, broadly democratic rule by focusing and inviting serious public debate over constitutional issues, debate that is in effect moderated by the Court. Maybe. Much depends on the quantity and quality of interactions among the Court, the other branches of government, and the people in general.

Larry Kramer asks what Martians observing American democracy for the past two hundred years or so would say if asked to describe its trajectory. On Kramer's view, they would describe a tradition that started as "popular constitutionalism," in which fundamental constitutional issues were genuinely resolved over time by the people themselves and the Court limited itself to enforcing the legal constitution as understood in light of the popular political constitution as given by the people, but that has developed into "jurocracy" or "judicial elitism," in which fundamentally political constitutional issues are resolved by a judicial elite that effectively governs the people. Worse, Kramer continues, they would say that the people themselves have acquiesced to this change, effectively ceding control over their body politic and abandoning their democratic political (if not legal) constitution.

Kramer, no doubt, overstates the case. But he and Waldron have helped rekindle interest in alternatives to strong judicial review, especially weak judicial review and departmentalism. According to weak judicial review, though the Supreme Court may invalidate legislation, Congress, or on some views the president, may effectively overrule the Court. According to departmentalism, though the Supreme Court may invalidate legislation on constitutional grounds, its constitutional judgments are binding only for the judicial branch. The other branches are free to come to their own judgments about the relevant constitutional issues and how best to move forward. Departmentalism leaves all three branches of government co-equal when it comes to the meaning and implications of the Constitution.

Notwithstanding the recent rekindling of interest in these alternatives to present practice, there is unlikely to be any radical shift in practice. Departmentalism suffers from the fact that there must be some way to resolve with finality disputes at the federal level between the executive and legislative branches, as well as disputes between the federal government and individual states, at least if we're to have a relatively smooth functioning government. This doesn't entail judicial supremacy or strong judicial review, of course. But it does undermine the appeal of a departmentalist approach to reform.

Weak judicial review, or judicial review with legislative supremacy, is a more likely candidate for reform initiatives. And some steps have been taken in recent years to put the issue on the political agenda. (The issue has been raised in congressional committees, and some legal scholars have pushed in this direction. Mark Tushnet has recently argued for a constitutional amendment establishing weak judicial review.) But much of the political steam for this initiative is driven by concern over particular issues and is unlikely to be long lasting. Instead, debate and reformist pressures are likely to focus on how the Court exercises its authority under strong judicial review. The fight is likely to center on when and how the Court ought to exercise its authority, not over whether it should or does have the authority it claims for itself in the first place. Those made uneasy by the authority given to the Court under strong judicial review may be mollified by a Court reticent to exercise its authority or committed to interpreting the Constitution in a manner they regard as favorable. We turn now to those issues.

INTERPRETING THE CONSTITUTION

There are many views with respect to the criteria that the Court ought to use when deciding whether to exercise judicial review. Whatever the view, the criteria affirmed will necessarily reflect, to some degree, the overall justification for judicial review that is taken as sound. Those giving a substantive moral defense of judicial review will be able to include substantive moral criteria among those the Court ought to use when deciding whether to exercise judicial review. Those giving proceduralist defenses will not. But there are other criteria independent of the particular justification given for judicial review. Prudential or pragmatic considerations regarding the impact or effect of judicial action may be given more or less weight. Constitutional consensus within or between the other branches of government may be given more or less weight. Considerations concerning the limitations of the Court's expertise or ability to sort through the relevant information may be given more or less weight. Conflicts between lower court jurisdictions may be given more or less weight. And so on. Generally speaking, the Court can be more active or more restrained in its exercise of judicial review. And there are arguments to be made for or against giving more or less weight to any of the considerations just mentioned. But rather than focus on the criteria determining the number and range of cases the Court decides to address, we shall focus here on the approaches to constitutional interpretation and reasoning judges do take, or ought to take, when deciding a constitutional case. However, here too, perhaps unsurprisingly, the general justification one gives for judicial review will inevitably shape, though not fully determine, one's views as to which modes of constitutional interpretation are appropriate.

The U.S. Constitution—indeed, every legal constitution, whether written or unwritten—requires interpretation. Constitutions necessarily often invoke general or highly abstract terms requiring interpretation, including due process of law, cruel and unusual punishment, commerce among the several states, and so on. And they often contain apparent conflicts or tensions between provisions requiring principled mediation. Further, they're necessarily intended to apply to at least some circumstances other than those under which they were immediately drafted and ratified and likely unforeseen by those who did the drafting and ratifying. So there is no avoiding constitutional interpretation. The question is how legal constitutions ought to be interpreted.

It makes a difference whether the constitution is written or unwritten. The interpretation of a written constitution, like the U.S. Constitution, can be guided by the common law legal traditions governing the interpretation of other written legal documents—contracts, wills, and so on. Of course, interpreting a constitution is not the same as interpreting a contract. Constitutions are intended to last much longer and serve different purposes than are contracts. It also makes a difference whether the constitution is easily amended. Where it is easily amended, allowing interpretive errors to be more easily corrected, there may be less pressure to settle on interpretive approaches likely to preserve consensus or minimize disagreement.

In the American legal tradition, there are roughly six kinds of interpretive argument commonly made with respect to constitutional questions. The first appeals primarily to the words of the Constitution itself. Of course, these words are not self-interpreting, so arguments focused simply on the wording of the Constitution take different forms, depending on how meaning is assigned to the interpreted terms. Broadly, meaning may be assigned on the basis of either the intentions of the drafters, the common usage at the time the language was ratified and made legally operative, or contemporary usage.

The second common sort of interpretive argument appeals primarily to the structure of the Constitution as a complete charter for a successful, or at least feasible, constitutional democracy subject to the rule of law. Here the focus is not primarily on the words of the text, but rather on the Constitution's purposefulness and integrity as a political charter. For example, the Constitution is structured so as to make possible a federalist system of constitutional democracy. This may be asserted as the justification for reading the Constitution so that its meaning yields further conclusions—for example, that individual states cannot tax a federally chartered bank or that Congress cannot encroach unduly on the internal sovereignty of individual states. These conclusions find their justification not in the words but rather in the federalist structure of the Constitution.

The third sort of argument draws on historical facts surrounding the relevant provisions—the conditions that led up to their enactment, Congressional and public debates, and so on—to resolve the meaning of the provisions being interpreted. So, for example, the historical circumstances surrounding the American Revolution might be made central to an argument interpreting the right to bear arms specified in the Second Amendment. Or the record of congressional and public debate surrounding the ratification of the Reconstruction amendments might be made central to an argument interpreting the due process or equal protection clauses of the Fourteenth Amendment.

The fourth sort of argument makes traditional constitutional doctrines and fidelity to past judicial precedent central to the interpretive undertaking. On this approach, interpreting the Constitution is an ongoing adjudicative activity pursued in roughly the same common law spirit as any other within a common law system. Arguments of this sort may, but need not, draw on substantive moral principles thought to animate traditional doctrines or past precedents. They may be more or less arguments from legal convention.

Arguments of the fifth sort draw on substantive moral principles. They appeal to the moral spirit or animating principles of the Constitution or our constitutional tradition (or perhaps even just moral principles thought to be true, regardless of their relationship to our Constitution or constitutional tradition). Dworkin's "moral reading" of the Constitution is one such argument. It reads the Constitution in light of those moral principles essential to the Constitution's status as the moral charter of our community of principle. But substantive moral principles may also be drawn from tradition, as well as from the contemporary moral ethos, without any direct critical inquiry into their truth or soundness as such.

Finally, arguments of the sixth sort read the Constitution in light of fundamentally forward-looking pragmatic or prudential considerations. Such arguments cannot be excluded from constitutional interpretation, because whatever else the Constitution is, it is not "a suicide pact." How much weight or influence ought to be accorded such arguments where the prospect of national suicide is not in play is a matter of significant controversy. But pragmatic arguments have sometimes carried the day. During the Great Depression, the Supreme Court authorized legislative action to alter the terms of otherwise valid contracts (mortgages etc.), pragmatically interpreting the pretty plain constitutional language denying Congress the authority to alter valid contracts.

Although there is plenty of talk about originalist or historicist approaches to interpretation versus pragmatic or moral approaches, the fact is that it is impossible to sustain any practice of constitutional adjudication across the full range of constitutional issues faced by the Court without making use of and taking into account interpretive arguments of each of the foregoing sorts at one point or another. What is at stake in the debates over constitutional interpretation is which modes of argument constitute, or should constitute, the center of gravity or point of departure within constitutional adjudication. Should judges always begin with and organize their thinking around textual or historical arguments? Or should they begin with and organize their thinking around a moral reading of the Constitution?

Those inclined toward a generally positivist conception of the law typically favor arguments centered on the Constitution as a past political act that is conventionally made the fundamental or master rule within the legal system. On their view, legal rights are given by the conventionally identified legal rules, and thus constitutional rights are given by the conventionally identified Constitution. Those more inclined toward a natural law conception of the law typically favor arguments centered on the Constitution as a past political act the force of which turns on its moral content or nature as presently assessed. Realists adopt a more eclectic and instrumentalist approach to constitutional interpretation.

All I want to do here, in drawing this chapter to a close, is highlight the incompleteness of so-called originalist approaches that take the words of the Constitution to be the first and usually last word when it comes to interpreting the Constitution. The first thing to notice is that when interpretive questions arise the words of the Constitution themselves cannot settle them, because it is those words that give rise to interpretive questions in the first place. Thus, to give meaning to the words of the historical text, we must appeal to something other than the words themselves. Suppose we appeal to the meaning subjectively intended by the drafters and ratifiers. But here we begin to face difficult questions. Should we favor the intentions of the drafters or of the ratifiers? They're different groups and need not—and often will not—have shared the same intentions. Suppose we find reason to favor one or the other. What then are we to do when we discover, as in many cases we inevitably will, that the individual drafters or ratifiers themselves intended different, perhaps incompatible, things? Are we to construct some shared intention? If so, do we simply look for that intention most widely shared? But that likely will often turn out to be a sort of lowest common denominator of little use to settling the interpretive question at hand. Do we then look to that intention we think the drafters or ratifiers should have shared? But that is a moral or evaluative question inconsistent with any positivist motivation to adopt an originalist approach to constitutional interpretation. Perhaps we should just appeal to the common linguistic usage of the relevant time period. But why think we can capture the original meaning of fundamental legal texts drafted and ratified by the legal and political elite and often making use of specialized terminology by reading them against the common linguistic usage of the time, assuming we can identify that usage with any substantial degree of confidence.

The upshot here is that while the modes of argument emphasized by originalists are and should be important and recognized modes of interpretive argument in constitutional adjudication, they are, by themselves, essentially incomplete. The turn to other modes of argument is unavoidable in many cases.

A FINAL THOUGHT

Even if strong judicial review is in some sense antidemocratic, it is not contrary to the rule of law, at least on a Hartian conception of the rule of law—so long as judges are engaged in genuine rule-following behavior when they exercise their official authority, so long as judicial review is always constrained by internalized norms that serve for judges as reasons for deciding constitutional cases one way rather than another. Of course, given the plurality of interpretive strategies just surveyed, as well as the more general concerns over indeterminacy surveyed in the previous chapter on legal realism, one might wonder whether even the rule of law is safe from strong judicial review.

SELECTED BIBLIOGRAPHY

On Constitutionalism, Democracy, and Judicial Review

Ackerman, Bruce. *We the People: Foundations.* (Cambridge: MA: Harvard University Press), 1991.
———. *We the People: Transformations.* (Cambridge, MA: Harvard University Press), 1998.

Bickel, Alexander. *The Least Dangerous Branch: The Supreme Court at the Bar of Politics,* 2nd ed. (New Haven, CT: Yale University Press), 1986.

Bobbitt, Philip. *Constitutional Interpretation.* (New York, NY: Oxford University Press), 2006.

Choper, Jesse. *Judicial Review and the National Political Process.* (Chicago, IL: University of Chicago Press), 1980.

Dahl, Robert. *Democracy and Its Critics.* (New Haven, CT: Yale University Press), 1989.

Dworkin, Ronald. *Law's Empire.* (Cambridge, MA: Harvard University Press), 1987.

———. *Freedom's Law: The Moral Reading of the American Constitution.* (Cambridge, MA: Harvard University Press), 1997.

Eisgruber, Christopher. *Constitutional Self-Government.* (Cambridge, MA: Harvard University Press), 2001.

Ely, John Hart. *Democracy and Distrust: A Theory of Judicial Review.* (Cambridge, MA: Harvard University Press), 1980.

Griffin, Stephen. *American Constitutionalism: From Theory to Practice.* (Princeton, NJ: Princeton University Press), 1996.

Kramer, Larry. *The People Themselves: Popular Constitutionalism and Judicial Review.* (Oxford, UK: Oxford University Press), 2004.

Raskin, James. *Overruling Democracy.* (New York, NY: Routledge), 2003.

Rosenberg, Gerald. *The Hollow Hope: Can Courts Bring About Social Change?* (Chicago, IL: University of Chicago Press), 1993.

Shapiro, Ian. *The State of Democratic Theory.* (Princeton, NJ: Princeton University Press), 2003.

Thayer, James. "The Origin and Scope of the American Doctrine of Constitutional Law." *Harvard Law Review* 7 (1893).

Tushnet, Mark. *Taking the Constitution Away From the Courts.* (Princeton, NJ: Princeton University Press), 2001.

Waldron, Jeremy. *Law and Disagreement.* (Oxford, UK: Oxford University Press), 2001.

Weschler, Herbert. "Toward Neutral Principles of Constitutional Law." *Harvard Law Review* 73 (1959).

6

On Punishment

SURVEYING THE PROBLEM

The coercive face of the law is perhaps no more clearly visible than it is with the criminal law. Citizens may run afoul of the law in many ways, but only when they run afoul of the criminal law do they risk being prosecuted and punished. Inquiry into when, why, and how we do or ought to use the authority of the state to punish citizens for violating the criminal law is one of the central tasks of the philosophy of law.

We are today in desperate need of a sound theory of criminal punishment. The documented prison population in the United States is the largest, both absolutely and proportionately, in the world. There are more than 2 million persons in prison in the United States, almost 1 of every 100. According to the U.S. Department of Justice, as of 2001, 5.6 million adults living in the United States had served time in prison. At current incarceration rates, roughly 1 of every 15 persons now living in the United States will at some point serve time in prison. Many of them will be drug offenders, the most significant factor in the rising incarceration rates. And many of them will be repeat offenders, whether for drug-related or other crimes. Roughly 40 percent of those in prison now are in prison for a third (or more) offense.

These figures are troubling enough. But equally troubling are the costs associated with these figures—the costs to taxpayers (including the opportunity costs of not being able to put scarce resources to other uses) who must fund the building and staffing of prisons, the court system, the police, and so on; the costs imposed on all those innocent persons (spouses, children, employers, etc.) who suffer indirectly when a person on whom they rely or for whom they care is incarcerated; the costs of diminished social solidarity and fellow feeling among citizens; the costs of lives, talents, and productivity lost to a life in prison; and so on. What explains and what could possibly justify this massive and expensive social undertaking we call punishment?

There are, of course, other important issues associated with the problem of punishment. Can the death penalty be justified? (Roughly four thousand now sit on death row.) Is public shaming a morally acceptable form of punishment? Is corporal punishment (e.g., caning) acceptable? Is the lifetime surveillance of convicted sex offenders who have already served their sentence morally acceptable? Is it morally permissible to punish a convict who becomes mentally ill subsequent to his conviction but before his punishment? May so-called hate crimes be punished more severely than otherwise identical non-hate crimes? Are mandatory minimum and three-strike sentencing rules morally acceptable? May juveniles be punished in the same manner as adults? When, if ever, should mercy temper punishment? What kinds of conduct may properly be criminalized and punished? Is strict criminal liability to punishment (punishment predicated solely on an agent performing an act and irrespective of his or her mental state) ever justified? Should unsuccessful criminals ("I tried to kill him but failed.") be punished less than successful criminals? What about criminals who necessarily fail to succeed ("I tried to kill him by casting spells on him.")? Who should determine the punishment given a particular offender? To what extent should punishment aim to compensate victims of crime or facilitate reconciliation between victims and offenders? And so on. But there is not much point in taking up these issues unless and until we have some sense of what our system of state-sponsored punishment is for and whether it is justifiable, and so on. And so it is to these matters we must first (and, given our limited space here, exclusively) attend.

In so doing, we face several tasks. First, we must get clear on what we are talking about when we talk about punishment. What distinguishes a punishment from, for example, a mere penalty? Second, we must identify what Hart termed the "general justifying aim" of any rule-governed institution of state-imposed punishments. What good or value or principle explains, or justifies, or perhaps even requires, the existence of such an institution? Third, we must identify, explain, and justify the criteria in terms of which one becomes eligible or liable to be punished by the state. What conduct, and committed with what mental states, is to be criminalized and thus subject to punishment? And which individual offenders ought, in fact, to be punished? Finally, we need to justify both the kinds and amounts of punishment we impose on offenders. Why incarcerate offenders rather than sever a few digits? Why five years of incarceration for this offense or offender and ten years for that?

A complete and adequate theory of punishment will answer all these questions in a consistent way. Such a theory may be either a pure or a mixed theory. A pure theory will coherently answer all these questions from a single, well-defined, theoretical point of view and by reference to a single or small set of unified principles. A mixed theory will answer different questions from different theoretical points of view or by reference to different principles without contradiction. Of course, to the extent that the answers given by a mixed theory can be made to hang together, to cohere, beyond simple consistency, that is a theoretical advantage.But a mixed theory need not cohere in this way; it need only be internally consistent.

The most enduring and popular pure theories are instrumentalism (utilitarianism or some other consequentialist theory that treats punishment as a necessary or appropriate means to some other good) and retributivism (which treats punishment, when deserved, as an intrinsic good). There are a variety of mixed theories. Some supplement a generally instrumentalist orientation by incorporating retributivist considerations. Others supplement a generally retributivist orientation by incorporating instrumentalist or utilitarian considerations. Still others draw on considerations neither clearly instrumentalist nor retributivist to answer at least some of the questions a complete theory must address.

There are two ways in which serious moral doubt about existing punishment practices may arise. First, some theory of punishment might succeed as a complete and adequate theory and thus provide an evaluative standard against which existing practices turn out to require substantial reform. Second, we may find that every theory of punishment carefully considered fails as a complete and adequate theory. Assuming we have not overlooked obvious theoretical possibilities, this must at least count as compelling prima facie evidence for the need to rethink our existing practices. This rethinking must range over the possibility that what is required is total abolition rather than mere reform of our existing punishment practices.

PUNISHMENT AND CRIME: DEFINITIONS AND BASIC CONCEPTS

Defining punishment under law is not as easy as it might appear. But some definition is needed, not only for constitutional purposes (e.g., the Eighth Amendment's prohibition on "cruel and unusual punishment" applies only to punishments) but also for philosophical purposes. For example, punishment of any sort seems especially inappropriate when imposed for matters entirely outside the control or agency of the person punished. But fines or penalties often do not. There's nothing especially morally problematic about being assessed a late fee when your taxes arrive late to the government office due to a postal service error entirely outside of your control. But there would be something morally problematic about being punished, even if the punishment were not very severe. So, there is a difference between punishment and mere penalties. But what is the difference?

Punishment is coercive; people are made to do or suffer things they likely regard as harmful and do not want to do or suffer. But this is not peculiar to legal punishment. The law often claims and exercises the authority to coerce persons to do or suffer things they likely regard as harmful and do not want to do or suffer. Contract law limits the means available to persons for securing certain desired results, and it sometimes forces people against their will to pay money to or perform acts for others. So too does tort law (which concerns the legal liability of persons for the harms they cause to others). Yet, as with the penalty fee imposed by the tax office for your late filing, the problem of punishment does not arise with respect to contract or tort law (at least not generally—punitive damages are a special problem within contract and tort law). We need to be able to explain and justify the authority of contract and tort law, of course. But by so doing, we will not have shed any light on the problem of punishment, for the problem of punishment is not simply the problem of coercive (and unwelcome or harmful) state action under the law. As a species of coercive (and unwelcome or harmful) state action, punishment is special.

We need not spend time parsing competing definitions. For present purposes, we only need a definition good enough to sustain and orient our initial philosophical inquiry. Here is one: predicated on a legal determination of guilt for violating a criminal statute, legal punishment is an official or authoritative coercive state action that deprives a person of some good, to which she otherwise has a right, for the twin purposes of imposing hard treatment and officially expressing some general social condemnation of her criminal behavior. Several features of this definition deserve brief comment.

First, punishment presupposes a legally valid (though perhaps erroneous) conviction (or a valid guilty plea) for a criminal law violation. So, although it is legally possible to punish persons who are in fact innocent, so long as they have been legally found guilty, it is not legally possible to punish persons never legally found guilty, even if they are in fact guilty. Second, punishment essentially and publicly condemns the behavior and person being punished. This is one thing that distinguishes punishment from administrative penalties or fines, damage awards, orders to perform certain actions, and many other familiar exercises of the law's authority to coerce. In these latter cases, although the law coerces, it does not necessarily condemn. Many penalties and fines are generally understood simply as the costs of certain kinds of behavior. They are perhaps meant to create particular incentives, but they express no general social condemnation. Punishment, on the other hand, always expresses, or is always intended to express, general social condemnation.

Consider a standard case of damages for breach of contract. When the law makes one party to a contract pay damages to the other for a breach of some material term, it typically does not thereby condemn the breaching party or conduct. Indeed, the law will often favor, or will at least be neutral, toward such breaches, so long as damages are paid. (This is because such breaches may facilitate economically efficient interaction between contracting parties. If the breaching party can pay sufficient damages to offset the total loss to the other party and still come out ahead, then breaching the contract and paying damages for the breach leaves each party better off, or at least no worse off, than they would otherwise have been under the terms of the contract—a Pareto efficient result, in economic terms.) In contrast, when the law punishes, even if it punishes only by imposing a financial loss, it fundamentally condemns the behavior and person punished.

But legal punishment is not just the official condemnation of those found guilty of some criminal violation. It also involves the coercive imposition of some sort of hard treatment. Of course, the hard treatment coercively imposed may be the means through which the condemnation is publicly expressed. But it need not be. Condemnation may be publicly expressed without any hard treatment at all, perhaps through public notices. Where there is only public condemnation, but no hard treatment, there is no punishment. Where there is only hard treatment, but no public condemnation, there is no punishment. Both are necessary to punishment, and they are analytically distinct. It is at least possible to imagine a system of criminal law within which those found guilty of violating its provisions were publicly condemned for doing so but were not subject to any further hard treatment. This would be a system of criminal law without punishment. The case for legal punishment cannot be made, then, simply by appealing to the social need to condemn publicly certain kinds of behaviors. For punishment involves hard treatment and the hard treatment must also be justified. It cannot be justified merely by reference to its role as a conventional mode of expressing public condemnation. Conventions do not justify themselves, and public condemnation can be expressed in other ways.

This is a crucial point, for there are many good reasons to have a legal practice aimed at publicly condemning certain behaviors defined as criminal. Such a practice would signal to persons both inside and outside the community that the behavior is officially renounced as unacceptable, and it would ensure that those innocent of such behaviors are not stained by the behaviors of others, and so on. It is not the symbolic public condemnation side of legal punishment that raises the most serious concerns; it is the coercive imposition of hard treatment. It is the hard treatment that must be justified, and whether it can be justified is what we focus on throughout much of this chapter.

Criminal behaviors or crimes are generally specified by reference to *actus reus* and *mens rea* requirements. The former specify the prohibited act; the latter, the mental state with which the prohibited act must be performed to make the person performing it eligible for punishment. Both are typically complex. For example, the *actus reus* requirements of burglary include, first, breaking and entering a residence, and second, doing so for the purpose of committing a felony therein.

The most basic requirement of *mens rea* is that the agent acted voluntarily (rather than being coerced or having acted due to an unexpected seizure). But *mens rea* requires more than mere voluntariness. In general, it requires also that one of four possible further conditions be satisfied. The agent must perform the *actus reus* either purposefully, knowingly, recklessly, or negligently. In the first case the agent purposefully commits the criminal act. An agent who shoots another for the specific purpose of killing him (and not for purposes of self-defense) commits intentional or purposeful homicide. This agent is more culpable than the agent in the second case. In the second case the agent commits the criminal act knowing that he will, or will likely, be committing a crime but without the specific purpose or intent to commit that crime. An agent who leaves a person bound and gagged in the desert with no specific intent to kill, but knowing that death will or will likely follow, knowingly (rather than purposefully) commits homicide if the victim does in fact die. This agent is not so culpable as the first, but more culpable than the agent in the third case. In the third case the agent acts in reckless indifference to the potentially criminal nature or consequences of his conduct. An agent who fires a gun into the air in a populated area not intending to kill anyone or knowing that anyone will or will likely die, but still aware of and recklessly indifferent to the risk posed by such activity, commits a reckless homicide or manslaughter if someone is killed by a bullet he fires. In the fourth case, acting negligently, the agent acts without even knowing of the risks he is imposing on others, but under conditions in which he should have known of and attended to those risks. This is the lowest degree of culpability recognized by the law. In general, the criminal law does not punish merely negligent conduct, but there are a few exceptions.

Satisfying one of the foregoing *mens rea* requirements, usually one of the first three, is almost always a necessary condition of criminal liability to punishment. In very rare cases, however, punishment may be imposed even though none of the foregoing requirements are met. When this happens, criminal liability to punishment is said to be strict, for it is predicated solely on the fact that the *actus reus* conditions are satisfied. (While strict criminal liability is rare, strict liability for one or another *actus reus* requirement is less rare. For example, with respect to the crime of statutory rape, offenders need not even be negligent with respect to the age of the victim. *Mens rea* requirements attach, of course, to the other *actus reus* requirements—for example, that certain sorts of sexual contact be made.)

Strict criminal liability authorizes punishment irrespective of culpability, and this we're generally unwilling to accept. But why? Is it because we think persons ought to get what they deserve and that only the culpable deserve punishment? Or is it because we think there is no real point, say, no deterrence or reformative value, in punishing persons for conduct only barely tied to their own moral agency? Whatever our theory of punishment, presumably it should coherently explain our unwillingness to make criminal liability to punishment strict (even as we sometimes make liability to forms of nonpunitive treatment strict).

A person is liable to criminal punishment when the state can prove each of the *actus reus* and *mens rea* requirements of the crime beyond a reasonable doubt. A failure to prove any element is sufficient to justify acquittal. Sometimes when the *actus reus* elements are proved but not the *mens rea* requirements, the otherwise criminal conduct is said to be excused. This may be for any of several reasons. The conduct may not have been voluntary at all. It may have been a matter of involuntary reflex, or the result of coercion, or mental illness. Or it may have been voluntary, yet the agent may fail some necessary condition of culpability. (Wherever the law recognizes excusing conditions for criminal liability to punishment, that liability is not strict. Thus, the reasons for our unwillingness to accept strict liability may best be revealed indirectly through an inquiry into our reasons for wanting the law to recognize specific excusing conditions.)

Excuses are not justifications. An excuse establishes that the agent is not responsible or culpable for illegal conduct. A justification establishes that the conduct itself was not illegal. Consider two killings. In the first, the killer is mentally ill and has no idea what it is she is doing or that it is wrong. She has a legal excuse sufficient to immunize her from criminal liability to punishment (though not, perhaps, to preventative detention or nonpunitive treatment). Her conduct is properly prohibited by the criminal law, and *it* merits condemnation, though *she* does not. In the second, the killer acts out of reasonable self-defense. He has a legal justification sufficient to render his conduct noncriminal. The criminal law does not prohibit killing in reasonable self-defense; neither he nor his conduct merits condemnation. Excuses and justification both block liability to punishment, but in very different ways.

A BRIEF HISTORICAL SKETCH

In the English-speaking world, utilitarian thinking dominated political philosophy and public policy during the first half of the twentieth century. Accordingly, it dominated philosophical and policy-oriented thinking about punishment. Further, criminals were typically seen as essentially rational (even if unreasonable) agents, whose criminal conduct reflected either cold calculations with respect to self-interest or a weakness of will. Punishment policy reflected these assumptions. Punishment was justified on instrumentalist grounds as a necessary or rational means to desirable ends. Specifically, it was justified as a way of giving rational agents clear and ever-present, self-interested reasons to obey the law.

By the 1950s, however, the picture of criminals as essentially rational agents responding out of self-interest to various incentives was increasingly displaced by a picture of them as more often than not less than fully rational patients suffering from one or another psychological or psychiatric (or even cultural or social) pathology. In short, with the rise of psychology and psychiatry and related fields of inquiry, criminals came to be viewed as ill. This was thought to explain the then just emerging evidence that punishment was, in fact, not a very effective deterrent to crime.

Given the generally utilitarian or consequentialist commitments still dominant within public policy and political philosophy, it was no doubt inevitable that with this new picture of the criminal as ill, the instrumentalist approach to punishment would be reoriented toward the new end of providing offenders with state-mandated, nonpunitive treatment for the pathological conditions lurking behind their criminal behavior. This "enlightened instrumentalism" found prominent spokespersons and gained a significant audience for several years. In England, it was championed by Lady Barbara Wootton; in the United States, by Karl Menninger. It challenged both instrumentalist and retributivist justifications for punishment. Punishment could not deter those who were ill, and those who were ill could not deserve to be punished.

This new orientation led, from the late 1950s until the mid-1970s or so, to many experiments in punishment practice and policy. But by the 1970s, patience was running thin. It seemed that nothing worked, neither the new-fangled attempts at treatment, rehabilitation, and reform nor the old-fashioned attempts to use punishment as a means to deter. Punishment just seemed not to do any real good. So why punish?

Perhaps inevitably, by the late 1970s, the retributivist idea that punishment is ultimately good in itself, at least when genuinely deserved, began slowly to gain both proponents and subscribers within both philosophical and policy circles. In philosophical circles, its case was encouraged first by John Rawls's emphasis on the moral requirement that states must respect the independent moral status of persons, a requirement utilitarianism presumably failed to satisfy, and second by a renewed interest in Immanuel Kant and Georg Hegel as moral and political theorists committed to the priority of the person as a responsible agent. In policy circles and the general public, the case was encouraged by the renewed emphasis on individual responsibility so central to the Ronald Reagan and Margaret Thatcher political "revolutions" in the United States and England.

By the 1990s, retributivism was clearly the dominant approach to punishment in the general public's political culture, as well as in the specialized worlds of public policy and political philosophy. There were, of course, dissenting voices. In the late 1970s, Michel Foucault published his well-known *Discipline and Punish,* in which modern punishment practices were cast as the embodiment of the mystifying ideologies through which the modern state maintained the power relations essential to its own being. In the 1980s, Friedrich Nietzsche's indictment of punishment as arising from and giving expression to vicious, debased, even sadistic emotions gained renewed attention. Retributivism also met with resistance from liberal theorists, even those sympathetic to the sort of broadly Kantian liberalism advanced by Rawls.

The consensus today seems to be that no pure theory of punishment, whether instrumentalist or retributivist, will survive critical examination. And so the debate has largely moved to new ground, focusing on mixed theories as well as abolitionist arguments for the end of punishment altogether or its radical transformation into something essentially nonpunitive under ideals of reparative or restorative justice.

PURE INSTRUMENTALIST THEORIES

Many have sought to justify legal punishment on purely instrumental grounds as a means to some desired end extrinsic to punishment itself. For utilitarians, this desired end is the maximization of aggregate or average utility (usually understood as pleasure, agreeable consciousness, or preference satisfaction). But for nonutilitarian instrumentalists about punishment, the end in terms of which punishment is justified may be any number of other goods extrinsic to punishment itself. For example, punishment may be justified as necessary or conducive to securing the rights of persons. What is central about instrumentalist arguments for punishment is that punishment be justified as a *means* to some good extrinsic to punishment itself; punishment is not good in itself. Instrumentalist justifications are therefore essentially forward-looking. What justifies punishment is the good it yields.

It is easy to get confused here. Unlike instrumentalists about punishment, retributivists argue that punishment is intrinsically good, at least when it is deserved. But it does not follow that retributivists must reject all consequentialist thinking about punishment. Of course, they might think of punishment as the kind of intrinsic good that imposes a duty to punish, regardless of the consequences. But they might alternatively think of it as a good, perhaps just one of many, to which we should attend as we endeavor to choose actions or create institutions with the best consequences. If they take this view, they might think punishment to be in some particular case unjustified, all things considered, even though deserved, because it would prevent the realization of other weightier intrinsic goods in play. So what distinguishes instrumentalists from retributivists about punishment is not that the consequences of punishing matter only to the former, but rather that only the latter counts punishment, when deserved, as intrinsically good.

Instrumentalists defend punishment as a necessary or appropriate means to some good independent of punishment itself, usually social control broadly understood. This provides the general justifying aim of our punishment practices. The specific candidate goods most often discussed include general deterrence, specific deterrence, reform and rehabilitation, and incapacitation. General deterrence refers to the good of overall crime reduction within society. Specific deterrence refers to a reduction in future criminal conduct by the punished offender. Reform and rehabilitation refer to the good of altering the offender's preferences, beliefs, or character traits so as to reduce the likelihood of future criminal activity. Incapacitation refers to the good of preventing an offender from committing any offense during the term of his punishment.

In general, instrumentalists about punishment focus on the institution or rules of punishment rather than on specific instances of punishing particular offenders. This is because it is implausible to think that particular sentencers (say, judges) in individual cases will always have enough time or information to make well-founded judgments about whether punishment in this or that case is necessary or appropriate to securing any of these goods. Sometimes they will, and when they do, they should punish only if and as needed to secure the desired goods. If punishing a particular offender, or punishing her in a particular way, will do no good, then punishing her is not justified. But typically, sentencers will not have sufficient information to make such judgments. They will then simply have to apply the rules. Thus, the primary focus for instrumentalists about punishment is on justifying the institution and general rules of punishment on instrumentalist grounds.

Standard instrumentalist justifications for punishment depend crucially on there being good empirical evidence to support the relationship between the institution (and its rules) of punishment and the goods that institution is thought to secure. Notwithstanding common suspicions, the fact is that the empirical evidence regarding the deterrent effects, general and specific, of punishment is mixed at best. We like to suppose that without punishment, criminal behavior would sky-rocket. But the fact is that most people obey the criminal law for reasons that have nothing to do with the threat of punishment. And recidivism rates suggest that many criminals are more or less immune to punishment as a specific deterrent. Recent studies suggest that when punishment deters, it does so only insofar as it unambiguously and immediately communicates to potential offenders severe social condemnation. The prospect, even the probability, of hard treatment in the future seems not to have much deterrent effect at all. Whatever the deterrent effects of the criminal law today with punishment, they may be roughly the same under a reformed system of criminal law without punishment. Simply by virtue of publicly proclaiming certain conduct forbidden and then publicly censuring those who engage in it, the criminal law may deter (at least as well as it does presently), irrespective of whether offenders are punished. If the hard treatment essential to punishment is to be justified on deterrence grounds, it must deter persons over and above the degree to which they would be deterred by the criminal law without that hard treatment. Uninformed intuitions notwithstanding, there is little hard evidence for thinking this the case. So although there might be—indeed, surely is—an instrumentalist justification for a criminal law under which criminal conduct is publicly condemned, it's not at all clear that there's an instrumentalist justification for the hard treatment essential to punishment. The hard treatment may well be gratuitous.

Instrumentalist arguments for punishment must establish not just that punishment, and thus hard treatment, secures some desired good (like deterrence), but also that it is necessary or especially conducive to securing that good and that the overall costs associated with it don't outweigh the overall benefits. This is a tall order to fill. Even if existing punishment practices, including hard treatment, could be shown to have some deterrent effect, what is the likelihood that they could be shown to be necessary or especially conducive to that effect? More problematically, what is the likelihood that they would prove the most cost-efficient means to that effect?

Similar worries arise for other instrumentalist arguments. If the goal of punishment is reform and rehabilitation, what reason do we have for thinking punishment a necessary or effective or cost-efficient means to this end? Ditto for incapacitation. Incarceration may seem an especially effective means to incapacitate a person from committing criminal offenses. It surely incapacitates offenders from committing some offenses. But any survey of criminal activity within prisons will reveal that it is far less effective on this front than is commonly supposed. In any case, what is the likelihood that incarceration is a necessary or cost-effective way to incapacitate offenders? It may be necessary or cost-effective for the most dangerous offenders, but surely not for all. Instrumentalists about punishment cannot afford to brush these questions aside. Their position depends on the empirical evidence regarding the relationship between punishment and the goods punishment is meant to secure.

The most common objection raised against instrumentalist arguments for punishment, especially utilitarian arguments, is that they allow for, and might even sometimes require, purposefully convicting and punishing a person known to be innocent or, perhaps less dramatically, punishing a guilty person much more than she deserves. Because instrumentalists justify punishment not in terms of giving offenders what they deserve, but rather in terms of securing some good extrinsic to punishment itself, their view suggests that it might be morally right, or even required, to punish an innocent person, or to punish a guilty person much more than he deserves, knowingly or purposefully, if that is what is needed to secure the desired extrinsic good. Indeed, if the extrinsic good justifying punishment is an aggregative good (such as overall crime reduction or total utility), then punishing an innocent person quite severely might be justified by the sum total of very small but still desirable effects on others (everyone commits one less minor offense or gains a small amount of utility). Where the extrinsic good at which punishment is aimed is an aggregative good, no one individual need be benefited enough to offset the harm suffered by the person punished. It is enough that the sum total of benefits offset the harm.

Instrumentalists often reply by arguing that in the real world, circumstances would never arise under which the punishing of innocents or excessive punishing of the guilty would in fact deliver the goods at which punishment is aimed. Convicting and punishing an innocent person, or punishing a guilty person much more than she deserves, might make good instrumentalist sense under highly implausible or fantastic scenarios. But it would never, or almost never, make sense in the real world; it just wouldn't produce the desired effects of deterrence, reform, whatever. Suppose the institutional rules of our punishment practices included a rule that allowed for the purposeful punishing of known innocents, or the excessive punishing of the guilty, under circumstances in which this was judged very likely to improve overall deterrence. This would seriously undermine the effectiveness (whatever the level) of our system of punishment. Of course, it does not follow that this is why our existing punishment practices do not allow for the purposeful punishing of known innocents or excessive punishing of the guilty. We may disallow these things for noninstrumentalist reasons. The point is that instrumentalists about punishment think they have good reasons for disallowing these things as well, so it is not obvious that they're committed to the permissibility of punishing the innocent or excessively punishing the guilty.

But, the critic will charge, surely we can imagine a particular circumstance where there are very good instrumentalist reasons to break such a rule prohibiting the purposeful punishing of a known innocent. Perhaps we know that by doing so secretly and without public knowledge, we can produce a substantial deterrent effect with no adverse consequences. It is not important whether such a circumstance would ever really arise. What is important is that its bare possibility reveals that the only reason instrumentalists have for not punishing known innocents is that doing so isn't likely to yield the desired benefits, and this is the wrong reason, or at least not the best moral reason, not to punish known innocents.

The instrumentalist might here appeal to the nature of a rule-governed practice like punishment. Rule-governed practices are not possible unless the rules constitutive of the practice are followed and are taken as binding rather than as rules of thumb or general guidelines, especially by those exercising official authority conferred by the practice itself. Our punishment practice may be justified on the grounds that it is instrumentally well suited to securing general deterrence or other extrinsic goods. But if so, that is at least in part because it is a rule-governed practice within which the costs and benefits of various forms of conduct are known in advance, so that expectations are relatively stable and rational choice is possible. But if punishment must be rule-governed to deliver the goods that justify it, then judges, lawyers, and others exercising official authority under our punishment practices must follow the rules. Of course, the rules may grant them official discretion in various domains. That is fine. But if the rules prohibit the purposeful punishing of known innocents, as they must if the practice itself is to deliver the desired goods of general deterrence and so forth, then all those participating in the practice must follow the rules. Thus, there is no official room for the purposeful punishing of known innocents, even secretly, in particular cases where it might be judged conducive to securing some extra degree of general deterrence or other extrinsic good.

But whatever the merits of the foregoing as an analysis of the nature of rule-governed practices, one aspect of the critic's point still stands. Even if instrumentalists can ensure that known innocents are never purposefully punished, they still misunderstand the reason why known innocents are not to be purposefully punished. It is wrong to convict and punish an innocent person—and not only because the institutional rules forbid it. It is also wrong to do so, regardless of whether it is necessary or conducive to securing some extrinsic good, such as overall crime reduction. It is wrong, in itself, apart from the rules and regardless of the consequences, because it gives the criminal something he doesn't deserve and thereby counts as a basic injustice. And this the instrumentalist, unhappily, simply cannot acknowledge.

Of course, instrumentalists might simply dig in their heels and insist that there is no basic justice with respect to punishment apart from following those rules constitutive of a punishment practice optimally aimed at some important good extrinsic to punishment itself. If purposefully punishing known innocents turned out to be necessary or especially conducive (and overall cost effective) to securing some such good, then that's just the way it is. The same might be said for the adoption of strict criminal liability to punishment—that is, punishment predicated solely on the external actions of an agent and without any regard for her internal mental states. If there are good instrumentalist reasons for strict criminal liability, then that's just the way it is. If our moral intuitions point in the other direction, well then, so much the worse for our moral intuitions.

But this is a position few are willing to take, and not just because they lack the moral courage to do so. It is rather because they have good reasons for thinking that purely instrumentalist approaches to punishment are morally mistaken in a particular way. By framing the justification of punishment purely in terms of the instrumental relationship between punishment and ends extrinsic to it, instrumentalists make the morality of how we treat individual persons turn entirely on matters extrinsic to their moral status. Instrumentalists thereby fail to incorporate into their theory of punishment any constraints or requirements tied to the moral respect due to persons simply because they are persons. They do not acknowledge persons as ends in themselves. But this is a bedrock moral notion not so easily dismissed by flip remarks like "so much the worse for our moral intuitions."

Purely instrumentalist theories of punishment may be in part correct. That state-sponsored punishment yields some good extrinsic to punishment may be a necessary condition of its being justified, but it is not likely a sufficient condition. And that means that purely instrumentalist theories must fail as complete and adequate theories of punishment.

SIDE-CONSTRAINED INSTRUMENTALIST THEORIES

One possible way to improve on purely instrumentalist approaches to punishment is to introduce independently justified side constraints on the practice of punishment. A side constraint is a moral consideration that functions in moral deliberation as something like a trump card— it has the power to override or constrain a generally higher or more basic moral consideration. The two obvious side constraints are that only those properly convicted of and reasonably believed to be guilty of a criminal offense be punished and that they be punished only in a manner and amount fitting their offense. These side constraints may be justified on retributivist or nonretributivist grounds. A retributivist might justify them on the grounds that basic justice demands that a known innocent never be purposefully punished. A nonretributivist might justify these constraints on the grounds that they are necessary to protect the value of human agency, for if innocence did not entail an immunity to punishment, it would be impossible for persons to plan their lives rationally; they'd never know what to expect. Or a nonretributivist might justify them on fairness grounds, because surprising innocent people with punishment would seem unfair.

Whichever way the side constraints are justified, side-constrained instrumentalist theories are a kind of mixed theory of punishment.

Consider first a side-constrained instrumentalism where the side constraints are given by a retributivist justification. Known innocents are not to be purposefully punished because they are not culpable and thus cannot deserve punishment. Nor are the guilty to be punished more than they deserve. Justice requires that persons get what they deserve. But if giving people what they deserve is important enough to justify these side constraints on our punishment practices, why is it not important enough to constitute the general justifying aim of our punishment practices?

The tension between the instrumentalist's general justifying aim and retributivist side constraints can be brought out easily enough. If retributivist considerations are sufficient to make it inappropriate to punish an innocent, even if so doing might realize some extrinsic good, then why wouldn't they be sufficient to make it appropriate to punish a guilty offender, even if so doing would realize no extrinsic good? How can desert-based concerns be sufficient to override instrumentalist considerations when it comes to punishing the innocent but not sufficient when it comes to punishing the guilty? The problem is that an instrumentalist who commits to punishing all and only the deserving is no longer an instrumentalist. An instrumentalist about the general justifying aim of punishment must be prepared to forgo punishing some who deserve to be punished if their being punished would generate no good extrinsic to the punishment itself. But it's not clear that this is compatible with refusing to punish any innocent, no matter how significant the extrinsic good so doing might generate.

If punishing people who don't deserve it is intrinsically bad, then punishing people who do deserve it would seem to be intrinsically good. But then there is always at least a prima facie reason to punish a culpable offender. There may, of course, be other goods to consider as well. And so it may sometimes turn out that in the final analysis, a culpable offender otherwise deserving of punishment ought not be punished. But this kind of reasoning belongs not to a side-constrained instrumentalism but rather to a complex, perhaps even a side-constrained, retributivism that takes punishment (when deserved) as intrinsically good and thus as at least prima facie justified, regardless of any further considerations, instrumental or otherwise.

A side-constrained instrumentalism in which the side constraints are given a nonretributivist justification presumably won't be vulnerable to this difficulty. But it will remain vulnerable on other fronts. If our punishment practices, including constraints on punishing known innocents or excessively punishing the guilty, are justified solely by virtue of their forward-looking instrumental relationship to goods extrinsic to punishment itself, then whether and how persons are punished under the practice will still be a function of something (respect for their rational agency as such, or basic justice, for example) other than considerations of desert. It is one thing to say that the legal rules governing punishment must require proof of an *actus reus* and *mens rea*, recognize various excuses, prohibit the purposeful punishment of known innocents, and so forth, if persons are to be able to plan their lives rationally or avoid unexpected or unfair surprises. It is another thing to say these rules are necessary so that persons are given what and only what they deserve or are shown the respect they are due as responsible, moral agents or persons. A side-constrained instrumentalism where the side constraints are given a nonretributivist justification can say only the former.

There are at least three troubling implications here. First, because desert-based considerations are not salient on this version of side-constrained instrumentalism, the side constraints must be interpreted as addressed to the *legally* innocent (those not duly convicted) rather than the *morally* innocent (nonculpable). Of course, the legally innocent will sometimes be morally innocent as well, but not always. And on this version of side-constrained instrumentalism, the constraint on punishing the innocent applies to the legally innocent. This may seem inadequate.

Second, since, on this view, goods extrinsic to punishment provide both the general justifying aim of and the side constraints on our punishment practices, we need some priority rule for deciding cases when these goods come into conflict. For example, strict criminal liability might sometimes yield significant goods in terms of general social control, but at the expense of the ability of agents to predict the consequences of their conduct and thereby rationally plan their lives. How do we know which good controls the issue here?

Third, when the legally guilty are punished on this view, they are punished not because they necessarily deserve it in any moral sense (for the legally guilty might not be morally culpable), but rather because their being punished will serve some good extrinsic to the punishment itself (it will deter others, etc.). But this would seem to involve treating the guilty as mere means to some general social end rather than as ends in themselves. It is no use to argue that the guilty are respected as ends in themselves, because their punishment depends on their having been found legally guilty under rules that require *mens rea*, recognize various excuses, and so forth. Legal guilt, even under such rules, is not the same thing as moral culpability. While the two may often overlap, they need not. So it looks like this version of side-constrained instrumentalism treats the guilty merely or primarily as means to other goods rather than as ends in themselves. It's true that insofar as it requires punishment rules that require *mens rea*, recognize excuses, and so forth, this version of side-constrained instrumentalism will respect persons as rational agents who have an interest in being able to plan for the future rationally, avoiding unpredictable and harmful surprises, and so on. But this is not the same as treating persons as responsible moral agents who may come to deserve being treated in particular ways by virtue of their own conduct.

Here the side-constrained instrumentalist might argue that it is okay not to treat or respect the guilty as ends in themselves. Perhaps through their illegal conduct, by violating the social contract, the guilty forfeit their right to be treated as ends in themselves. But surely this overstates the matter. Illegal conduct by itself cannot plausibly be seen as triggering a full-fledged forfeiture of all the rights predicated on one's status as a person or an end in oneself. It cannot even be seen as triggering forfeiture of all the rights of citizenship. So it must be that only certain rights are forfeited. But which ones? And how is punishing the guilty for the sake of securing general deterrence consistent with those rights that are retained? This view leaves the criminal offender in an unstable or ambiguous position. Having forfeited some of his rights through his illegal conduct, he is no longer a full member of the political community and entitled to be treated as such. But he is still a moral person possessed of some rights and in a special relationship to the political community that is punishing him and to which he presumably is to be restored after his punishment is complete. Clearly, if we're to argue that it's okay not to treat the guilty as ends in themselves, because by virtue of their criminal conduct they forfeit some key rights, but not all their rights, then we must make some clear sense of this in-between moral status the criminal occupies. I'm not sure it can be done.

In the end, side-constrained instrumentalists face something of a dilemma. If they offer a retributivist justification for their side constraints, then they must explain why retributivist considerations are important enough to override instrumentalist considerations in particular cases but not important enough to supply the general justifying aim of our punishment practices. If they offer a nonretributivist justification for their side constraints, then they must explain, among other things, how the punishment practices they endorse respect the status of all persons as responsible moral agents who may come to deserve being treated in particular ways by virtue of their own conduct, even though those practices ignore desert-based considerations altogether.

PURE RETRIBUTIVIST THEORIES

According to pure retributivists, the justification for punishing criminal offenders for their offenses is that it is intrinsically good to do so. Punishment is not justified as a means to any other end, such as crime reduction or the reform of offenders. It is an end in itself. This is because the morally culpable criminal offender deserves to suffer and to suffer punishment in particular, and it is just and therefore intrinsically good that she get what she deserves. This intrinsic good is one the state has the authority and obligation to secure. For the pure retributivist, this is the general justifying aim of our punishment practices. Pure retributivist theories of punishment are, then, essentially backward-looking rather than forward-looking in their justificatory logic. Punishment is justified not by reference to what it will secure in the future, but by reference to what requires it from the past. That a person is a morally culpable criminal offender is, for the retributivist, a necessary—and the only sufficient—condition of her properly being punished. It is also the only consideration relevant to the manner and amount of punishment to which she is properly subject.

Though retributivism is sometimes said to collapse into little more than an argument for institutionalized vengeance, it is structurally quite different. Retributivists maintain that it is intrinsically good that morally culpable criminal offenders be given the punishment they deserve, apart from any psychological effects on victims or within the community. Further, they can, and often do, condemn as vicious or debased, even if explainable, the desire to exact vengeance.

Retributivism is also sometimes said to collapse into little more than *lex talionis,* "an eye for an eye and a tooth for a tooth." But *lex talionis* is not about the reasons why persons are to be punished but rather about the kind and amount of punishment those who are to be punished should suffer. While pure retributivists must hold that persons should receive the punishment they deserve in both kind and amount, they need not adopt *lex talionis* as the proper measure of that punishment.

Pure retributivists must provide philosophically sound and compelling answers to at least four questions. First, why do morally culpable criminal offenders deserve anything? Second, why do they deserve to suffer punishment, and exactly what punishments do they deserve to suffer? Third, in what sense is it intrinsically good that they suffer the punishments they deserve? Fourth, why is the state authorized and obligated to secure this intrinsic good?

With respect to the first question, retributivists hold that criminal offenders ordinarily satisfy the conditions of responsible moral agency and therefore may be said to deserve something in light of their conduct. It is sometimes said that if it turns out that the natural world, and thus human persons, are subject to causal determinism, then the conditions of responsible moral agency cannot obtain. But this is probably false. Responsible moral agency is consistent, on the dominant view, with a causally determined natural world (though it should be noted that what scientists mean when they speak of a causally determined natural world is often not what comes to mind for the person off the street or even the philosopher without some knowledge of the philosophy of science; for one thing, causal determinism refers to a property of scientific laws, not of the world itself). Causal determinism and moral responsibility are compatible, because responsible moral agency requires no more than that persons be causally linked to effects in the world through voluntary (uncoerced) conduct arising out of their own deliberations and choice, or some other internal mechanism responsive to the weight and force of competing reasons for acting in different ways. Whether Sally could have acted other than she did is irrelevant to whether she's morally responsible for her action. Whether Jim's decision to act as he did is itself an effect of causal factors external to him, perhaps even antedating his birth, is similarly irrelevant. What is relevant is whether Sally and Jim acted for reasons and whether they are causally linked through their action to that which they are being held responsible for. But this is a matter we cannot pursue here. We need only note that retributivists need a philosophically plausible conception of responsible moral agency, one that could survive the truth of causal determinism (if it is true), but that here they are in no worse position than anyone else.

So, why do culpable criminal offenders, as responsible moral agents, deserve to suffer and to suffer punishment in particular (regardless of any external effects such punishment might produce)? And how do we know exactly what punishment particular offenders deserve to suffer? These are difficult questions to which retributivists do not have altogether satisfactory answers.

That those who commit terrible moral wrongs deserve to suffer is perhaps a basic truth for which no argument may be given. There is certainly a strong sense in which suffering would seem to fit or be an appropriate response to moral culpability. If I imagine myself having committed a vicious murder or rape, I find it almost impossible to think of myself as deserving anything other than suffering by virtue of my vicious conduct. But what do those who commit terrible moral wrongs deserve to suffer? They surely deserve at least blame and resentment from others, as well as the pain of guilt from their own self-assessment. But do they deserve to suffer the hard treatment of punishment above and beyond this? That is not so clear; it does not follow from the fact that one deserves to suffer blame, resentment, or the pain of guilt that one also deserves to suffer the hard treatment of legal punishment.

But just suppose it did. We'd still face something of a riddle. For murderers and rapists deserve to suffer blame, resentment, and the pain of guilt not because of the illegality of their conduct, but rather because of their crime's immorality and because of their moral culpability. Even if there were no criminal laws prohibiting murder and rape, murderers and rapists would still deserve to suffer blame, resentment, and the pain of guilt. So even if their deserving these things entailed that they also deserved to suffer the hard treatment of legal punishment, the connection between their deserving punishment and the *illegality* of their conduct would remain unclear. The illegality of their conduct would seem to play no role in accounting for their deserving punishment. But this is problematic, for it suggests that *legal guilt* is not a necessary condition of justified legal punishment. That cannot be right. Immoral conduct that is legally permissible ought not be legally punished, regardless of moral desert. And morally acceptable conduct that is legally impermissible possibly ought to be punished. It is not clear how a pure retributivist can account for this.

One reason sometimes advanced for the claim that genuine criminal offenders deserve punishment, regardless of the morality of their underlying conduct, is that punishment is necessary to annul or negate the criminal act as a violation of legal right. The criminal law establishes legal rights. The existence of these rights entails that there is or must be some legal act triggered by their violation. If legal rights could be violated without any consequence, then it would be silly to claim that they existed in any real sense in the first place. It would be silly to say that the criminal law provides me with a legal right to bodily integrity if others could physically attack, even kill, me without legal consequence. There is something to this line of argument, but it establishes neither that punishment must be the necessary legal act triggered by a violation of the criminal law (why isn't a criminal conviction and significant public condemnation enough?) nor that criminal offenders are properly punished because they deserve it (rather than because of the conditions that must be satisfied if legal rights are to exist in any meaningful sense).

Another argument sometimes made here is that criminal offenders deserve to be punished because by violating the criminal law, they wrongly derive some benefit or advantage that they do not deserve, and punishment is needed to strip them of this undeserved benefit or advantage. Justice demands that criminals be punished. This sounds like an appealing claim at first. It would seem to provide a reason for the hard treatment of punishment (rather than just censure), as well as punishment for all and only criminal (rather than just moral) offenses. But it fares less well upon closer inspection. The problems come once we try to spell out the benefit or advantage that criminal offenders wrongly derive by violating the law and that punishment is meant to remove or erase.

Suppose we say that it is the psychological benefit or advantage of feeling unrestrained by the criminal law and thus free to act on one's desires, a benefit or advantage not enjoyed by law-abiding citizens. This sounds plausible at first. But the fact is that most law-abiding nonoffenders feel no desire to violate, and thus do not feel restrained by, the criminal law. And so it's hard to see how the criminal offender enjoys a benefit or advantage here. Suppose we say instead that the criminal offender enjoys the benefit or advantage of an objective increase in freedom or liberty over and against the rest of us who obey the criminal law. This greater freedom or liberty might be understood or measured simply in terms of noncompliance with the criminal law. But then all criminal offenders would be equally culpable and thus equally deserving of punishment, even equally deserving of the same punishment, because they all violate the criminal law. But it can't be that all criminal offenders are equally culpable and equally deserving of the same punishment. (Indeed, some may not even be culpable or deserving of punishment at all—for example, those who for good moral reasons violate deeply unjust laws.) So it must be that the greater freedom or liberty the criminal offender enjoys over and against the rest of us is to be understood or measured by reference to the particular law she ignores or violates. The murderer wrongfully enjoys a freedom or liberty over the life of another that the rest of us give up and do not enjoy. The rapist wrongfully enjoys a different freedom or liberty over the body of another, but also one the rest of us give up and do not enjoy. And so on. By putting the matter this way, we can avoid being driven to the claim that all criminal offenders are equally culpable and equally deserving of the same punishment.

But we still have problems. If criminal offenders deserve punishment because through their criminal conduct they secure a measure of freedom or liberty not enjoyed by those who obey the particular law in question, then punishment is deserved only if the criminal law already exists. The criminal law sets the benchmark in terms of which criminal offenders arrogate to themselves an extra measure of freedom or liberty. But this would seem to get things backward. The criminal law arguably exists so that persons guilty of certain sorts of conduct may get the punishment they deserve as a matter of law. Furthermore, it seems odd to say that a murderer or rapist deserves punishment because of some extra amount of freedom or liberty wrongly arrogated to himself over and against his law-abiding peers, rather than because of the evil nature of his act or the suffering directly and wrongfully imposed on his victim. The underlying moral wrongfulness of the conduct, the harm wrongfully imposed on others, would seem better to account for the fact that the criminal offender deserves punishment than would any alleged advantage or benefit gained relative to law-abiding citizens in general. (Indeed, if it is not the underlying moral wrongfulness of the conduct—the harm wrongfully imposed on others—that calls for punishment, then perhaps those who violate a deeply unjust law for good moral reasons still *deserve* to be punished. After all, they secure for themselves a measure of freedom or liberty those of us who obey the law do not enjoy.)

Retributivists must look beyond any unfair advantage or benefit derived by criminal offenders to defend their claim that criminal offenders deserve the punishment they get. If legal punishment is justified because it gives the criminal offender what he deserves, then criminal offenders must deserve their punishment by virtue of the immorality of their illegal conduct and their culpability for engaging in it. But the nature of their culpability or the immorality of their conduct need not be the same in all cases. Sometimes it may be a function of the underlying conduct in itself, as it is with murder and rape. Such conduct is said to be *mala in se,* or bad or evil in itself, and those who engage in it without an excuse are usually regarded as morally culpable to some degree. Other times, the culpability of a criminal offender or the immorality of her conduct may be a function of a general social need for compliance with some conventional rule or other essential to a collective good or to social coordination. There is nothing intrinsically immoral about driving 85 miles an hour, and a person may, in principle, nonculpably engage in such behavior without an excuse. But driving faster than the posted speed limit is immoral, and doing so without an excuse is morally culpable, insofar as some speed limit rule is needed to secure the collective good of minimizing the costs of auto traffic, including traffic fatalities, and otherwise coordinating social conduct so that persons can get where they want to go. So if the posted speed limit is 60 miles an hour, then driving 85 without an excuse is immoral and blameworthy conduct. Such conduct is said to be *mala prohibita,* or bad or evil because conventionally prohibited. Conduct *mala in se* or *mala prohibita* is immoral, and persons who engage in such conduct without an excuse are to some degree morally blameworthy. If being morally blameworthy is sufficient to deserve punishment, then such persons deserve punishment.

But why think that being morally blameworthy is at least sometimes sufficient to deserve punishment? Perhaps the best reason is that it fits and explains, better than any alternative, persistent intuitions we have about what it means to treat persons as responsible moral agents—intuitions not only about what others deserve when they culpably engage in immoral conduct, but also about what we think we ourselves would or do deserve for such conduct. Those who culpably engage in certain kinds of immoral conduct deserve blame, resentment, and the pain of guilt *as well as the hard treatment* essential to punishment. This may be a kind of foundational moral principle. There may be no argument for it other than that it fits and explains our persistent intuitions and considered judgments. After all, when we engage in culpable wrongdoing, don't we think we deserve to suffer some loss – to be punished – as a result?

There are two difficulties with this line of argument. First, not everyone shares the intuition that those who culpably engage in immoral conduct deserve anything more than blame, resentment, and the pain of guilt. Intuitions regarding the hard treatment of punishment are varied, even among persons who take desert seriously. Second, even if we ignore those who do not share the intuition, the fact is that the intuition can be explained in more than one way. True, one way to explain it would be to point to a moral principle connecting culpability, desert, and the hard treatment of punishment. But another way would be to point to various features of our own psychology. Perhaps we all secretly envy the power of the criminal but find ourselves too cowardly to exercise such power, other than anonymously through the collective action of state-sponsored punishment. Or perhaps state-sponsored punishment affords us a socially acceptable way to satisfy our ineliminable sadistic desires. Or perhaps we're so driven to sublimate our own criminal tendencies that we cannot see the criminal offender as anything other than radically evil, something no longer human and thus undeserving of respect. Or perhaps we seek indirect expiation for our own sins through the punishment of others. I could go on, but you get the picture. The retributivist must show that his foundational moral principles fit and explain our intuitions and judgments better than these rival psychological and emotional explanations. Of course, the retributivist might object here that even if our intuitions and judgments about punishment did arise from such vicious psychological or emotional bases, this would not in itself necessarily falsify the intuitions or judgments. To think that it would, at least without further argument, would be to fall victim to the genetic fallacy. But then again, sometimes the psychological or emotional roots of our moral judgments do bear on their truth or falsity. And this may be one of those cases.

Suppose we were somehow able to get past these difficulties and establish that those who act immorally in ways prohibited by the criminal law do in fact deserve the hard treatment essential to punishment. We would still need to be able to specify the appropriate kind and amount of punishment for particular offenses and then for particular offenders found legally guilty of such offenses. But this would seem to be an impossible task. We can perhaps arrange punishments of a single kind from the least to the most severe. And we can perhaps arrange crimes (again, probably only of a single kind—say, violent assaults or property crimes) from the least to the most serious. We might then simply superimpose the first scale on the second. But we'd have no reason to think we were punishing offenses or offenders even roughly in accord with desert unless we had some independent reason for thinking that at least one point on this superimposed scale correctly correlated a particular offense with a particular punishment. Pure retributivists must be able to do more than rank offenses and punishments from the least to the most serious and severe. They must be able to establish independently, for at least some offense or offender, that this or that particular punishment is the deserved punishment. But how is this to be done?

One possibility would be to appeal to the rule of lex talionis—an eye for an eye, a tooth for a tooth. But this is implausible. First, it supposes that offenders deserve to be punished solely for the harm they cause rather than for their moral culpability. But retributivists must hold that offenders deserve to be punished for their moral culpability; even if the harm they cause is ingredient in their moral culpability, it is not the sole ingredient. So retributivists cannot be satisfied with a literal application of the "eye for an eye" rule. They must correlate the kind and amount of punishment imposed with the degree of moral culpability. And lex talionis provides poor guidance here. Second, it cannot be that what rapists deserve is to suffer the moral wrong of being raped by a culpable offender (or any comparable moral wrong culpably done). Whatever the punishment deserved by a rapist, the rapist receiving it must be a moral right, not a moral wrong. So it looks like lex talionis is insufficient to correlate offenses or offenders with determinate punishments on the basis of desert. But if this is so, then how are retributivists to know whether we are ever punishing people as they deserve? Retributivists can't just assign the most severe punishment to the most serious offense or the worst offender, for there's no reason to think that so doing would give offenders what they deserve. The worst offense or offender may deserve more or less than that imposed by the most severe punishment.

The fact is that while genuine criminal offenders may deserve to suffer, even deserve to be punished, there is no way to know, independently and without reference to a given punishment scale, what kind or amount of punishment any offender or offense intrinsically deserves. How would one justify any particular punishment as intrinsically deserved for counterfeit, or kidnap, or falsifying tax records, or murder, or trespass, or burglary, or . . . (the list goes on)? Matters grow more problematic for the retributivist when we direct our attention away from types of offenses and toward particular offenders, for the range of considerations bearing on individual desert are simply too many and too varied: past history, the context of the action, mental and moral capacities, and so on.

This is a serious problem for the retributivist. If it turns out that we never know or have well-justified beliefs about the punishment a particular offense or offender deserves, then even if the retributivist is right about the intrinsic goodness of giving criminal offenders the punishment they deserve, this is an intrinsic good we cannot ever hope to realize. So if retributivism provides the only sound justification for our punishment practices, then we should abolish our practice of legal punishment!

There is another way in which a purely retributivist orientation toward punishment may ultimately justify the abolition of existing punishment practices. Even if we knew exactly what particular offenses or offenders deserved by way of punishment, we would almost never find ourselves able to impose that punishment without harming other innocent persons in various ways related to the person being punished. The tax cheat who goes to jail for ten years has an innocent wife and children who suffer. Perhaps he was also an excellent and rare medical doctor in a rural community, so his patients suffer. Even the serial rapist who serves a life sentence may have an innocent spouse, children, parents, an employer, customers, clients, and so on, any or all of whom will be harmed indirectly by the punishment he is given. By giving the criminal offender what he deserves, the retributivist inevitably gives some, and often many, innocent persons suffering that they do not deserve, often suffering as great as that endured by the criminal offender. If it is not possible to give criminal offenders the punishment they deserve without imposing substantial undeserved harms on the rest of us, then arguably retributivists ought to endorse the abolition of existing punishment practices.

This raises yet another difficulty for the pure retributivist. The pure retributivist is committed to the view that punishing criminal offenders who deserve to be punished is an intrinsic good that the state has an obligation and the authority to realize. But even if it was an intrinsic good, why think it is one the state has an obligation or the authority to realize? In general, we think the state has an obligation to realize only goods that all or nearly all citizens have a fundamental interest in securing but likely cannot reliably secure by themselves. Security from various harms is such an interest. And so the state may have an obligation and the authority to punish, if so doing proves necessary or especially conducive to providing citizens with security from assault, deception, and other harms. But the pure retributivist cannot follow this instrumentalist path. The pure retributivist must maintain that the intrinsic good realized when those deserving punishment are given the punishment they deserve is a good that all, or nearly all, citizens have a fundamental interest in, one appropriately is realized through state action. Given the scarcity of resources available to any state and the many other goods and interests to which those resources might be devoted, it follows that pure retributivists must maintain that realizing the intrinsic good of punishing those who deserve it is generally weightier or more important than the many other goods and interests to which citizens might otherwise devote scarce state resources.

But it's just not plausible to think that punishing those who deserve it is as important as, or more important than, securing for citizens the good of or their interest in an adequate education or affordable health care or a clean environment. If punishment is to be justified—at least absent superabundant state resources—then it must be because it is or does some good (apart from giving persons what they deserve) sufficient to justify devoting to it a substantial share of scarce state resources that might be used for these other purposes. The mere intrinsic goodness of giving the culpable the punishment they deserve is surely not enough to justify state-sponsored punishment. But this means a purely retributivist theory cannot be a complete and coherent theory of punishment. Some reference to goods extrinsic to punishment itself must be invoked to provide the general justifying aim of punishment practices. And so we're pointed back toward a mixed theory.

What does pure retributivism get right? One thing it gets right is that insofar as punishment is meant to communicate to criminal offenders a general social condemnation of their conduct—and surely punishment (and the criminal law more generally) serves this expressive function—it necessarily presupposes of criminal offenders a capacity for responsible moral agency sufficient to support deserving blame or censure for their conduct. Punishment practices must respect and treat criminal offenders as responsible moral agents, not as mere opportunities for realizing general social goods like crime reduction.

COMMUNICATIVE THEORIES OF PUNISHMENT

Punishment practices might be justified, while still respecting and treating criminal offenders as responsible moral agents, if they were aimed at affording criminal offenders the public opportunity to reestablish their commitment to the values of, and to reaffirm their membership in, the political community whose criminal law they violated and to which they belong. If the criminal law was limited to matters of serious common concern to the members of a body politic, if it expressed a sort of minimal shared morality, then those who violate it will have not just caused harm but also will have offended public morality to some degree. As responsible moral agents and members of the body politic whose public morality they have violated, they should respond appropriately to the wrongfulness of their conduct. This means doing more than just compensating and seeking reconciliation with their victims, where that is possible. It also means offering some sort of public apology to the community and taking on some sort of additional burden or hard treatment—something like "secular penance," to use Anthony Duff's expression—to signal their ownership of and their responsibility for the wrong done. This punishment might take many forms, including extraordinary service to the community.

On this view, punishment is justified neither as a good in itself nor as a means to some other good extrinsic to punishment (whether general deterrence or the moral education or development of the offender). Rather, it is justified as a constitutive or essential ingredient in the only sort of moral communication appropriate between responsible moral agents and the bodies politic to which they belong. Bodies politic—even diverse and tolerant liberal bodies politic committed to individual autonomy, privacy, and so on—necessarily commit themselves to some shared public morality, typically expressed through the criminal law. Through the criminal law, they communicate to their members shared public values. Among these will or ought to be a commitment to treating all members of the body politic as responsible moral agents. But because even responsible moral agents may reasonably be expected to violate the criminal law sometimes, and because when they do, they will rightly want and need publicly to reestablish their commitment to shared public values and reaffirm their membership within the body politic, the criminal law must include provisions for some sort of "penitential punishment," appropriately scaled to reflect the kind and degree of wrongfulness or offense being addressed by the penitent.

If justified, then, punishment must do more than express condemnation running from society to the offender. It must also express back to the community the offender's acceptance of and, through the hard treatment voluntarily endured, appropriate response to that condemnation. It must, therefore, instantiate a kind of reconciliatory communication as between society and criminal offenders. As such, the justification for punishment is neither purely backward-looking nor purely forward-looking. It is both.

This is an attractive approach to rethinking punishment. But several difficulties must be addressed. First, it is not at all clear how the coercive imposition of punishment on offenders is consistent with their communicating remorse or anything else to society. If offenders are to communicate anything to society, it would seem that they must do their punishment or "secular penance" freely and voluntarily. But surely criminal offenders should not be at liberty to accept or reject their punishment. Communicative theories of punishment must justify its coercive imposition.

Second, because this communicative approach ties punishment to wrongfulness (as a penitential expression of remorse appropriate to the wrong committed), it must be able to correlate specific punishments with specific offenses in something other than an ad hoc manner. But, as we have seen, though we can perhaps rank offenses and punishments each along a separate scale from least to most severe, we have no reason for thinking that any two particular points along these scales correlate.

Third, this approach to punishment presupposes a conception of bodies politic as bound by something like a shared, even if thin, public morality. Moreover, it presupposes that criminal offenders are otherwise recognized and treated as full members of the political community against whose public morality they offend. But neither of these presuppositions, certainly not the latter, is likely fulfilled in the United States or many other modern states. Even if the criminal law really does express something like a shared public morality—rather than either a mere modus vivendi between otherwise hostile individuals and groups or the particular morality of a politically dominant group—the fact is that too many individuals and groups are neither recognized nor treated as full members of the political community allegedly committed to that public morality. They are economically, socially, culturally, and/or politically marginalized, exploited, oppressed, excluded, and so forth. Under such conditions, punishment necessarily reduces to an action that some take against others. It cannot take the form of a respectful two-way communication between equal and responsible moral members of a genuine "we." That punishment might be justified as "secular penance" were these social conditions realized is perhaps a point of mainly academic interest.

THE ABOLITIONIST CHALLENGE

All of the aforementioned justifications for something like our existing punishment practices have proved less than compelling in one or another way. Some are vulnerable to objection on empirical grounds, others on moral or conceptual grounds. This raises the possibility that nothing like our existing punishment practices—practices that coercively impose hard treatment on offenders—can be justified. If our existing punishment practices cannot be justified, then they should be abolished. Of course, we might have good reason to approach the abolitionist task with great care. Too rapid abolition of existing practices may upset settled expectations and vested interests to so great a degree that more damage than good is done. Further, since many today conventionally link the coercive imposition of hard treatment with symbolic public condemnation of criminal behavior, preserving the symbolic public condemnation of criminal behavior without the coercive imposition of hard treatment presents some short-term challenges during the transition to a post-punishment regime. But surely, if our existing practices or something like them cannot be justified, we must begin to think seriously about how best to move forward with the abolitionist undertaking. We cannot stand silent before a legal system we know to be significantly unjust in important ways.

This will strike some as crazy talk. But if it is, then we should be able to do better than we've been able to do so far at justifying our penal practices. And if we cannot do better, then philosophers of law must turn their attention to the abolitionist challenge. They cannot settle for simply giving bad reasons for what we assume we must and will continue to do, regardless of the reasons for or against.

Three final thoughts: First, notice that we have said nothing at all about distributive patterns of punishment, patterns that often appear to be arbitrary or to reflect racial or economic discrimination. Even if punishment could, in principle, be justified, we would still have to ensure that it was administered in a nonarbitrary and nondiscriminatory manner consistent with the rule of law. It is not clear that we have managed to accomplish this yet, and this is a problem regardless of whether punishment is justified. Second, as we contemplate the abolitionist challenge, we ought not lose sight of Hart's important conceptual insight: there is no necessary conceptual connection between law and coercive sanction or hard treatment. Finally, remember that we have said nothing to suggest that criminal behaviors ought not be publicly condemned through some legal practice or other. Indeed, we have assumed throughout this discussion that in every society there will be good reasons to create legal institutions aimed at realizing the public condemnation of certain kinds of behavior deemed criminal. What we have called into question is the coercive imposition of hard treatment. Because there are many ways to publicly condemn criminal offenders without imposing hard treatment on them, our doing so must be justified. Yet it's not clear that it can be.

SELECTED BIBLIOGRAPHY

On Punishment

Braithwaite, J. *Crime, Shame, and Reintegration.* (Cambridge, UK: Cambridge University Press), 1989.

Davis, Michael. *To Make the Punishment Fit the Crime.* (Boulder, CO: Westview Press), 1992.

Duff, R.A. *Punishment, Communication, and Community.* (Oxford, UK: Oxford University Press), 2001.

Feinberg, Joel. *Doing and Deserving.* (Princeton, NJ: Princeton University Press), 1970.

Fletcher, George. *Rethinking Criminal Law.* (Boston, MA: Little Brown), 1978.

Hart, H.L.A. *Punishment and Responsibility.* (Oxford, UK: Oxford University Press), 1968.

Husak, Douglas. *Philosophy of Criminal Law.* (Lanham, MD: Rowman and Littlefield), 1987.

Ignatieff, Michael. *A Just Measure of Pain.* (New York, NY: Random House), 1978.

Lacey, Nicola. *State Punishment: Political Principles and Community Values.* (New York, NY: Routledge), 1988.

Matravers, M. *Justice and Punishment.* (Oxford, UK: Oxford University Press), 2000.

Moore, Michael. *Placing Blame: A Theory of Criminal Law.* (Oxford, UK: Oxford University Press), 1997.

Norrie, Allen. *Punishment, Responsibility, and Justice.* (Oxford, UK: Oxford University Press), 2000.

Sher, George. *Desert.* (Princeton, NJ: Princeton University Press), 1987.

Ten, C.L. *Crime, Guilt, and Punishment.* (Oxford, UK: Oxford University Press), 1987.

von Hirsch, A. *Censure and Sanctions.* (Oxford, UK: Oxford University Press), 1993.

7

On International Law

The philosophy of international law is a topic not usually addressed in philosophy of law textbooks. Indeed, there are very few canonical texts or constitutive debates within the philosophy of international law. Hart relegated the topic to the final chapter of his classic *The Concept of Law* on the grounds that international law was a peripheral or marginal or nonparadigmatic case of law, unfit to serve as a focal point for the philosophy of law. Since Hart, the philosophy of international law has remained a rather underdeveloped area of inquiry, notwithstanding the fact that several centuries ago many prominent thinkers, including Grotius, Pufendorf, Vattel, and Kant, devoted a great deal of attention to it. Today there are rich bodies of literature devoted to normative issues regarding ideals of global or international justice and to empirical and doctrinal issues regarding the practice and content of international law. But there isn't much devoted to a general *philosophy* of international law. And so, when it comes to an introductory text of this sort on the philosophy of law, international law does not serve well as a point of departure. Thus, it comes not at the beginning of this book, but at the end. But its position in this book ought not be read as a claim regarding international law's status as peripheral, marginal, or nonparadigmatic.

In any event, when it comes to international law, change is at hand. For many reasons, not least the end of the Cold War, international law for the past decade or so has been, almost paradoxically, in a period of both rapid development and increasing instability. Accordingly, philosophers of law have begun to turn their attention to it. This is all to the good.

Any adequate philosophy of international law must address both analytic and normative issues. With respect to the former, we need to know whether and in what sense what we commonly call international law is really *law* capable of underwriting legal rights and imposing legal obligations; whether there is a necessary conceptual connection between international law and morality; and how international law and domestic law are related as systems of law. On the normative side, we need to identify what international law ought to be as a matter of both ideal and nonideal theory. We will need to determine how ideals of justice, legitimacy, freedom, the rule of law, equality, human welfare and flourishing, virtue, and peace and stability, among others, ought to figure in and determine international law. As we shift from the context of independent domestic legal systems to that of an international legal order, we may find it necessary to shift or adjust our understanding of these ideals. A sound normative philosophy of international law might look quite different from a sound normative philosophy of domestic law.

We begin with a brief overview of just what it is we're talking about when we talk about international law. Because few persons are as familiar with the international legal order as they are with their own country's domestic legal system, this is a necessary preliminary. Then we take up our two central inquiries in turn, addressing analytic issues first and normative issues second. The discussion is necessarily incomplete and preliminary, both because of space constraints and because the philosophy of international law is an underdeveloped area of philosophical inquiry. I close with a few thoughts about the relationship between international law and international politics.

WHAT IS INTERNATIONAL LAW?

The Romans distinguished between *jus civile* and *jus gentium*. The former refers to the domestic law governing a tribe or people or other bodies politic with their own legal jurisdiction. The latter refers to the law governing the relations between such tribes or peoples and other bodies politic within the Roman Empire. International law today, especially as it concerns the legal relations between states, traces its origins to Roman *jus gentium*.

While much international law today concerns legal relations, obligations, and so on governing interactions between states as independent and legally recognized corporate agents or actors, it also extends beyond the straightforwardly international in this sense of state-to-state relations. It governs interactions between a wide range of agents or actors on the international stage even when they are not all subject to a common domestic legal jurisdiction. So, for example, it often governs interactions between corporations incorporated in different countries or between states and international organizations like the World Bank. It also often governs stateless agents or actors—for example, stateless refugees or pirates living (and working) on the high seas. (Yes, there are still pirates, though they rarely wear eye patches or wooden legs.) Finally, to some small degree, international law today governs the internal affairs of independent states apart from any interaction between them. Increasingly, it governs issues of human rights, civil war and secession, and related matters, thus functioning as a legal constraint on the internal affairs of states, apart from any interactions those states may have with other states. In this sense, it is no longer just *international* law; it is also *transnational*.

International law, then, must and does deal with a wide range of specific issues. It governs the legal recognition and continuity of states within the international order. It deals with conflicts over territorial and jurisdictional boundaries, the legal relations between distinct domestic legal orders, and the diplomatic relations between states and their representatives. It governs the international movement of persons, money, and goods, and thus sets the legal framework for all international trade, as well as for international labor, capital, currency, and commodity markets. It regulates the use of international or shared resources, such as the seas and seabed, shared waterways, Antarctica, the atmosphere and outer space, and in some cases even specific animal species. It provides the legal framework for making and interpreting treaties, sets the legal rules governing warfare, and specifies the conditions under which a state or other international actor may be liable to another state or international actor for compensatory damages as a result of harm inflicted. It makes possible and constrains the activity of many international associations, from the World Health Organization and International Monetary Fund to Human Rights Watch and the Red Cross. Finally, it assigns all individual human persons certain basic rights that no state or other actor may violate free of legal consequence.

WHO DOES INTERNATIONAL LAW GOVERN?

International law recognizes three kinds of legal subjects or actors: states, international organizations, and individual human persons. States govern a permanent population in a fixed territory. Traditionally, any sort of stable or enduring system of government, no matter how vicious, was sufficient to underwrite the existence of a state under international law. But today, international law is slowly moving toward requiring a legitimate government as a condition of legal recognition. Very roughly, a legitimate government is one in which, minimally, the rulers rule without gross domination or oppression and through something like the rule of law. They attend to what they sincerely regard as the common good of those they rule; they communicate with them, hearing and responding to their complaints; and they act always through or within a system of public law. At a minimum, a legitimate government respects certain very basic human rights.

This is one of the most unstable areas of international law today. The legal practice of restricting legal recognition to legitimate states is only just emerging, and the criteria for recognition are still evolving. There is a robust debate underway as to what those criteria ought to be. The main disagreement seems to be between those who favor relatively robust criteria requiring something like a liberal democratic order (and thus fidelity to a pretty comprehensive list of human rights) and those who favor less demanding criteria requiring only, say, a constitutional republican form of government (and thus fidelity to a less comprehensive list of human rights). Nevertheless, there is a rather substantial, but not unanimous, agreement over the need to incorporate into international law some substantive criteria of legitimacy that states must meet in order to earn legal recognition. This criteria is more demanding than the traditional standard of mere effective control of a territory and population and includes respect for at least the most important and basic of human rights. But the incorporation of such criteria into international law as a matter of legal fact is still incomplete, though certainly underway. Why it is taking so long is discussed below. But the obvious explanation is that there is, in the international legal system, no legislative authority analogous to that found in most domestic legal systems. International law is made in different ways.

This ongoing shift in international law toward recognizing only legitimate states is a source of much current difficulty. Many existing states are not legitimate, even by the less robust criteria of having a constitutional republican form of government. Yet they have traditionally enjoyed recognition as legal subjects within international law. It is not clear whether or how international law could provide for withdrawal of that recognition. It is clear that any summary withdrawal would likely produce some very bad consequences. The challenge, then, is to find some way within international law to formalize a particular standard of state legitimacy while simultaneously allowing currently illegitimate states time to comply with that standard, all without engendering a political or legal crisis within the international legal order.

International organizations have long enjoyed legal status within international law. The best known are post-World War II developments: the United Nations, the World Trade Organization (previously GATT), the International Monetary Fund, the World Bank, the World Health Organization, the World Meteorological Organization, and so on. But many international organizations enjoyed legal status under international law prior to World War II. One of the earliest was an international commission formed in Europe several centuries ago to regulate the use of the Rhine River. Through the nineteenth and early twentieth centuries, international organizations were created and legally recognized to deal with the international delivery of mail, international telegraph and eventually telephone communications, international civil and commercial aviation, ocean transport, and so on. Today, international organizations fall into roughly three categories. There are those whose members are all states sharing a common public purpose (e.g. the UN). There are those whose members are all states joining in a shared public commercial enterprise (e.g. OPEC). And there are those whose members are not exclusively states and whose purposes are exceedingly diverse. These include many familiar nongovernmental organizations, such as Amnesty International and the Red Cross.

Individual human persons have not long enjoyed legal status within international law, except as the representatives or agents of states or other recognized international organizations. Traditionally, they have enjoyed legal status only under domestic legal systems. This fact is still manifest within international law in many ways. For example, individual persons cannot file a complaint or initiate proceedings with the International Court of Justice. But here too international law has been changing. Today, international law recognizes individual persons as legal subjects when they are refugees, asylum seekers, or stateless persons. It also recognizes them as legal subjects if they commit various specified crimes against humanity or war crimes (they can be prosecuted as individuals) or if their most basic human rights have been violated (they can seek remedies as individuals). Whether and the extent to which international law will develop so as to confer on individual human beings full recognition as independent legal subjects is an open question.

WHAT ARE THE SOURCES
OF INTERNATIONAL LAW?

The two primary sources of international law are treaties and custom. Treaties include both bilateral and multilateral treaties, as well as general conventions like the Charter of the United Nations or the Convention on Civil and Political Rights. International law has long recognized the right of states to ratify treaties subject to expressed reservations. When this happens, the treaty's legal force is limited by the expressed reservation. Many states ratify general conventions only after expressing reservations about particular provisions. To know whether and how a state is bound by a treaty, one must know not only whether it ratified the treaty but whether it did so with any expressed reservations.

Treaties do not include documents or undertakings signed or affirmed under the express understanding that they are not treaties. The Universal Declaration of Human Rights is just such a document or undertaking. It is not a treaty; rather it is a joint resolution or declaration and does not, therefore, have the force of law as a treaty under international law. So it does not follow from the fact that a state fails to comply with the UDHR that the state is violating international law. To be sure, many UDHR provisions have been integrated into later treaties, and these do bind state parties. But the UDHR itself does not bind as a treaty.

Custom is the second primary source of international law. It refers to those generally followed practices within the international order that have been internalized and accepted as law by those engaged in them. Custom does not have the force of law until it has been internalized and accepted as law. Whether it has been so accepted is shown by the behavior of those engaged in the customary practice. Thus, merely habitual behavior is not sufficient to give rise to a customary norm within international law, nor is reflective rule-following behavior that is not internalized and accepted as having the force of law. Custom becomes international law only when those engaged in it affirm it as law through some reflective act of will. A great deal of international law arises, or originally arose, through custom—the law governing piracy, for example. Some human rights norms may be said to have arisen in this way, too, in particular those the violation of which would "shock the conscience of all mankind." Arguably, significant portions of the UDHR are now acquiring the status of law within the international order—not just by virtue of being integrated into subsequent treaties, but also by virtue of being integrated into the customary practice of states in the necessary way.

The primacy of treaty and custom as sources of international law suggests something like an Austinian voluntarist understanding of international law. Both treaty and custom foreground the will of apparently sovereign states as the source of international law's normative authority. But things are not quite that simple. Treaty and custom are fundamental sources of international law only because states and other international actors have internalized a kind of rule of recognition validating them as such within a shared practice. To be sure, this rule of recognition is rather thin and underdeveloped as compared with what one might find in a mature domestic legal system. Indeed, the international legal order is generally rather thin and underdeveloped as compared with domestic legal systems. It lacks a fully integrated and well-developed set of secondary rules governing legislation, adjudication, and enforcement. Accordingly, the international legal order exists independent of anything like a world state or even a unified global federation. Still, there is an international legal order. Those exercising authority within and through it do so subject to internalized rules setting out criteria of legal authority and validity. The normative force of those criteria arises not from their unconstrained wills but from their joint resolve to use them as the basis of ongoing, rule-governed interaction. Mere might can make legal right no more in the international than in the domestic context.

The extent to which the independent states whose rule-following behavior gives rise to international law are themselves "sovereign" is determined by the international law they make and to which they bind themselves. Thus, the nature and content of international law, on the one hand, and the nature and content of state sovereignty, on the other, have been mutually constructed through the rule-following behavior of states. Today, newly formed states are simply "born into"

191

an already existing international legal order. That legal order then underwrites whatever "sovereignty" those states possess and has normative force for them, irrespective of their consent or voluntary undertaking.

Because international law arises through the joint commitment by already existing states to shared criteria of legal authority and validity, it is perhaps no accident that the primary sources of international law—treaty and custom—are those to which the subject parties may be reasonably thought to have consented. Traditionally, states have committed only to criteria of international legal validity that leave them with a nearly unlimited sovereignty over their own internal affairs and something like a right to veto any proposed international "law" with which they might disagree. Thus, they settled on a system that enabled them to avoid obligations under international law simply by refusing to take them on through treaty or by voicing objections to customary practices. In this sense, the traditional international legal order shared both the merits and demerits of a unanimous consent decision procedure. Unanimous consent decision procedures are highly conservative, because they make it very difficult to move from the status quo. But they are also highly successful in yielding only changes to the status quo likely to endure over time. It should thus come as no surprise that international law has seen its greatest periods of growth—substantive and doctrinal, as well as institutional—only after very serious international crises of a global or nearly global reach. It often takes such crises to push all or nearly all states toward new treaty undertakings or new customary practices reflectively affirmed as law—the Treaty of Westphalia in 1648 ending the Thirty Years War, the Articles of Definitive Peace of 1763 ending the Seven Years War, the Final Act of 1815 ending the Napoleonic Wars, the Treaty of Versailles ending the First World War, and so on. Indeed, without the very great crises of the latter half of the twentieth century, there would not likely be the current movement within international law toward granting legal recognition only to legitimate states and toward affording individual human persons legal standing for some purposes. Nor would there be the United Nations and its associated institutions.

Beyond treaty and custom, there are two traditional sources of international law. The first is the common judicial ethos of civilized states. Legal doctrines or practices common to all civilized states may be and often are incorporated into international law apart from any arguments from treaty or custom. Many norms of due process have been incorporated into international law in this way. All civilized states commit themselves to one or another conception of due process and usually to certain fundamental due process requirements, for example, persons are to be informed of the charges against them, they are to have an opportunity to defend themselves, ex post facto applications of legal rules are to be avoided, and so on. As international legal practice has developed, these norms have been incorporated into international law on the grounds that they reflect shared understandings of how legal systems are to operate.

The final traditional source of international law—beyond treaty, custom, and the judicial ethos of civilized peoples—are rulings by authoritative judicial bodies, reports from recognized international commissions, and so on. Thus, past decisions by the International Court of Justice or the European Court of Human Rights function as sources of law. They generally lack weight sufficient to outweigh treaty, custom, or even the judicial ethos of civilized states, but they do have weight and sometimes determine what international law requires.

All these traditional sources of international law reflect the genetic fact that international law is parasitic on or secondary to domestic legal systems. International law is, or at least has been, created by and for states. But notwithstanding this genetic fact, a very different source of international law has begun recently to receive more sustained and widespread recognition. This is the so-called higher law of *jus cogens,* which refers to those principles or norms of international law necessarily binding on all states or other international actors regardless of their treaty undertakings or the shape of, or their attitude toward, customary practices. *Jus cogens* requirements are said to be mandatory or nonderogable. Some *jus cogens* principles or norms are said to give rise to *erga omnes* obligations, or obligations owed by all states not to any other particular state but to the international community as a whole. To affirm *jus cogens* norms or principles and *erga omnes* obligations as something like the morally necessary content of any system of international law capable of yielding genuine legal obligations is to affirm something like a natural law theory of the international legal order.

It was arguably *jus cogens* norms or principles to which the Nuremberg Court referred when it tried Nazi officials for crimes against humanity, crimes against peace, and war crimes. While the court made some references to traditional sources of international law, many commentators, then and now, understood it to be invoking *jus cogens*. While the Nuremberg Court's actions were not entirely unprecedented (in 1482, the Burgundian Knight Peter Hagenbach was tried on war crimes as a violation of what appear to have been something like *jus cogens* norms of international law), they were sufficiently at odds with international legal practice at the time to engender a robust debate. Some philosophers of law, including Hart, saw the Nuremberg Court as either engaging in an ex post facto application of new legal norms or exacting little more than victor's justice. Others, including Gustav Radbruch, defended the court's action from natural law and *jus cogens* principles as consistent with the rule of law.

Today, *jus cogens* is increasingly recognized as a valid source of international law, though the notion is still controversial. Naturally, *jus cogens* has come to play an important role in the defense of various legitimacy criteria to be met by states as a condition of their legal recognition within the international order. These criteria, especially those setting out the more controversial of human rights, are sometimes difficult to defend as law from any of the traditional sources of international law, such treaty, custom, and so forth. Accordingly, they are argued for on the grounds of *jus cogens* as legal obligations binding on all states, regardless of treaty, custom, and so on. Here several questions arise.

The first and most obvious question concerns the content of these *jus cogens* principles, norms, or obligations. It seems perhaps noncontroversial to say that regardless of treaty or custom or any other source of international law, states may not slaughter large, peaceful, law-abiding segments of their own populations. States that do so may be subject to various sanctions, even coercive intervention, within the international order, because *jus cogens* principles prohibit genocide. But what about liberalism or democracy? Do *jus cogens* principles require liberal democracy? Should nondemocratic or nonliberal states arranged as something like more or less decent constitutional republics—say, the way some of the medieval Italian city-states (Venice, Florence, Pisa, Sienna) were organized—also be at risk of sanction or coercive intervention within the international order, because *jus cogens* principles prohibit nonliberal or nondemocratic political regimes? What, exactly, is this higher law that all states must honor regardless of what the traditional sources of international law say? And how do we know it?

A second but perhaps less obvious question concerns the validity and normative authority of *jus cogens* norms, principles, or obligations as international *law*. It is one thing to argue that international law ought to include *jus cogens* norms, principles, and obligations if it is to be good law. It is quite another to argue that international law already includes them and does so irrespective of any of the traditionally recognized sources of international law. Can we affirm the latter without taking a natural law stance toward international law as law? And if we commit ourselves to a natural law stance toward international law, must we also commit ourselves to a natural law stance regarding domestic legal orders? Do we risk incoherence if we do not?

Finally, as a normative matter, we need to inquire into the costs and benefits of introducing *jus cogens* norms into international law. International law already provides for the introduction of various transnational norms—for example, basic human rights norms—through custom. As already noted, provisions of the UDHR are often enforced as international law on just this basis. What *jus cogens* allows is the rapid introduction into international law of norms not yet entrenched in customary practice. With *jus cogens* as a source of international law, the content of international law is cut free from the status quo. International law is therefore made into a potential tool of progressive change, but not without costs. Its normative force as law will no longer be derivable solely from the internalization of the constitutive norms of a shared practice, and its criteria for legal validity will undoubtedly prove more controversial, potentially destabilizing the international legal order.

HOW IS INTERNATIONAL LAW ENFORCED?

Enforcing international law is a complex business given the absence of a unified world state possessed of supreme executive power. A great deal of international law is enforced informally and without overt force. There are three basic modes of noncoercive enforcement. The first and most obvious is through some form of adjudication. The parties to many disputes arising under international law may submit their dispute to an appropriate tribunal—say the International Court of Justice or the newly formed International Criminal Court—for resolution. But adjudication within international law is almost always limited by the fact that no state is necessarily subject to the jurisdiction of any tribunal. Jurisdiction is almost always dependent on the voluntary consent of the parties. The same is generally true for nonadjudicative forms of dispute resolution, such as arbitration and mediation. This gives state parties a great deal of wiggle room. For example, when the United States was brought before the International Court of Justice by Nicaragua on charges that the CIA mined Nicaraguan ports, the United States argued that it had never consented to ICJ jurisdiction either generally or over cases concerning U.S. actions in Central America. The ICJ found that the United States had consented to jurisdiction. In response, the United States declined to participate in the proceedings and refused to recognize the ICJ ruling against it as valid. Still, many disputes are resolved, and international law is often enforced through adjudication, arbitration, mediation, and so forth, notwithstanding the fact that jurisdiction is voluntarily conferred by the parties.

Sometimes international tribunals are created on an ad hoc basis, and nonconsensual jurisdiction is asserted. This is usually only in cases of war crimes or crimes against humanity and is defended increasingly in terms of *jus cogens* norms and *erga omnes* obligations. The United Nations has established such tribunals to deal with war crimes in the former Yugoslavia and in Rwanda, for example. The Nuremberg and Tokyo tribunals, created in the aftermath of World War II, are models here. In the future, most cases of war crimes, crimes against humanity, and so forth will be brought before the newly formed International Criminal Court, if they are not prosecuted in an appropriate domestic jurisdiction. But like all standing international tribunals, the ICC's jurisdiction, even though it is only a kind of backup jurisdiction, is still consensual. Most states have consented to ICC jurisdiction. The United States has not.

The second mode of enforcing international law without overt force involves the use of diplomatic pressure. States may withdraw diplomats or embassies or cut off various forms of diplomatic or trade relations to enforce what they understand to be international law. This is sometimes an effective way to enforce international law. The third mode is to subject the noncompliant state to some sort of reprisal for its violation of international law by committing against it some act also in violation of international law. So, if one state tortures prisoners taken from another state during wartime, the latter may in turn torture prisoners taken from the former as a reprisal. Illegality is met with illegality. The same often occurs in trade relations. Illegal tariffs meet illegal tariffs. This often results in fuller compliance with the relevant requirements of international law.

Sometimes international law is enforced through overt force. The use of international force, including international sanctions enforced by force, is regulated by the Security Council of the United Nations subject to the Charter of the United Nations. The Charter limits the Security Council to authorizing the use of force only when necessary to preserve peace and security within the international order (though the Charter also commits all the states within the United Nations to appropriate action aimed at fully securing the human rights of all). Under the Charter, states are free to act in self-defense when under threat of immediate attack and without the time to seek authorization from the Security Council. But they are obligated to seek that authorization as soon as they are able and to abide by the decisions of the Council.

This arrangement has had limited success. The problem is not simply that the five permanent members of the Security Council— the United States, England, France, Russia, and China—all have a veto over any proposed Security Council action, though this most certainly paralyzed the Security Council during the Cold War years and still sometimes paralyzes it today. The problem is also that it remains unclear whether the Security Council has the authority to authorize the use of force to enforce human rights norms within a state that poses no direct threat to any of its neighbors. Whether— and, if so, when—the Security Council should have the authority to authorize so-called humanitarian interventions (the forceful intervention into the domestic affairs of a state engaged in no international aggression) is a theoretical and practical problem of the first degree within international law. So long as this problem remains unresolved, and it is not likely to be resolved without some sort of reform of the Security Council itself, international law will sometimes be enforced through unilateral or multilateral uses of force without Security Council authorization. It is important to emphasize, however, that any state or "coalition of the willing" undertaking to enforce international law through military force without Security Council approval must do so without violating any other provisions of international law, including those that govern the legal conduct of warfare, treatment of prisoners, and so on, whether they arise out of treaty or customary practice.

While military action is no doubt the most visible mode of enforcing international law, it is probably the least important when it comes to the day-to-day operations of the international legal order. Indeed, we have yet to mention the most important way in which international law is enforced: within and by domestic legal systems. Everyday and around the world, international law is enforced within and by domestic legal systems. Every mature legal system recognizes some significant segment of international law as genuine law and enforces it within its own system as such, though subject to its own procedures and practices.

Sometimes international law is enforced by domestic courts, because the content of the relevant bit of international law has already been fully integrated into the domestic legal order. For example, the United States incorporates into its own domestic law many basic human rights under international law. It does this in two ways. First, it secures many basic human rights for its citizens as constitutional and civil rights within its own domestic legal system. Second, it secures many basic human rights for noncitizens under the Alien Tort Claims Act, which gives federal courts in the United States jurisdiction over civil suits for monetary damages initiated by aliens for violations of international law. In 1980, a man from Paraguay successfully used the act to sue the policeman who had tortured his son to death in Paraguay. Suits under this act are rarely successful, however, and when they are, they often leave plaintiffs with no more than an unsatisfied damage award. Nevertheless, there have been some recent attempts to use the act to sue multinational corporations for alleged violations of international law committed outside the United States.

Sometimes international law is enforced by domestic courts, not as international law already integrated into the domestic legal order and thereby transformed into domestic law, but rather simply as international law binding in the context or circumstance at hand. Courts in the United States routinely enforce provisions of international law governing trade relations or maritime issues without those provisions having been fully integrated into the domestic legal order as domestic law. They enforce those provisions simply as international law. Of course, they enforce them only against parties over whom they have jurisdiction.

Some states have asserted what is known as *universal jurisdiction* with respect to certain domains of international law. Universal jurisdiction gives the courts of any domestic legal system jurisdiction over the parties to a dispute under the relevant domain of international law, regardless of the nationality of the parties or the geographical site of the dispute. Belgium has asserted universal jurisdiction with respect to certain crimes against humanity and human rights violations. In general, however, universal jurisdiction seems to be regarded as posing a threat to international stability sufficient to lead most to favor the development of international tribunals.

In any case, we should not lose sight of the crucial role already played by domestic legal systems in the enforcement of international law. Domestic legal systems, along with noncoercive enforcement measures, constitute the lion's share of enforcement activity within the international legal order. International tribunals and coercive international action play a much smaller, though more visible and still important, role.

This brings us to something of a puzzle regarding the relationship between domestic and international law within the existing order. It is not clear whether the relationship is one in which all domestic legal systems are essentially nested within one overarching system of international law, or one in which the world's many domestic legal systems and the one international legal system run on something like parallel tracks, with the former sometimes enforcing the latter.

On the former view, there is really just one legal system, a complex international system that provides for many diverse but subordinate domestic legal systems. On this view, domestic legal systems should enforce international law so long as it applies; they are not directed by international law to do otherwise. Very few states today take this view of the relationship between the domestic and international legal systems, though one or two (e.g., the Netherlands) come close.

On the latter view, shared by many states today, the domestic and international legal orders exist on two separate planes. Domestic legal systems are neither necessarily subordinate to nor nested within the international legal order. They may incorporate or otherwise recognize international law as binding and accordingly enforce it, but they need not do so simply because it is international law and they cannot do so without the appropriate domestic authority. Thus, in the United States, courts may enforce those provisions of international law, the content of which is explicitly incorporated into domestic law (as is true for many human rights incorporated as constitutional or civil rights). They may also enforce those provisions explicitly recognized as binding international law within the domestic legal system (the Constitution recognizes treaties as binding and the Alien Tort Claims Act recognizes other provisions of international law as binding). But they need not otherwise enforce international law simply because it is international law. And, in fact, they cannot do so unless the Constitution grants them that authority. On this latter view, then, a state—say, the United States—may have a genuine legal obligation under international law that its courts cannot enforce within its domestic legal order because they lack the legal authority to do so. (Of course, if the Supreme Court has final and binding authority to determine the limits of its own authority under the Constitution, then ... well, it's time to reread the chapter on judicial review.)

IS INTERNATIONAL LAW REALLY LAW?

Given the foregoing description of the international legal order, it might seem odd to ask whether international law is really law. But, indeed, for generations, many political and legal philosophers and theorists, and more than a few politicians, have more or less sneered at the idea of international law, insisting always on putting "law" in scare quotes. Some were skeptical about the possibility of anything like a rule-governed international order. Others insisted that on any realistic view, the international "legal" order was just another name for that which the powerful imposed on the weak. To determine whether international law is really law, challenges from such skeptics and realists must be examined in turn.

One argument sometimes made is that because there is no global sovereign able to impose sanctions for violations of international law, there is no international law properly speaking. But this is a bad argument. As we learned from Hart in the chapter on positivism, legal systems require neither a sovereign in the traditional sense nor sanctions for noncompliance to exist as legal systems. Rule-following behavior of the sort necessary to constitute a legal system and give rise to legal obligations depends not on sovereigns and sanctions but on critical and reflective social pressure to comply with the relevant rules—both primary rules of obligation and secondary rules of legal validity—within a shared practice. And this surely exists within the international legal order. States pressure one another in a variety of ways to comply with international law, as well as with shared criteria of international legal validity. And although states sometimes violate international law, when they do, they generally try to hide the fact that they have done so or undertake to justify their conduct to other states by reference to international law itself—arguing, for example, that what others claim to be a valid bit of international law is in fact not valid or not binding in the case at hand.

Another argument sometimes made is that states comply with and pressure other states to comply with international law only out of self-interest, not because they think they have any moral obligation to obey international law as law. But even if this is true, it is beside the point. So long as states behave in ways that evidence the internalization of the norms governing the validity criteria and positive primary obligations of international law, why they in fact comply with international law is beside the point. If it turned out that most Americans obeyed the law only out of self-interest, that would not count against the existence of the American legal system as a bona fide legal system able to impose genuine legal obligations.

Yet another argument often made is that there can be no international law because states are necessarily absolute sovereigns and thus cannot themselves by bound by any law. But this argument rests on an implausible Hobbesian-Austinian concept of sovereignty. We need only recall that constitutional states exist and possess genuine legal systems, even though there is no absolute sovereign in a constitutional state. The argument might, then, be recast in the following way: there can be no international law because states are necessarily independent and subject to no authority other than that which constitutes their domestic legal orders and thus them as states. Here the argument is that international law is inconsistent with the independence and autonomy of constitutional states. But this argument is no better. Whether international law is consistent with the independence and autonomy of constitutional states turns on the content of international law, not on the fact that it is international. There is no reason why international law cannot recognize as independent and autonomous, for example, all constitutional states that satisfy certain standards of legitimacy.

A more sophisticated argument is that while there may be primary rules of obligations within the international "legal" order, there is no secondary rule of recognition and thus no "valid" law. But this cannot be seriously maintained today. The behavior of states and other international actors today evidences internalized criteria of legal validity applicable to the international legal order. To be sure, the international legal order still lacks the sort of well-developed rule of recognition one might expect to find in a mature domestic legal system. Accordingly, it lacks the sort of unity characteristic of mature domestic legal systems. But there are surely secondary rules covering adjudication, lawmaking, and enforcement, as well as an increasingly well-developed and shared understanding within key institutions of the criteria of legal validity.

We might also note here that if we accept Dworkin's criticisms of Hart's "model of rules," then we ought not suppose that there can be no international law unless there is a well-defined rule of recognition latent within the shared practice of international actors. All we need to find, to be justified in saying that there is an international legal order, is a preinterpretive consensus among the key actors within the international order sufficient to sustain an interpretive social practice distinctively legal in nature by virtue of its concern to regulate and legitimate coercion.

From the perspective of both Hartian positivism and Dworkinian constructivism, then, international law looks very much like real law. States increasingly behave in such a way as to evidence the internalization of something like a basic rule or recognition, or at least a preinterpretive consensus, that validates treaty, custom, and so on as binding international law. They criticize one another for noncompliance with international law and issue those criticisms in the name of the law, indicating that they think the law has normative force. And they pretty clearly regard that normative force as neither simply moral nor merely prudential. Many parts of international law are regarded as normative even though they concern matters that are intrinsically morally indifferent—for example, how the territorial waters of states are to be determined. States are expected to comply with international law even if it is not in their immediate self-interest to do so.

But there are other objections to the claim that international law is real law, objections ventured from the perspective of natural law theory. For example, one might argue that all law must be aimed at the common good of those subject to it and given by one possessed of legitimate authority over them. But that morality does not extend to international relations, so, in that context, the "common good" and "legitimate authority" are necessarily empty notions, rendering international law impossible. But if morality governs the internal domestic relations of members within a state, why would it not extend to international relations? Some have argued that it would not extend to international relations because morality is necessarily relative; there is no universal morality. But this is a bad argument.

There are several different relativist theses. Descriptive relativism holds that, as a matter of fact, there are no moral norms shared by all people, states, or cultures worldwide. But though the world obviously contains considerable diversity of moral belief and practice, descriptive relativism is not obviously true. It is very likely that there are some universally shared moral norms, even if they are highly abstract principles. In any case, descriptive relativism is a purely descriptive claim that by itself entails no normative conclusions. To put the point differently, even if there are now no universally shared moral norms, it could still be true, universally true, that there ought to be. Thus, descriptive relativism provides no basis for a natural law objection to the possibility of international law existing as genuine law, because "the common good" and "legitimate authority" are natural law notions given content not by the moral beliefs people happen to have but by the beliefs they should have.

A second relativist thesis might be called skeptical relativism, which holds that the reason our world has so much moral diversity is that there are no rational or objective cross-cultural bases for resolving moral disagreements. Without access to such bases for resolving moral disagreements and assessing the truth or falsity of conflicting moral claims, we cannot know or prove the content of any universal moral truths, even if they happen to exist. Thus we could never be sure that international law was genuine law by virtue of its necessary connection to universal moral truths regarding the common good or the legitimacy of authority claimed by those who make international law. But do we have any reason to endorse skeptical relativism?

The argument for it is that it's the best explanation of our current experience of intractable moral disagreement. But why isn't the difficulty of the issues faced the best explanation of our intractable disagreement? Why think there are no universal standards at all for assessing the truth and falsity of moral claims or resolving moral disagreements? What, after all, accounts for the stable points of moral agreement we seem to find between people, states, and cultures? And even if descriptive relativism is true and there are no such points, why appeal to skeptical relativism as the best explanation for that fact? Aren't there other and better explanations, including demographic and institutional diversity? Perhaps we find some moral disagreements intractable not because we lack any shared standards of moral reasoning but rather because we find ourselves unavoidably tied to different starting points when we engage in moral reasoning. In any case, it seems premature to affirm skeptical relativism. If there is a path to a clearer sense of shared standards of moral reasoning, it is the path of a continued international moral conversation, dialogue, and so forth. International law may prove an important site for such activity and thus help us develop a clearer sense of our shared standards of moral reasoning.

A third relativist thesis might be called prescriptive relativism, which holds that there are good cross-cultural reasons for claiming that tolerance ought universally to govern the relations between morally diverse peoples. On the strongest version of prescriptive relativism, tolerance of moral diversity is the only moral value or norm for which there are good objective moral reasons of universal application. This seems too strong. Weaker versions allow for additional universally binding values or norms, but insist that they are few in number and so narrow or abstract that they do not undermine the commitment to tolerating a very wide range of morally diverse value systems, cultures, ways of life, and legal and institutional arrangements.

Prescriptive relativism is not incompatible with seeing international law as genuine law from a natural law perspective. But it does suggest that international law ought to leave a great deal of room for diverse and largely autonomous domestic legal systems; indeed, it suggests that there would be something fundamentally unjust about a system of international law that did not tolerate a fairly wide range of largely autonomous domestic legal systems. The common good at which international law ought to aim is to be understood in the relatively thin terms of peaceful relations between diverse and independent states. Yet, the tolerance to which prescriptive relativism is committed need not, indeed ought not, be an unlimited tolerance. Thus, prescriptive relativism is consistent with refusing to recognize under international law the legitimacy of states that do not deserve to be tolerated, either because they fail to respect basic human rights or because they engage in expansionist acts of international aggression.

There are no good reasons of a relativist sort, then, for thinking that international law cannot be genuine law, because there is no morality international in reach from which it might draw its notions of the common good or legitimate authority. But what sort of natural law reasons could there be, then, for thinking international law cannot be genuine law?

Some critics argue that international law is not real law unless all states have a moral reason to obey it. But this, they maintain, all states can never have. States exist to serve their members, and it is accordingly to the national interest that state officials are morally bound. All states might participate in an international legal order as a kind of modus vivendi, complying with its demands out of prudential self-interest. But they lack the capacity to be morally bound to or by international law. States have moral obligations only to their own members.

This argument also fails. It is true that states exist and are morally bound to serve their members. But it is also true that their members have moral interests that reach beyond state borders, and states must serve these interests. If these interests include the realization of basic human rights worldwide within a system of international law that all states have good moral reasons to obey, then the officials of every state ought to serve those interests, among others. Whether the international legal order is able to exist as anything more than a modus vivendi, whether states will ever have a moral reason to obey international law as law, will depend, then, on whether and how successfully states are able to serve the interests of their members and bring into existence an international legal order sufficient to underwrite genuine moral obligations to obey.

There is one final objection from the natural law perspective to the idea of international law as genuine law. It is that international law simply does not serve the common good of all peoples or states because it inevitably becomes just another weapon in the arsenal of the most powerful states keen on expanding their power and influence. Thus, out of a moral concern for the common good of all, we should reject international law and work as best we can for a peaceful international order secured through a modus vivendi balance of powers, nonlegal practices, and so forth. This argument draws on the suspicion, shared by critical legal studies in the domestic context, that the law—in this case international law—is always really just politics and power by another name, always just a tool through which domination may be legitimated or hidden from view.

International law has long been and is still vulnerable to this objection in a much more obvious way than the domestic law of mature legal systems. It is simply less well developed and thus less able to resist being turned into a tool of the powerful. But the future of international law is open, and it seems premature to suppose that it is not possible for international law to develop the ability to constrain rather than merely to serve politics and power. It is too early to give up hope for the rule of law within the international order.

From a natural law perspective, international law is surely imperfect as law. It has been too long dominated by a statist orientation that gives legal recognition to all states, including those that fail to serve the interests of their individual members. It has only recently begun to approximate anything like the rule-of-law ideal. Enforcement has been inconsistent. But still, it seems fair to say that today it must count as genuine law from a natural law perspective. And if it counts as genuine law from both a positivist and natural law perspective, then perhaps it is time we finally to put to rest the question of whether international law is really law. It is. The real question today is what it ought to be.

WHAT OUGHT INTERNATIONAL
LAW LOOK LIKE?

It would take another book or two to say much in detail about what international law ought to look like. But we can set the stage and identify some of the main topics to be addressed.

The first thing we need to do is distinguish two theoretical frameworks within which the question "What ought international law look like?" arises. The first is that of ideal theory. Here we ask what international law should look like under the best possible conditions—that is, illegitimate or outlaw states no longer exist, all states are reasonably developed and possessed of mature domestic legal systems, all states are disposed voluntarily to comply with the demands of international law, there are few if any violations, and so on. The second is that of nonideal theory. Here we ask what international law should look like under something closer to our present conditions—that is, illegitimate and outlaw states still exist, some states are not very developed or have only an immature domestic legal system, not all states are disposed voluntarily to comply with the demands of international law, there are regular violations, and so on.

We need to answer the "what ought international law look like?" question for both ideal and nonideal theory. The answer we give within ideal theory sets the target at which we ought to aim. It specifies what we can reasonably hope for and thus ought to work to bring about. The answer we give within nonideal theory gives us normative direction as we undertake the transitional work of moving the international legal order toward the ideal. We need the normative direction given by nonideal theory, because we know that ends do not justify any and every means to them. For example, if war or coercive humanitarian intervention are to be means of moving us closer to the international legal order ideal theory sets for us as a reasonable hope, then we need to know what the international law governing war or humanitarian intervention ought to look like now.

Surely not everything aimed at realizing the ideal ought to be permitted. Our means should conform to what international law ought to look like under nonideal conditions. And under nonideal conditions, international law will set the limits of just war and humanitarian intervention, protecting innocent civilians from intentionally inflicted harm, outlawing gross human rights abuses, insuring against the use of war or humanitarian intervention for expansionist or imperialist ends, and so on.

The second thing we need to do is get clear on the relationship between international and domestic law. We cannot answer the question "What ought international law look like?" without addressing this matter at the outset. But we must take care to address it within both ideal and nonideal theoretical contexts, for there is no *a priori* reason for thinking that it ought necessarily be the same within both theoretical contexts. It is here that we confront directly the question of whether we have good reasons to hope for an international legal order possessed of the sort of unity and scope common to unified states with mature domestic legal systems, as well as what role we envisage for *transnational* norms binding internally on domestic legal systems (e.g., human rights norms).

Beyond these initial inquiries, we will need to inquire into a wide range of areas of international law, asking in each case what international law ought to look like in both ideal and nonideal theoretical contexts. What ought international law require with respect to human rights? How should those rights be enforced or protected? Should there be a distinction between those human rights eligible to be enforced or protected through coercive force and those marking shared goals or aspirations not eligible to be so enforced? What ought international law look like with respect to international economic activity, the movement of people, currency, capital and commodities, international investment, and so on? Should international law serve a particular conception of global distributive justice? If so, which one? Or is the idea of global distributive justice out of place in the international context? What ought international law look like with respect to the use of common or shared resources, the seas and seabed, the atmosphere, outer space, species, ecosystems, genetic information, and so on? What ought it look like with respect to such collective goods as public health or global security? Should mutual aid between states be required by international law? If so, under what conditions and subject to what limits? What should international law require with respect to secessionist movements or civil wars? Should there be an international criminal law beyond that dealing with war crimes? How should it be enforced? Ought there be a system of international punishment? For states as well as individuals? Or is a system of nonpunitive reparations preferable? What institutional arrangements ought to be realized for the sake of the international legal order? Should the United Nations be reformed or replaced? Should there be new international courts? Philosophers of law need to join those already working in international relations, political science, law, and related disciplines to address these pressing normative issues. There are few tasks more important.

INTERNATIONAL LAW AND POLITICS

Many universities offer classes in both international relations or politics and international law, as if each constituted a discrete and insular phenomenon to study. But increasingly, this distinction seems inappropriate. For nowhere perhaps is the gap between law and politics narrower than in the international arena. Overtly political actions, clearly outside the bounds of uncontested legality, are often taken precisely to shape customary practice and thus determine the future course of international law. And international law is itself routinely deployed as a resource within political contests. Whether it is the activity of the U.N. Security Council prior to the Iraq War or U.S. policy in the "war on terror" or the extradition by Spain of former Chilean dictator Augusto Pinochet, there seems to be but the finest of lines separating law and politics in the international setting.

This may seem surprising and peculiar. But we ought not forget the lessons learned from earlier chapters in this book. Even within mature domestic legal systems, the line between law and politics is often thinner than it may first appear. Law and politics are, in both the domestic and the international legal orders, forever engaged in reciprocal interplay, each shaping the other.

What does this mean for us? Within our domestic legal systems, it means that all of us, even those who are neither lawyers nor judges nor legislators nor voters, have some influence over and must assume some responsibility for the legal order. Of course, those with more influence must assume more responsibility. But the legal system of every state rests ultimately on the political order its members achieve or tolerate. And so all members share some responsibility for it. The same is true for the international legal order. All states have some influence over and must assume some responsibility for it. But those with the most influence—the United States first among them—must assume more responsibility. They must act purposefully for the sake of securing a more fully adequate international legal order. Still, in the end, the international legal order rests ultimately on the international political order achieved or tolerated by member states. It is a joint undertaking, involving the collective submission of state power to the rule of law.

The interpenetration of law and politics in both the international and the domestic legal spheres need not be a source of dismay or disappointment. And it need not count against the rule-of-law ideal. After all, the contrast between the rule of law and the rule of man was always one ripe for overreading. The law cannot rule but through individual persons. It is neither self-originating nor self-interpreting nor self-executing. It is made, interpreted, and enforced by and for humans, who happen to be first and foremost social and political animals. The question, then, is not whether through law we humans might escape politics and power and overcome our nature as social and political animals. The question is rather whether we might, over time and through the interplay of law, politics, and power, increasingly tame the worst while setting free the best elements of our social and political nature.

SELECTED BIBLIOGRAPHY

On International Law

Bederman, David J. *International Law Frameworks.* (Cincinatti, OH: Foundation Press), 2001.

Beitz, Charles. *Political Theory and International Relations,* 2nd ed. (Princeton, NJ: Princeton University Press), 1999.

Buchanan, Allen. *Justice, Legitimacy, and Self-Determination: Moral Foundations for International Law.* (Oxford, UK: Oxford University Press), 2004.

Donnelly, Jack. *Universal Human Rights: In Theory and Practice,* 2nd ed. (Ithaca, NY: Cornell University Press), 2003.

Kelsen, Hans. *Principles of International Law,* 2nd ed. (New York, NY: Holt, Rinehart and Winston), 1966.

Martin, Rex and David Reidy, eds. *Rawls's Law of Peoples: A Realistic Utopia?* (Oxford, UK: Blackwell Publishers), 2006.

May, Larry. *Crimes Against Humanity: A Normative Account.* (Cambridge, UK: Cambridge University Press), 2005.

Nardin, Terry. *Law, Morality, and the Relations of States.* (Princeton, NJ: Princeton University Press), 1980.

Nickel, James. *Making Sense of Human Rights.* (Berkeley, CA: University of California Press), 1987. (Revised second edition forthcoming from Blackwell Publishers.)

Rawls, John. *The Law of Peoples.* (Cambridge, MA: Harvard University Press), 1999.

Reidy, David and Mortimer Sellers, eds. *Universal Human Rights: Moral Order in a Divided World.* (Lanham, MD: Rowman and Littlefield), 2005.

Reus-Smit, Christian. *The Politics of International Law.* Cambridge University Press, 2004.

Steiner, Henry and Philip Alston. *International Human Rights in Context: Law, Politics, Morals*, 2nd ed. (Oxford, UK: Oxford University Press), 2000.

Talbott, William. *Which Rights Should Be Universal?* (Oxford, UK: Oxford University Press), 2005.

Teson, Fernando. *A Philosophy of International Law.* (Boulder, CO: Westview Press), 1998.

Walzer, Michael. *Just and Unjust Wars*, 3rd ed. (New York, NY: Basic Books), 2000.

The **WADSWORTH PHILOSOPHICAL TOPIC SERIES** is dedicated to providing both philosophy students and general readers with insight into the background, development, and current scholarship in the discourse on great philosophical topics. More than a simple guide, each of the volumes has the goal of helping to empower the reader when analyzing and discussing original works. For North American college and university adopters, any of these volumes may be bundled with each other or with any other Wadsworth titles at a substantial discount. Contact your local Wadsworth representative for bundling assistance. For more details about this series and other related titles, join us at **philosophy.wadsworth.com**

Volumes in this series will soon include:

CPSIA information can be obtained
at www.ICGtesting.com
Printed in the USA
FFOW02n0818070117
31113FF